D0607611

WITHDRAWN
FROM THE RECORDS OF THE
MID-CONTINENT PUBLIC LIBRARY

746.43 SH83
Shrader, Valerie Van Arsdale
Blue ribbon afghans from
 America's state fairs

MID-CONTINENT PUBLIC LIBRARY
Raytown Branch
6131 Raytown Road
Raytown, MO 64133

RT

Blue Ribbon Afghans
from America's State Fairs

Blue Ribbon Afghans
from America's State Fairs

40 Prize-Winning Crocheted Designs

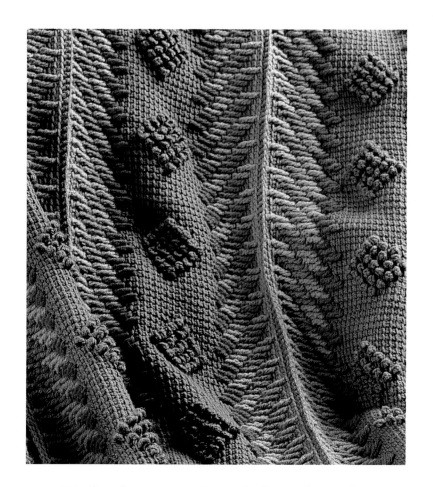

Valerie Van Arsdale Shrader

LARK BOOKS
A Division of Sterling Publishing Co., Inc.
New York

ART DIRECTOR: **Kathleen Holmes**

PHOTOGRAPHER: **keithwright.com**

COVER DESIGNER: **Barbara Zaretsky**

ILLUSTRATOR: **Orrin Lundgren**

ASSISTANT EDITOR: **Veronika Alice Gunter**

EDITORIAL ASSISTANT: **Anne Wolff Hollyfield**

PRODUCTION ASSISTANCE: **Jeff Hamilton, Shannon Yokeley**

EDITORIAL ASSISTANCE: **Cindy Burda, Delores Gosnell, Rosemary Kast,
  Nathalie Mornu, Rain Newcomb, Marissa Y. Thompson, Nicole Tuggle**

ART INTERN: **Avery Johnson**

EDITORIAL INTERN: **Rebecca Lim**

TECHNICAL CONSULTANT: **Marilyn Hastings**

MID-CONTINENT PUBLIC LIBRARY
Raytown Branch
6131 Raytown Road
Raytown, MO 64133

RT

MID-CONTINENT PUBLIC LIBRARY

3 0000 12456603 9

10 9 8 7 6 5 4 3 2 1

First Edition

Published by Lark Books, a division of Sterling Publishing Co., Inc.
387 Park Avenue South, New York, N.Y. 10016

© 2003, Lark Books

Distributed in Canada by Sterling Publishing,
c/o Canadian Manda Group, One Atlantic Ave., Suite 105
Toronto, Ontario, Canada M6K 3E7

Distributed in the U.K. by Guild of Master Craftsman Publications Ltd., Castle Place, 166 High Street,
Lewes, East Sussex, England BN7 1XU, Tel: (+ 44) 1273 477374, Fax: (+ 44) 1273 478606,
Email: pubs@thegmcgroup.com, Web: www.gmcpublications.com

Distributed in Australia by Capricorn Link (Australia) Pty Ltd.,
P.O. Box 704, Windsor, NSW 2756 Australia

The written instructions, photographs, designs, patterns, and projects in this volume are intended for
the personal use of the reader and may be reproduced for that purpose only. Any other use, especially
commercial use, is forbidden under law without written permission of the copyright holder.

Every effort has been made to ensure that all the information in this book is accurate. However, due
to differing conditions, tools, and individual skills, the publisher cannot be responsible for any injuries,
losses, and other damages that may result from the use of the information in this book.

If you have questions or comments about this book, please contact:
Lark Books
67 Broadway
Asheville, NC 28801
(828) 253-0467
Manufactured in China

All rights reserved

ISBN 1-57990-414-9

table of CONTENTS

Introduction

Photo by Michael J. Okoniewski,
courtesy of the New York State Fair

COME ONE, COME ALL, to the state fair! Could anything be more exciting?

When state fairs were begun in the 1800s, there truly was *nothing* more exciting for the farm family: these fun-filled events offered a respite from the year's toil and a chance to visit with friends and neighbors. Officially, the purpose of the fair was to encourage and promote sound agricultural practices as well as introduce new products and processes. The early fairs were a great success, so rural folk continued to gather at these events to rejoice in the year's bountiful harvest and learn about advances in agriculture. While the advent of the information age has diminished this function, the state fair remains the perfect place to have a ball, see amazing new products, eat yummy food, and marvel at our American way of life.

A trip to the fair is still an eagerly awaited event, because there's so much to see, so much to do! You experience the thrill of the midway, swirling with neon and ringing with laughter. The tantalizing food is impossible to resist: cotton candy or funnel cake, barbecue or roasted corn? Heck, maybe all of it at once. The livestock barns teem with magnificent creatures, the finest and most pampered of their breeds—stately Guernsey cows, giant Poland China hogs, feisty Rhode Island Red roosters, silky Angora rabbits, noble Arabian stallions, and exotic Nubian goats.

And the exhibit halls hold the state's best—of everything! From traditional homestead crafts like woodworking and knitting to modern-day pursuits like website design and sports photojournalism, the finest examples are on display at the fair. To honor this heritage of excellence in handicraft, *Blue Ribbon Afghans from America's State Fairs* showcases the art of crochet, in particular the time-honored afghan. Needle arts were not a hobby but a necessity for farm families, because none could afford the luxury of store-bought blankets, socks, shawls, or mittens. Crocheting was a practical duty; it kept the family warm during long, cold winters. But the crocheted item was a thing of beauty, too, showcasing the skill of its creator. It's the perfect blend of functionality and creativity, the hallmark of American ingenuity.

Today, this traditional art flourishes, and presented here are its most talented practitioners—blue ribbon winners at our state fairs. The composition of this group demonstrates that crochet continues to attract diverse enthusiasts: the winners include high school students, Ivy League graduates, professional women, stay-at-home moms, great-grandmothers—and a gentleman who learned to crochet while serving in the United States Coast Guard.

Not only does the book honor our American agrarian heritage, but it also celebrates fine craftsmanship, the best our states have to offer. Learn a little bit more about the development of our agricultural expositions—the history is colored with downright fascinating facts and trivia—then ooh and ah at the skill of the blue ribbon winners. So, as you leaf through this book, imagine this: you've passed through the main fair gate and paused for a moment to absorb the spectacle that surrounds you. Where to go first? Maybe you were tempted by the cotton candy stand, but now you're heading for the exhibit hall. Step inside and begin your day at the fair now!

How It All Got Started

THE STATE FAIR was born of agriculture. In the mid-nineteenth century, the vast majority of Americans relied on farming for their livelihood. Recognizing the importance of sound agricultural practices to the country's growth, many states began to form agricultural societies or state boards of agriculture to encourage and support farmers. The main objective of many of these organizations was the creation of a state fair, where farmers and their families could learn how to work more efficiently, raising bigger and better crops and livestock. The thrill of competition at these events—and the resulting cash prize—was a strong incentive. The fairs supported agriculture by introducing new ideas, products, and processes, and came to be major economic influences in the states as well by improving the business of farming.

Courtesy of the Indiana State Fair

THE FIRST FAIR

Where did the idea of an agricultural fair originate? The concept of a trade fair or festival is thousands of years old. In this country, fairs were held to sell livestock during colonial times. In 1807, Elkanah Watson organized an exhibition of two imported Merino sheep in Pittsfield, Massachusetts, and applied a little Yankee ingenuity to the old trade fair idea, because he wasn't *selling* anything. Rather, he hoped to interest local farmers in raising these sheep to create a supply of their high-quality wool for his mills, because the domestic animals produced just half the fleece of his Merinos. The success of this event delighted Watson, who later wrote that "farmers and even women were excited" by his show. From this humble beginning, the

Father of the American Fair

In addition to his enterprising work in establishing the model for the state fair, Elkanah Watson (1758–1842) was an important figure in the early history of the United States. A descendant of the *Mayflower* pilgrims, he helped convey gunpowder shipments to General George Washington during the Revolutionary War. Later, he served as an envoy to France on behalf of Benjamin Franklin. He became a merchant there and developed a keen interest in the canals of Europe.

After his return to the United States, he explored the rivers of the Northeast in a flat-bottomed boat called a *bateau*. After these experiences, Watson envisioned building a system of artificial waterways that would link together the region's various centers of commerce. In fact, he claimed to have conceived the idea for the Erie Canal and was a vocal proponent of the project.

Watson dabbled in land speculation and banking, eventually opening the State Bank of Albany in 1803. He also wrote extensively about his travels. After his retirement in 1807, Watson organized the modest sheep show and agricultural exposition for which he is best known.

agricultural fair in the United States was born. (For some of Watson's other accomplishments, see page 7.)

By 1811, the Berkshire (County, Massachusetts) Agricultural Society had organized to sponsor the event that evolved from Watson's first exhibit; competitive prizes were introduced at this fair. Thousands of farmers were in attendance. Just one year later, prizes were awarded for women's domestic goods, recognizing the importance of these handicrafts to the success of the farm family. The blueprint for the state fair was created from these early county shows—an annual event that allowed farm families to socialize, exchange information, display their finest products, and learn about innovations in agriculture.

Watson's notion of a fair promoting agriculture spread throughout the young country. In 1841, the state of New York sponsored a fair that drew in excess of 10,000, by some estimates. (In contrast, the New York State Fair attracted over a million visitors in 2001.) One by one, events were organized in other states: Georgia in 1846, Michigan in 1849, Ohio in 1850, Pennsylvania in 1851, Indiana in 1852, Illinois and North Carolina in 1853, Iowa and California in 1854. Nebraska held a Territorial and Mechanical Fair in 1859—before it *became* a state. In fact, many of the western states had fairs or expositions long before they attained statehood.

Courtesy of the N.C. Office of Archives and History

HOW THE FAIRS DEVELOPED

Agriculture and farm life was the focus of the earliest state fairs, with exhibits on raising crops and demonstrations of new machinery and tools. Home arts were included, too, and a $2.50 premium for the best loaf of bread would have been a welcome prize in the 1880s. More than a century ago, the exhibits were in tents or rustic wooden buildings; for example, the precursor to the Kansas State Fair was held in a downtown livery stable. Fairgoers could see livestock such as horses, cows, sheep, swine, and poultry; crops such as corn, wheat, oats, sugar cane, potatoes, and carrots; staples such as cheese, butter, preserves, honey, and baked goods; farm machinery and implements such as wagons, buggies, plows,

The grand champion mare from the 1912 Oregon State Fair.
Courtesy of the Oregon State Fair & Expo Center

turnip drills, and root slicers; and domestic goods, such as clothing and quilts. You could take a gander at fine arts, too: painting and drawing were included in some of these early events, as well.

The dining hall at the North Carolina State Fair of 1884. Courtesy of the N.C. Office of Archives and History

The fairs also offered an opportunity for recreation, to relax and escape the never-ending chores required to run a farm. Entertainment often included horse, mule, or pony racing, with the track as the central feature of the fairground. (The racing was taken quite seriously—carrier pigeons were employed to distribute the results from Maryland's early state fairs.) Even today, racing and horse shows continue to be an important component of state fairs. Other early attractions included baseball games and sack races, plowing and oxen contests. Many a greased pole was climbed—or at least attempted. Just like today, music was involved, with the local brass band performing. The pageantry of Native American dancing was featured at many of the western fairs. The highlight of the day's festivities was often a spectacular fireworks display.

Speechmaking and politicking came to be integral parts of the activities. In 1854, Senator Steven Douglas and his challenger, Abraham Lincoln, spoke on successive days at the Illinois State Fair. New York had two former presidents, Martin Van Buren and Millard Fillmore, speak in 1858. Famed orator William Jennings Bryan addressed the crowd at the North Carolina State Fair during one of his unsuccessful runs for the presidency in the early 1900s. Not to be outdone, local dignitaries also took a turn at the podium.

By design, many of the early fairs were held in a different location each year, because of the difficulty of long-distance travel in the 1800s. Moving the events from city to city allowed more residents of the state to attend and participate in the fair. (A century ago, it was common for families to camp in or near the fairgrounds, and some

Famous (and Infamous) Blue Ribbon Winners

Let's start with the well-behaved: Mormon leader Brigham Young, who led his fellow believers to a permanent home in Utah, was also a participant in the state's fair. He won a blue ribbon for Best Celery and took home $25 for Best Stallion.

Many famous (and well-behaved) animals were first exhibited at state fairs, but perhaps the most historically significant was an iron-gray yearling that won a blue ribbon in 1858. This colt was named Traveller, and of course he achieved great fame as the beloved mount of Confederate general Robert E. Lee. The colt was awarded the top prize at the precursor to the State Fair of West Virginia.

Now, to the not-so-well-behaved: Frank James, outlaw and brother to notorious bandit Jesse James, lived in Tennessee under an assumed name when he was on the lam. He claimed to have been awarded a blue ribbon during that time, but not for thievery—for raising champion Poland China hogs.

This proud winner poses with her prize—and her bull—in 1920. Courtesy of the Iowa State Fair

contemporary fairs still offer camping accommodations.) While some of the events settled rather quickly into a central location, others continued to be held in different parts of the state; as many as 12 cities hosted the Illinois fair during its infancy.

Just as women's handicrafts and household goods were perceived as vital to the success of the farm family, fairs soon began to recognize the importance of encouraging young people to continue the traditions of farming and farm life. Competitive exhibits by children were important additions to the fair's events, including the raising of livestock and produce and the production of handicrafts; early youth contests featured such things as butter making and

A Fair Bite to Eat

A good many state fairs were born as a means of promoting their region's agricultural bounty and the resulting cuisine. In fact, the very name "fair" is derived from the Latin word for feast, *feriae*.

Today, of course, certain foods are synonymous with the state fair experience, no matter the locale: funnel cakes, elephant ears, cotton candy, candy apples, all kinds of foods-on-a-stick. Others got their start at the fair, but have since transcended the midway to become firmly entrenched in the American diet. The St. Louis World's Fair of 1904, for instance, lays claim (but not without contention) to the introduction of the ice cream cone and the hot dog. And the corn dog is alleged to have made its debut in 1942 at the Texas state fairgrounds, invented by fair concessionaires. (Corn dog historians speculate that the corn meal coating was a nod to that other Texas favorite, the tamale—a fair favorite in its own right in that part of the country.)

Some fair delicacies, however, remain unique to their region of origin. The Slug Burger—a hamburger made from ground beef blended with protein meal, then deep-fried—can be found only in Corinth, Mississippi, where it's always a big seller at the North Mississippi Tri-State Fair. (The burger's name, by the way, refers not to a creepy crawly but to its original price—a single nickel, also known as a "slug.")

Fairgoers in Alaska enjoy halibut tacos, caribou-steak sandwiches, buffalo bratwurst, and spicy reindeer Polish dogs. Frog legs and alligator-

on-a-stick are popular in Louisiana. Yakisoba—fried Japanese noodles—are a big hit in the Pacific Northwest. And in Michigan, the Upper Peninsula State Fair just wouldn't be the Upper Peninsula State Fair without pasties: meat-and-rutabaga-pie sandwiches.

Resourceful fair concessionaires are always trying new treats. No one knows for sure who first stuck a stick in a candy bar, dipped it in funnel-cake batter, deep-fried it, and dusted it with sugar, but fried candy bars swept the fair scene in the late 1990s. For the adventurous eater with saltier tastes, fried pickles-on-sticks have been showing up around the country in recent years, too.

Courtesy of the Middle Georgia Archives, Washington Memorial Library, Macon, Georgia

penmanship. These exhibits emphasized the essential contributions to the family made by farm children, who by necessity worked in the fields and the barns. Today, entries in junior class categories can comprise the majority of a fair's exhibits.

While fairs provided a social outlet for farm families, they also offered the city slicker an opportunity to appreciate the achievements (and old-fashioned hard work) of the farmer. This function still holds true today, as the many exhibits demonstrate the vital role of agriculture in our economy.

It's a bird… it's a plane… it's something wonderous in the sky.
Courtesy of the Iowa State Fair

HOW THE FAIRS HAVE CHANGED

Some of the events that are now officially designed state fairs evolved from earlier regional affairs organized by agricultural societies or private individuals. Florida's fair, for instance, did not get an official designation until 1975. After railroad tycoon Henry B. Plant hosted horse races and exhibits for guests at his hotel in Tampa in 1898, this event evolved into the South Florida Fair, which eventually became the Florida State Fair.

This transition from local to regional to state fair was rather common, and of course there was spirited competition amongst the regional events; there was much rejoicing in Hutchinson, Kansas, when its fair was able to call itself the legitimate state fair in 1903. Still other fairs developed through a different set of circumstances. The Alaska State Fair in Palmer, one of five fairs held throughout the enormous state, grew from the homesteading efforts during the early 1900s. After two earlier attempts failed to

Courtesy of The State Fair of Louisiana

Courtesy of the Iowa State Fair

populate the Matanuska Valley, the federal government in 1935 established a farming community to develop that region of the state, as well as provide economic opportunities for families during the Depression. After their first year on the frontier, the settlers organized a celebration that included the ever-present horse racing, boxing matches, a rodeo, and agricultural exhibits; that tradition continues today.

Many fairs have operated continuously since their inception—more or less. Interruptions have occurred, most often during wartime. The facilities themselves were often pressed into service during these times of crisis; the

State Fairs…By the Numbers

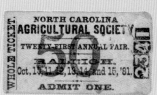
Courtesy of the N.C. Office of Archives and History

In 2000, the winning entry in the Alaska State Fair's Cabbage Weigh-Off was a record-breaking 106½-pound head. That's a *lot* of coleslaw.

There were over 50,000 lights on La Grande Wheel, the giant Ferris wheel at the 2002 Arizona State Fair. The ride accommodated 288 people at once, who took in the panoramic view from atop the 15-story structure.

It takes between 500 and 600 pounds of butter to sculpt the average butter cow. That's enough butter to slather about 50,000 biscuits! Early butter cows—which were made of solid butter, rather than butter packed on a chicken-wire frame—often required more than 800 pounds.

Georgia's first state fair, held in Stone Mountain in 1846, made a profit of $104. Admission was 10¢.

Wisconsin built a humdinger of an ice cream sundae at one of its recent fairs, using 20 gallons of Wisconsin ice cream and 14 pounds of hot fudge topping for the 100-foot-long concoction. It was estimated that you would need to lick 20,000 times to polish it off!

In 1894, the Illinois State Fair charged 50¢ for adults and $1.25 for a carriage of four. A person on horseback paid 75¢.

The hottest temperature ever recorded at the Iowa State Fair was 108°F. Unfortunately, it was on Older Iowans' Day, in 1983.

The private partners who purchased land for Michigan's state fair sold the 135 acres to the state agricultural society for $1 on April 18, 1905.

In addition to its state fair, Kansas held more than 240 events at its fairgrounds during 2001.

Hungry? Here are some impressive numbers from the 2002 Big E in Massachusetts: there were 34 tons of Maine potatoes baked; 18,200 pieces of blueberry pie sliced; 10,000 bread bowls filled with broccoli-cheese soup; and 6 tons of clam fritter mix fried.

The budget for the first Iowa State Fair was $323. The city of Raleigh, North Carolina, contributed $25 toward that state's first fair in 1853.

Michigan's Miracle of Life exhibit is a favorite with children, as you can well imagine. A couple of years ago, delighted kids watched 12 calves, 59 piglets, 300 chicks, 50 quail, 12 turkeys, and 40 lambs come into the world during the fair.

A 586-pound monster recently won the Great Pumpkin Contest, held every year during the Virginia State Fair. That's a *lot* of pies.

Confederacy seized South Carolina's state fair buildings and manufactured arms there, though Union forces later burned the buildings. In 1918, the United States Army established a camp for aviators at the Texas Fair Park, and no fair was held that year. During World War II, Kentucky's fairground became an assembly plant, and Oregon's facilities housed military personnel. Kansas's state fair supported the war effort in other ways: at the 1942 fair, participants sold war bonds and held a "Scrap Day," when free admission was offered for donations of scrap metal. Outbreaks of disease, like measles, have affected attendance through the years, and some fairs ceased operation during epidemics of influenza and polio.

Courtesy of the N.C. Office of Archives and History

PUTTING IT ALL TOGETHER

Even today, some states have no officially designed fair. Of this group, a few have more than one event that includes "state fair" as part of its name, but the central idea of all these remains the same: a celebration of the state, its products, and its citizens. Modern fairs are organized in a variety of ways. In Connecticut, the citizens enjoy a series of local fairs rather than one central event, and the Big E, held in West Springfield, Massachusetts, is unique in that it serves the six New England states. Each state owns its own structure and property along the fair's "Avenue of the States," allowing fairgoers to truly visit each participating state.

Courtesy of The State Fair of Louisiana

Funding and organization of the events differ from state to state. Many fairs are supported and funded by a state agency; others, like those in Georgia and South Carolina, are run by private organizations that distribute the fair's proceeds to charities. Still others are incorporated as nonprofit organizations, like the State Fair of Texas, which provides a

Courtesy of the Middle Georgia Archives, Washington Memorial Library, Macon, Georgia

Courtesy of The State Fair of Louisiana

number of college scholarships each year for both fair participants and students who attend local high schools.

Contemporary fairs continue to support the agricultural community, but their purposes have grown to include showcasing the entirety of the state, including its industrial and technological achievements. The legislation that governs Michigan's fair says that its event will "promote all phases of the economy…and encourage and demonstrate agricultural, industrial, commercial, and recreational pursuits." Indeed, a fair can have a tremendous economic impact on the state; Iowa's fair is the largest event (and tourist attraction) in the state and contributes an estimated $50 to $60 million to the state's economy. Facilities at the fairgrounds—like racetracks,

Mr. Ferris's Wheel

Americans just don't like to be outdone. So when the United States hosted the 1893 World's Colombian Exposition in Chicago, a team of engineers got together for some serious brainstorming. Their job was to come up with a project that would rival France's grand Eiffel Tower, which had been designed and built for the 1889 World's Fair in Paris. Unfortunately, the ideas presented were disappointing, failing to "meet the expectations of the people." Until, that is, George Washington Ferris Jr., bridge builder and owner of an iron- and steel-testing company, had an inspiration.

By some accounts, Ferris got his idea by looking at another carnival favorite, the carousel (or merry-go-round), despite that fact that a manually powered, 50-foot-tall wheel made its debut at the New York State Fair in 1849. Ferris, however, envisioned an enormous vertical wheel. He's said to have sketched the plan for the first Ferris wheel on a napkin at an engineers' banquet.

The completed wheel stood 264 feet tall. Two 140-foot steel towers supported its 250-foot-diameter wheel; twin

Courtesy of the Iowa State Fair

1,000-horsepower motors propelled it. Thirty-six wooden carts, carrying up to 2,160 passengers, moved a full revolution every 10 minutes. The entire mechanical marvel cost $380,000 to build, a fortune at the time. But at 50¢ a ride, Ferris's wheel paid for itself twice over by the end of the exhibition.

The original Ferris wheel made another appearance at the 1904 World's Fair in St. Louis, but was then disassembled and sold to metal dealers. Ferris's visionary design lives on at every fair in the United States and in many other countries, too. And today, the Ferris wheel is still in competition with the Eiffel Tower—for most romantic place to pop the question.

exhibit halls, and coliseums—are used throughout the year and continue to generate income and provide employment after the fair's run is over for the year.

Though it has changed with the times, the spirit of today's state fair remains the same. The fair is still the year's most thrilling event, full of family fun, quality entertainment, and innovative exhibits. While you can still hear hog calling, you'll also hear karaoke. You can watch a harness race as if it were 1885, or you can opt for the excitement of twenty-first-century motorcycle stunts. And the standard of excellence that was established in the early fairs continues today for the competitive exhibits, in which only the best entry is awarded the blue ribbon.

Courtesy of the Iowa State Fair

Courtesy of the Iowa State Fair

Courtesy of the Indiana State Fair

Courtesy of the Middle Georgia Archives, Washington Memorial Library, Macon, Georgia

Winning the Prize

An impressive display of afghans at the fair.
Photo by Steve Shaluta, courtesy of The State
Fair of West Virginia

COMPETITIVE EVENTS at the state fair were designed for inspiration and innovation, to reward quality and creativity in the production of goods or the raising of livestock. In a large modern fair, it's not unusual to have more than 50,000 exhibits, with around 30,000 blue ribbons awarded. In Elkanah Watson's 1813 show, 15 prizes were awarded to women, mostly for clothing items. Today, many fairs have more than 15 different categories for crocheted items alone! A needlework department may have over 200 classes, including everything from weaving to machine embroidery.

HONORING CROCHET

The focus of this book, crochet, is first mentioned as a competitive category in the 1880s. Interestingly enough, the development of state fairs and the widespread popularity of crochet occurred at roughly the same time, the middle of the nineteenth century. Theories vary on the development of the art of crochet itself, but by the 1820s patterns began to appear in Dutch magazines, and by the 1840s crochet books were published. Though there's little history on its introduction to this country, it was obviously embraced in the United States as it was in Europe. It was an inexpensive and relatively quick way to make both functional and beautiful items, like warm mittens, hats, and shawls, as well as to decorate clothing and linens with affordable lace. The tool—the hook—was easily made, and thread or yarn was relatively cheap, so it was a very appealing handicraft for women on the farm.

Fair Treat: Cotton Candy

Believe it or not, we have a dentist to thank for that perennial fair treat, cotton candy. In 1897, Dr. William Morrison of Nashville, Tennessee, and his partner, John C. Wharton, invented a contraption that melted sugar to liquid, then used centrifugal force to squeeze it through tiny holes in a metal plate. When the sugar came out the other side, it immediately solidified into thin, cottony threads, which the candy makers termed "fairy floss." (Short for "Tooth Fairy floss," perhaps?) The enterprising gentlemen introduced their concoction at the St. Louis World's Fair in 1904, where they sold over 68,000 boxes of the stuff—for 25¢ a pop. That was half the cost of admission to the fair!

Cotton candy, the name that came in vogue during the 1920s, is still a big moneymaker for fair concessionaires, and it's made in much the same way that Dr. Morrison devised. The average 3-ounce bag consists of nothing more than a few teaspoons of sugar blended with a hint of flavoring and color, yet it sells for as much as $3.50 a bag. That's a lot of cash for a spoonful of sugar.

In fact, the ever-popular granny square motif is an American innovation, thought to have developed from a need to utilize every available scrap of material. A warm afghan could have been made from many squares of differently colored yarn, intriguing in design and downright practical in creation. Today, it's hard to find a state fair without a granny square category in its crochet competitions, which still honor the contribution of that anonymous frontier craftsperson.

The blue ribbon winners in this book were judged on a number of criteria, varying from state to state, but excellence in execution is common to all. North Carolina's standards provide a good example: out of a total of 100 possible points, 25 can be awarded for the general appearance of the article, including design and color; 60 for workmanship, including uniformity and technique; and 15 for presentation. The standards for New York's Arts and Crafts Division are similar, with 60 percent of the total score allotted to workmanship. Skill and attention to detail are prerequisites, and accomplished crochet artists and designers judge the contests.

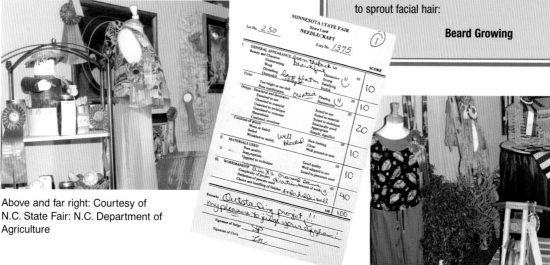

Above and far right: Courtesy of
N.C. State Fair: N.C. Department of
Agriculture

Fair Folly

Fastest pig, biggest pumpkin, cutest baby, best Elvis impersonation—these are all standard fare at many state fairs, including Iowa. But in the Hawkeye State, even if your dahlias droop or your cake crumbles, you still have dozens of opportunities to come home with a first-place prize in *something*. Following are just a few of the contests that have been open to Iowans with more unusual talents:

Rubber Chicken Throwing

Egg Rolling

Sidewalk Bowling

Bubble Gum Blowing

Cow Chip Throwing

Accordion Soloing

Solo Yodeling

Yo-Yo-ing

Joke Telling

Whistling

Pairs' Pie Eating

Hog Calling

Diaper Decorating

Children's Mom Calling

Ladies' Husband Calling

And finally, for those with no other talent than the ability to sprout facial hair:

Beard Growing

17

Presenting the

Blue Ribbon Afghans

Winners

NORTHEAST   DEEP SOUTH

MIDWEST   FAR WEST

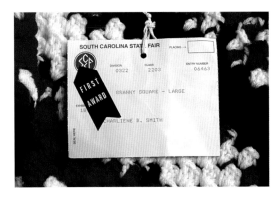

THE GIFTED CROCHETERS celebrated in *Blue Ribbon Afghans from America's State Fairs* epitomize the highest ideals of the state fair, where only the most talented, most innovative, and most skilled are awarded the highest honors. They're a diverse group, with representatives from every region of the country, and their stories and their talent unfold in the pages that follow. One winner took home a blue ribbon with her very first afghan, while others have had years of success, winning dozens of ribbons. Many, too, have won Best of Show awards. While some were self-taught, others learned the craft from a kind and patient loved one. Several of the blue ribbon winners are multitalented, taking home ribbons in other pursuits such as canning, tatting, baking, and gardening.

But it's their devotion to crochet that's honored here. While they no longer have to crochet from necessity like early farmwomen, they carry on the tradition of making useful, lovely items that are often gifts of the heart and hands. Indeed, many of these prize-winning afghans were made specifically for family or friends, and thus many of the blue ribbon winners have special anecdotes to share about them. Still others are eloquent spokespeople for their craft, hoping that their success inspires others to take up crochet.

Sixteen of the designs are original, so take some time to admire the pieces that have been created, not by professional designers, but rather by dedicated practitioners of the art. Other blue ribbon winners used patterns that were first published elsewhere, and these have been reprinted here with the gracious cooperation of the original designers. (For more on these companies, see page 157.) One prizewinner kept a pattern for 20 years, until a granddaughter's request for an afghan prompted her to use it for her blue ribbon project.

This isn't a learn-to-crochet book. Instead, the afghans included here showcase the craft, and all the classic stitches—ripple, afghan, popcorn, shell—are on display. Some feature cross-stitch, embroidery, or appliqué, and of course, there's an interesting selection of designs that feature our homegrown granny square. While most of these are full-size afghans, there are plenty of designs to keep baby warm and snuggly, too. The instructions assume that you are already proficient in the craft and don't need basic lessons in technique.

Many of these beautiful pieces were created several years before this book was written, with little thought of winning a blue ribbon, much less being published in a book. For instance, some of the prizewinners who created original afghans committed their instructions to paper only when they were selected for this book, and every attempt has been made to provide accurate instructions and yarn requirements. For your convenience, crochet abbreviations have been standardized to the greatest degree possible: see the abbreviation chart on page 158.

Courtesy of the New York State Fair

So, here's what you'll find in the pages ahead: First, instructions for 45 afghans. Many of the prize-winning crocheters added their own personal touches to the afghans; any variations to the pattern are noted also. As we have published the instructions as originally written, keep in mind that yarn requirements may vary if the artist altered the pattern. The afghan chapter is followed by profiles of the prizewinners; general information about each individual state fair, including contact information and dates of operation; and a section on the pattern designers and/or companies.

As you read the book, remember that these blue ribbon winners carry on a tradition of excellence that was established over a century ago, when the first piece of crochet was recognized as the finest in its class. Not only are these winners the very best at their chosen craft, they are also the pride of their state.

Grape Arbor

Samantha Kline

This beautiful granny square variation features three variegated rounds, followed by a fourth in a solid shade. The squares are artfully arranged in this memorable afghan.

Materials & Tools
Worsted-weight yarn, approximately:
- 42 oz. white
- 72 oz. variegated
- 30 oz. in each of two solid colors, chosen from variegated shades

Size F crochet hook

Gauge
5 sc = 1 in.; one square = 3¼ in.

Finished size
Approximately 73½ x 84 in.

INSTRUCTIONS
Pattern is four-round granny squares. The first three rounds are made from variegated yarn, while the fourth is a solid color.

GRANNY SQUARE
With variegated yarn, ch 8, join to form ring.

Rnd 1: Ch 3, 2 dc into round, making 3. (Ch 2, 3 dc) 3 times into ring, ch 2, join with sl st. Ch 3, turn.

Rnd 2: 2 dc into ch-2 sp. (Ch 2, 3 dc) into ch-2 sp around. Join with sl st.

Rnd 3: Ch 3, turn. Repeat rnd 2. Cut yarn and work into end.

Rnd 4: Repeat rnd 3 with solid color yarn. Cut yarn and work into end (280 squares with white border, 112 squares with dark sage border, 112 squares with dark plum border).

ASSEMBLY
Sew squares as shown in the photo, using white yarn when matching white squares. Use variegated yarn or solid color yarn as appropriate.

Original Design

Ripple Afghan

Thelma H. Berkley

This prizewinner is created from instructions passed down through Thelma's family. She adjusts the pattern each time she makes this design, depending upon the size of the afghan.

Materials & Tools
Worsted-weight yarn, approximately:
 10 oz. variegated
 20 oz. aqua

Crochet hook size F, or size
 to match gauge

Gauge
10 sc = 2½ in.

Finished size
Approximately 54 x 60 in.

INSTRUCTIONS
Note: Work in back loop only for ripple ridge, **except** *work under both threads in the first and last 2 sts of each row (to prevent edge from curling).*

Ch 305.

Row 1: Sk first ch from hook, work sc in next 2 chs, sk 1 ch. *Sc in next 11 chs, 3 sc in next ch, sc in next 11 chs, sk 2 chs. Rep from * 11 times, the last time sk only 1 sc at end of point and sc in the last 2 chs.

Row 2: Ch 1, turn, work sc in next 2 sc, sk 1 sc. *Sc in next 11 sc, 3 sc in next sc, sc in next 11 sc, sk 2 sc. Rep from * 11 times, the last time sk only 1 sc at end of point and sc in the last 2 sc.

Rep row 2 for the rest of the afghan, using color combination of your choice.

Traditional Design

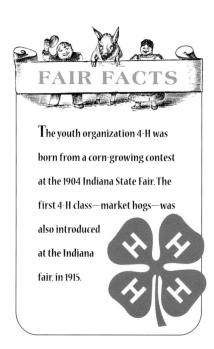

FAIR FACTS

The youth organization 4-H was born from a corn-growing contest at the 1904 Indiana State Fair. The first 4-H class—market hogs—was also introduced at the Indiana fair, in 1915.

Diamond Story

Vickie lets her muse lead her to design; this clever geometric afghan was inspired by a paint advertisement. She often looks to her environment for ideas.

Vickie P. Story

Materials & Tools

Worsted-weight yarn, approximately:
 54 oz. cream
 28 oz. blue

Crochet hook size E, or size to
 match gauge

Tapestry needle

Gauge
One granny square = 2 in.

Finished size
Approximately 44 x 70 in.

GRANNY SQUARE

Ch 4, join with a sl st to form a ring.

Rnd 1: Ch 3 (counts as first dc), 2 dc in ring; * ch 2, 3 dc in ring; rep from * twice more; ch 2, join with sl st in top of beg ch-3.

Rnd 2: Sl st in each of next 2 dc, sl st into ch-2 corner sp; ch 3, in same sp work (2 dc, ch 2, 3 dc); * in next corner sp work (3 dc, ch 2, 3 dc), rep from * twice more; join with sl st in top of beg ch-3; finish off and weave in ends.

AFGHAN

Following granny square instructions, make 401 squares with cream and 188 with blue. Afghan has 31 rows with 19 squares in each row. Following color arrangement chart (figure 1), join squares according to joining instructions that follow.

JOINING

Thread appropriate color yarn in tapestry needle. Holding 2 squares with right sides together, join with overcast st in outer loops only. Work across each square, carefully matching sts. Join all squares in this manner whether joining squares for a row or joining rows of squares.

EDGING

With right side facing you, join cream with a sl st in any corner sp of afghan, ch 3.

Rnd 1: Work 2 dc in same corner sp; ch 2, 3 dc in same sp—corner worked. Ch 1; 3 dc in ch-2 sp between groups of 3 dc. Continue in this pattern until you have completed cream around the whole afghan. Join with sl st; finish off and weave in ends.

Rnd 2: Join blue at corner, work sc in top of corner st; ch 1; sc in same st—corner made. Sc in top of each st working corner pat at the corners. When you have completed blue around the whole afghan join with sl st; finish off and weave in ends.

Original Design

□ white
■ blue

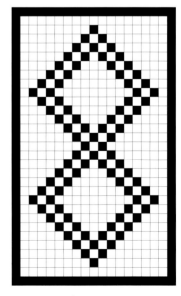

Figure 1

Blue Ribbon Afghans from America's State...

Samantha Kline

Purple Shades

Here's another blue ribbon afghan from Samantha. This one, in inviting shades of plum, features a multitude of granny squares in varying sizes.

Materials & Tools

Worsted-weight yarn, approximately:
 18 oz. black
 24 oz. each of lavender, light
  plum, and plum

Crochet hook size F

Gauge

5 sc = 1 in.; 5-rnd center
 black granny square = 4¼ in.

Finished size

Approximately 52 x 52 in.

INSTRUCTIONS

Make granny squares per Samantha's directions on page 22.

With black, make center square of 5-rnd granny square, surrounded by four 2-rnd granny squares of each color as shown in photo below.

With black, work 2 rnds of sc. Make four squares of each remaining color, with 3 rnds color, 1 rnd black, and 1 more rnd of same color.

Then, 3 rnds dc in black, lavender, light plum, plum, and black again, in that order.

Make eight squares each of lavender, light plum, and plum, with 3 rnds color, 2 black, and 2 color. Join with plum squares on corners. Then, using black, 3 rnds dc border.

Make 4-rnd granny squares (eight black and 16 of each color). Join with black on corners, then plum, light plum, lavender, plum, light plum, lavender, black in that order, alternating around the afghan.

FINISHING

With black, 2 rnds of sc. Add 6-in. fringe corresponding to the color of the square.

Original Design

Romantic Rose

Carol Joan Fritz

Carol's lovely afghan illustrates the simple beauty that a single color can lend; she says this was a pleasure to crochet.

Materials & Tools

Worsted-weight yarn, approximately:
  63 oz. rose pink

Size G crochet hook, or size
  to match gauge

Gauge
4 sc and 4 sc rows = 1 in.

Finished size
Approximately 46 x 62 in.

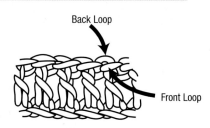

Back Loop

Front Loop

Figure 1

Working in front or back loops—To work "in front loop only" or "in back loop only," instead of working under both loops of the stitch, insert hook only under front loop (loop toward you) or only under back loop (loop away from you.)

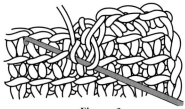

Figure 2

Double crochets and popcorn stitches are worked in the front loop of stitch of second row below one being worked.

INSTRUCTIONS

Note: Work each row separately, leaving about 6 in. of yarn at each end for fringe. Do not turn work. Fasten off at end of each row and cut yarn. All scs are worked in back loop of st (see figure 1). All dcs and popcorn sts are worked in front loop of st of second row below one being worked (see figure 2).

For ease in following, total number of sc and dc to work have been given—remember to fasten off at end of each row. To change length of afghan, work beg ch in a multiple of 22 and then add 7 more chs.

Popcorn st—yo, insert hook in front loop (fl) of st 2 rows below, yo, pull through st, yo, pull through 2 loops on hook, (yo, insert hook in same fl of st 2 rows below, yo, pull through st, yo, pull through 2 loops on hook) twice, yo, insert hook in same fl of st 2 rows below, yo, pull through st, yo, pull through 2 loops on hook, yo, pull through all loops on hook.

Row 1: Ch 249. Fasten off. Join with sc in first ch, sc in each ch across. Fasten off. (249)

Rows 2–4: Join with sc in first st, sc in each st across. Fasten off.

Row 5: Join with sc in back loop of first st, sc in back loop of next 13 sts, dc in front loop of next st 2 rows below, (sc in back loop of each of next 21 sts, dc in front loop of next st 2 rows below) 10 times, sc in back loop of last 14 sc. Fasten off.

From now on abbreviations will be used for ease in following. Remember to fasten off at end of each row.

Row 6: 13 sc, dc, sc, dc, (19 sc, dc, sc, dc) 10 times, 13 sc.

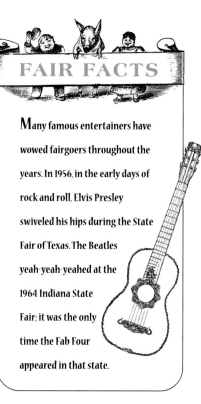

FAIR FACTS

Many famous entertainers have wowed fairgoers throughout the years. In 1956, in the early days of rock and roll, Elvis Presley swiveled his hips during the State Fair of Texas. The Beatles yeah-yeah-yeahed at the 1964 Indiana State Fair; it was the only time the Fab Four appeared in that state.

Row 7: 12 sc, dc, 3 sc, dc, (17 sc, dc, 3 sc, dc) 10 times, 12 sc.

Row 8: 11 sc, dc, 5 sc, dc, (15 sc, dc, 5 sc, dc) 10 times, 11 sc.

Row 9: 10 sc, dc, 7 sc, dc, (13 sc, dc, 7 sc, dc) 10 times, 10 sc.

Row 10: 9 sc, dc, (4 sc, dc) twice, *11 sc, dc, (4 sc, dc) twice, repeat from * 9 more times, 9 sc.

Row 11: 8 sc, dc, 4 sc, dc, sc, dc, 4 sc, dc, (9 sc, dc, 4 sc, dc, sc, dc, 4 sc, dc) 10 times, 8 sc.

Row 12: (7 sc, dc, 4 sc, dc, 3 sc, dc, 4 sc, dc) 11 times, 7 sc.

Romantic Rose

Row 13: 6 sc, dc, 4 sc, dc, (5 sc, dc, 4 sc, dc) 21 times, 6 sc.

Row 14: 5 sc, dc, 4 sc, dc, 7 sc, dc, 4 sc, dc, (3 sc, dc, 4 sc, dc, 7 sc, dc, 4 sc, dc) 10 times, 5 sc.

Row 15: (4 sc, dc) twice, 9 sc, dc, 4 sc, dc, (sc, dc, 4 sc, dc, 9 sc, dc, 4 sc, dc) 10 times, 4 sc.

Row 16: 3 sc, dc, (21 sc, dc) 11 times, 3 sc.

Row 17: (4 sc, dc) 5 times, *sc, dc, (4 sc, dc) 4 times, rep from * 9 more times, 4 sc.

Row 18: 5 sc, dc, 4 sc, dc, 2 sc, dc, sc, dc, 2 sc, dc, 4 sc, dc, (3 sc, dc, 4 sc, dc, 2 sc, dc, sc, dc, 2 sc, dc, 4 sc, dc) 10 times, 5 sc.

Row 19: 6 sc, dc, 4 sc, dc in front loop of each of next 2 sts 2 rows below, 3 sc, dc in front loop of each of next 2 sts 2 rows below, 4 sc, dc, (5 sc, dc, 4 sc, dc in front loop of each of next 2 sts 2 rows below, 3 sc, dc in front loop of each of next 2 sts 2 rows below, 4 sc, dc) 10 times, 6 sc.

Row 20: 7 sc, dc, 13 sc, dc, (7 sc, dc, 13 sc, dc) 10 times, 7 sc.

Row 21: 8 sc, dc, 11 sc, dc, (9 sc, dc, 11 sc, dc) 10 times, 8 sc.

Row 22: (9 sc, dc) twice, (4 sc, dc, sc, dc, 4 sc, dc, 9 sc, dc) 10 times, 9 sc.

Row 23: 10 sc, dc, 7 sc, dc, *4 sc, dc, (sc, dc) twice, 4 sc, dc, 7 sc, dc, rep from * 9 more times, 10 sc.

Row 24: 11 sc, dc, 5 sc, dc, (6 sc, dc, sc, dc, 6 sc, dc, 5 sc, dc) 10 times, 11 sc.

Row 25: 12 sc, dc, 3 sc, dc, (4 sc, dc, 7 sc, dc, 4 sc, dc, 3 sc, dc) 10 times, 12 sc.

Row 26: 13 sc, dc, sc, dc, (4 sc, dc, sc, dc, 5 sc, dc, sc, dc, 4 sc, dc, sc, dc) 10 times, 13 sc.

Row 27: 14 sc, dc, (6 sc, dc, 3 sc, popcorn st in fl of next st two rows below, 3 sc, dc, 6 sc, dc) 10 times, 14 sc.

Row 28: 13 sc, dc, sc, dc, (4 sc, dc, sc, dc, 5 sc, dc, sc, dc, 4 sc, dc, sc, dc) 10 times, 13 sc.

Row 29: 12 sc, dc, 3 sc, dc, (4 sc, dc, 7 sc, dc, 4 sc, dc, 3 sc, dc) 10 times, 12 sc.

Row 30: 11 sc, dc, 5 sc, dc, (6 sc, dc, sc, dc, 6 sc, dc, 5 sc, dc) 10 times, 11 sc.

Row 31: 10 sc, dc, 7 sc, dc, *4 sc, dc, (sc, dc) twice, 4 sc, dc, 7 sc, dc, rep from * 9 more times, 10 sc.

Row 32: 9 sc, dc, (4 sc, dc) twice, *4 sc, dc, sc, dc, 4 sc, dc, (4 sc, dc) twice, rep from * 9 more times, 9 sc.

Rows 33–164: Rep rows 11–32 six times.

Rows 165–175: Rep rows 11–21.

Row 176: 9 sc, dc, (9 sc, dc, 11 sc, dc) 10 times, 9 sc, dc, 9 sc.

Row 177: 10 sc, dc, (7 sc, dc, 13 sc, dc) 10 times, 7 sc, dc, 10 sc.

Row 178: 11 sc, dc, (5 sc, dc, 15 sc, dc) 10 times, 5 sc, dc, 11 sc.

Row 179: 12 sc, dc, (3 sc, dc, 17 sc, dc) 10 times, 3 sc, dc, 12 sc.

Row 180: 13 sc, dc, (sc, dc, 19 sc, dc) 10 times, sc, dc, 13 sc.

Row 181: 14 sc, dc, (21 sc, dc) 10 times, 14 sc.

Rows 182–184: Sc in each st across. Fasten off.

FRINGE

Pull a 12-in. strand of yarn halfway through each end of each row. Tie the three strands at the end of each row together with an overhand knot. Lay afghan on flat surface; comb out fringe with fingers. Trim evenly.

Designer: Carol Hegar for Shady Lane Original Crochet Designs. If you like this pattern, you will find similar ones from Shady Lane at their website, www.shadylane.com.

Sunbonnet Sue

Karen Marie Massey

Karen loves to see afghans come to life with color as seen in this vivid blue ribbon winner, with its bright blocks set against a black background.

Materials & Tools
Worsted-weight yarn, approximately:
> For background—34 oz. black
> For each block—25 yds. bonnet, sleeve, stocking color; 25 yds. dress, shoe color; 1 yd. hand color
> For border—80 yards of each color of choice (A and B)

Crochet hook size F, or size to match gauge

Gauge
4 dc = 1 in.; 2 dc rows = 1 in.

Finished size
Approximately 41 x 72 in. (Doll is 7 in. tall; block = 12 in. square.)

Notes: Work all loose ends in as you go and clip unless otherwise stated. This does not take on the shape of a square until rnd 4 of Background.

BLOCK
Sleeve
Row 1: With Sleeve color, ch 3, sc in second ch from hook, sc in last ch, turn. (2 sc made)

Row 2: Ch 1, sc in each st across, turn.

Row 3: Ch 1, 2 sc in first st, sc in last st, turn. (3)

Sunbonnet Sue

Row 4: Ch 1, sc in each st across, turn.

Row 5: Ch 1, sc in first sc, 2 sc in next st, sc in last st, turn. (4)

Row 6: Ch 1, 2 sc in first st, sc in next 2 sts, 2 sc in last st, turn. (6)

Row 7: Ch 1, sc in each st across, turn.

Row 8: Ch 1, sk first st, sc in next st, (sk next st, sc in next st) 2 times, turn. (3)

Row 9: Ch 1, sk first 2 sts, sc in last st. Fasten off.

Hand

Row 1: With Hand color, go back to beginning of Sleeve, sc in each of 2 rem loops of starting ch at bottom of sts on row 1, turn.

Row 2: Ch 1, sc in first st, sl st in last st. Fasten off. Lay Sleeve aside until called for in pattern.

Bonnet

Row 1: With Bonnet color, ch 11, dc in fourth ch from hook, dc in next 3 chs, 2 dc in next ch, hdc in next ch, sc in next ch, sl st in next ch, turn. (10 sts made)

Row 2: Sk first st, sl st in next st, sc in next st, hdc in next st, dc in next st, 2 dc in next st, dc in next 3 sts, 2 dc in last st, turn. (11 sts)

Row 3: (Ch 3, dc) in first st, (dc in next 2 sts, 2 dc in next st) 2 times, hdc in next st, sc in next st, sl st in next st, sl st in beginning of row 2, sl st in very first ch of Bonnet. (15 sts)

Row 4: There are seven rem loops of the starting ch across bottom of row 1, 2 hdc in each ch across, turn. (14 hdc)

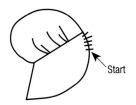

Figure 1

Row 5: (Ch 3, dc) in first st, (dc in next 2 sts, 2 dc in next st) 3 times, hdc in next st, sc in next st, sk next st st, sl st in next st, turn. (17 sts)

Row 6: Sk first 2 sts, hdc in each st across, turn.

Row 7: Ch 3, sk next st, dc in next st) 6 times, turn.

Row 8: (Sk next 2 sts, sc in next st) 2 times. Fasten off.

Dress

Row 1: With Dress color, starting at bottom edge of Bonnet brim (see figure 1), working in *back loops*, make 5 sc in bottom edge of Bonnet brim *(you will be working in the last 4 sts of row 3 and the first hdc of row 4)*, turn. (5 sc made)

Row 2: (Ch 3, dc) in first st, dc in next st; place top of Sleeve on other side of work (see figure 2), dc in next st and last st of Sleeve at same time (this joins Sleeve to Dress), dc in next st, 2 dc in last st, turn. (7 dc)

Row 3: (Ch 3, dc) in first st, dc in next 4 sts, 2 dc in next st, dc in last st, turn. (9)

Row 4: (Ch 3, dc) in first st, dc in next 6 sts, 2 dc in next st, dc in last st, turn. (11)

Row 5: (Ch 3, dc) in first st, dc in next 8 sts, 2 dc in next st, dc in last st, turn. (13)

Row 6: (Ch 3, dc) in first st, dc in next 10 sts, 2 dc in next st, dc in last st, turn. (15)

Row 7: (Ch 2, sc) in first st, sc in next st, hdc in next 3 sts, dc in next 2 sts, 2 dc in next st, dc in next 2 sts, hdc in next 3 sts, sc in next st, 2 sc in last st. Fasten off. (18 sts)

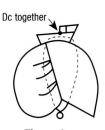

Dc together

Figure 2

Stocking

Row 1: With Stocking color, working in back loops, sc in middle 4 sts of last row of Dress, turn. (4 sc made)

Row 2: Ch 1, sc in each st across. Fasten off.

Shoe

Row 1: With Shoe color, work a sc in back loop of each st of last row, turn. (4 sc made)

Row 2: Ch 1, sc in first 3 sts, 2 sc in last st. Fasten off.

Tack Hand in place on Dress.

Background

Rnd 1: See figure 3 for the placement of stitches on this first rnd. Always try to work in a *back loop* when attaching background stitches to doll.

Dots are numbered to help you follow the directions on this first rnd. Starting at dot 1, with Background color, work the following in each dot:

Dot 1: 3 sc.

Dot 2: 3 dc.

Dot 3: 3 tr.

Dot 4: 3 dtr.

Dot 5: 3 ttr.

Dot 6: 3 dc.

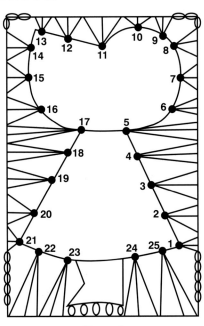

Figure 3

Dot 7: 3 hdc.

Dot 8: 3 dc, ch 3.

Dot 9: 3 hdc.

Dot 10: 3 hdc.

Dot 11: 3 dc.

Dot 12: 3 hdc.

Dot 13: 3 sc, ch 3.

Dot 14: 3 dc.

Dot 15: 3 dc.

Dot 16: 3 tr.

Dot 17: 3 ttr.

Dot 18: 3 dtr.

Dot 19: 3 tr.

Dot 20: 3 dc.

Dot 21: 3 sc, ch 6.

Dot 22: 3 ttr.

Dot 23: 3 dtr.

Sc in each of 5 sts across bottom of foot.

Dot 24: 3 dtr.

Dot 25: 3 ttr.

Ch 6, sc in first sc of dot 1.

Clusters of three have been formed down each side of doll.

Rnd 2: Ch 4, 2 tr in same place as ch-4, 3 tr in sp between each cluster of rnd 1 up to first ch-3, 2 tr in ch-3 sp, ch 4, 3 sc in ch-3 sp, sc in each of next 14 sts, 3 sc in ch-3 sp, ch 4, 2 tr in ch-3 sp, 3 tr between each cluster up to ch-6 sp, 3 tr in first ch, sk 1 ch, tr in each of next 3 chs, ch 4, sc in next ch, sc in next 3 ttr,

sc in next 3 dtr, sc in next 5 sc, sc in next 3 dtr, sc in next 3 ttr, sc in first ch, ch 4, tr in next 3 ch, join with sl st in top of first ch-4.

Rnd 3: (Ch 4, 2 tr) in first st, 3 tr between each cluster up to ch-4, ch 5, 3 sc in ch-4 sp, sc in each sc across, 3 sc in ch-4 sp, ch 5, 3 tr between each cluster up to next ch-4 sp, ch 5, 3 sc in ch-4 sp, sc in each sc across, 4 sc in ch-4 sp, ch 5, join. Fasten off.

Rnd 4: Join Bonnet color with sl st in last ch-5 sp, ch 3, 2 dc in same place, 3 dc between each cluster of rnd 3, (3 dc, ch 2, 3 dc) in ch-5 sp, (sk 2 sc, 3 dc in next sc) 8 times, (3 dc, ch 2, 3 dc) in ch-5 sp, 3 dc between each cluster down side, (3 dc, ch 2, 3 dc) in ch-5 sp, (sk 2 sc, 3 dc in next) 8 times, 3 dc in ch-5 sp, ch 2, sl st in top of ch-3. Fasten off.

Rnd 5: Join Dress color with (sl st, ch 3, 2 dc) in last ch-2 sp, 3 dc between each cluster of previous rnd and (3 dc, ch 2, 3 dc) in each ch-2 sp, ending with 3 dc in ch-2 sp, ch 2, sl st in top of ch-3. Fasten off.

Rnd 6: Join Background color with (sl st, ch 3, 2 dc) in last ch-2 sp, 3 dc between each cluster of previous rnd and (3 dc, ch 2, 3 dc) in each ch-2 sp, ending with 3 dc in ch-2 sp, ch 1, dc in top of ch-3—joining ch sp made.

Rnd 7: Ch 3, 2 dc in same place, 3 dc between each cluster of previous rnd and (3 dc, ch 2, 3 dc) in each ch-2 sp, ending with 3 dc in ch-2 sp, ch 1, dc in top of ch-3. Fasten off.

AFGHAN

15 blocks, three wide by five long. Sew or crochet together.

Border

Rnd 1: Join Background color with sl st in a corner ch-2 sp, ch 3, 2 dc in same place, 3 dc between each cluster, in places where Blocks are joined work 1 dc in ch-2 sp, 1 dc in seam where Blocks are joined together and 1 dc in next ch-2 sp, work (3 dc, ch 2, 3 dc) in all corner ch-2 sps. End with 3 dc in ch-2 sp, ch 1, dc in top of ch-3—joining ch sp made.

Rnd 2: (Ch 3, 2 dc) in first ch sp, 3 dc in between each cluster of last rnd and (3 dc, ch 2, 3 dc) in each ch-2 sp, ending with 3 dc in ch-2 sp—joining ch sp made. Fasten off.

Rnd 3: With color A, join with sl st in joining ch sp and repeat rnd 2.

Rnd 4: With color B, join with sl st in sp joining ch sp and repeat rnd 2.

Rnd 5: With Background color, join with sl st and repeat rnd 2.

Alteration: Since Karen loves color, she increased the size of this afghan to add one more row of blocks. This allowed her to create symmetry among the motifs.

Pattern Courtesy of Annie's Attic

Rosebud

Jacquelynn A. Copenhaver

Jacquelynn must be a fan of yellow roses, for she changed the colors in this pattern that was designed to highlight the beauty of the bloom.

Materials & Tools

Sport-weight yarn, approximately:
  11 oz. variegated
  12 ounces white

Crochet hook size G, or size to match gauge

Tapestry needle

Gauge

Triangle measures 6 in. along each side.

Finished size

Approximately 39 x 43 in.

TRIANGLE (Make 66)

With variegated ch 5; join with a sl st to form a ring.

Rnd 1: *Ch 3, 3 dc in ring, remove hook from loop, insert hook into top of ch-3 and into dropped loop, draw loop through ch—beg cluster made; ch 3; * 4 dc in ring, remove hook from loop. insert hook into first of the 4 dc and into dropped, loop, draw loop through dc—cluster made; ch 3; rep from * 4 more times; join to beg cluster (6 clusters). Fasten off.*

Rnd 2: Join white in any ch-3 sp. Ch 3, 8 dc in same sp, [ch 4, sk next sp, 9 dc in next sp] twice, ch 4; join to top of ch-3.

Rnd 3: Ch 3, dc in same ch as joining, * dc in next 3 dc, (dc, tr, ch 3, tr, dc) all in next dc, dc in next 3 dc, 2 dc in next dc, sc in next ch-4 sp **, 2 dc in next dc; rep from * around, end at **, join.

Rnd 4: Ch 1, sc in same ch as joining, sc in next st, * hdc in next st, dc in next 4 sts, (3 dc, ch 3, 3 dc) all in ch-3 sp, dc in next 4 sts, hdc in next st **, sc in next 5 sts; rep from * to last 3 sts, end at **, sc in last 3 sts; join to first sc. Fasten off.

Rnd 5: Join variegated in any ch-3 sp. Ch 3, 2 dc in same sp, [dc in next 21 sts, (3 dc, ch 3, 3 dc) all in next sp] twice, dc in next 21 sts, 3 dc in next sp, ch 3; join to top of ch-3. Fasten off.

Sew triangles together following diagram (figure 1), matching dc and leaving the ch-3 free.

CLUSTER MOTIF (Make 23)

With white work same as rnd 1 of Triangle. Sew to the intersection of 6 triangles, matching chs.

BORDER

Rnd 1: With right side facing, join variegated at arrow on figure 1 in the last dc before the first of 4 sps. Ch 1, sc in same st, * (sc, dc) in next sp, tr in each of next 2 sps, (dc, sc) in next sp, sc in next 27 sts, (sc, dc) in next sp, (dc, sc) in next sp, sc in next 27 sts; rep from * once more; (sc, dc) in next sp, (dc, sc) in next sp, [sc in next 27 sts, (sc, dc) in next sp, 2 tr in next sp, (dc, sc) in next sp] 4 times, [sc in next 27 sts, (sc, dc) in next sp, (dc, sc) in next sp] twice, sc in next 27 sts; rep from *around, working in last 26 instead of 27 sts; join to first sc. Fasten off.

Rnd 2: Join white in same sc as joining, ch 5, dc in same sc, * sk next 6 sts; *(dc, ch 2, dc) all in next st*—V-st made: [sk next 2 sts, V-st in next st] 19 times, sk next 6 sts, V-st in next st, [sk next 2 sts, V-st in next st] 97 times; rep from * around working sts in second set of brackets 96 instead of 97 times; join to third ch of ch-5.

Rnd 3: Ch 1, * (2 sc, ch 3, 2 sc) all in next ch-2 sp; rep from * around; join to first sc. Fasten off. Weave in ends.

Alterations: Jacquelynn crocheted the pieces together instead of sewing them, and she substituted yellow yarn for the variegated yarn—they turned out to be prize-winning changes!

Pattern Courtesy of Coats & Clark

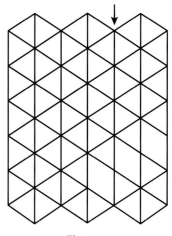

Figure 1

Sweet Baby Afghan Sampler

Dee Stanziano

This impressive piece of work combines 25 different stitches. No wonder it won the top prize!

Materials & Tools

Worsted-weight yarn, approximately:
    21 oz. white
    6 oz each of sky blue, pink,
        yellow, and green

Crochet hook size G, or size to
    match gauge

Tapestry needle

Gauge

Square = 7 in.

Finished size

Approximately 47 x 47 in.

SQUARES (Make 25)

See placement chart on page 45.

Using white: Lattice, Tall Fans, Cluster, Box, Filet Heart

Using sky blue: Tall Cables, Alternate, Reverse Filet Heart, Deezer, Bow Ties

Using pink: Spike, Tulips, Popcorn Heart, Sedge, Sweet Pea

Using yellow: Wattle, Herringbone, Leaf, Steps, Hugs & Kisses

Using green: Picot, Lacy V, Half-Double Puffs, Exchange, Crunch

All colors will be used in the afghan border.

Note: See instructions on page 44 for finishing each square.

White Squares

LATTICE

Ch 33.

Row 1: Hdc in fifth ch from hook, * ch 1, sk next ch, hdc in next ch; rep from * across (15 ch-sps).

Row 2: Ch 2 (will always count as the first hdc), turn; hdc in first ch-sp, * ch 1, hdc in next ch-sp; rep 13 times across; ch 1, hdc in last hdc. Rep row 2 until work measures 7 in.

TALL FANS

Ch 28.

Row 1: 2 dc in fifth ch from hook, ch 1, 2 dc in next ch, * sk next 3 chs, 2 dc in next ch, ch 1, 2 dc in next ch—shell made; rep from * across to last 2 chs, sk next ch, dc in last ch.

Row 2: Ch 3, turn; work shell in each ch-1 sp across, dc in top of turning ch.

Row 3: Ch 3, turn; work shell in next shell (in ch-1 sp), * ch 2, sc *tightly* around sp between shells of last 2 rows, ch 2, work shell in next shell; rep from * across, dc in top of turning ch.

Rows 4–5: Ch 3, turn; work shell in each shell across, dc in top of turning ch.

Rep rows 3–5 until work measures 7 in., ending by working either row 4 or 5.

CLUSTER

Ch 25.

Row 1: Yo, insert hook into third ch from hook, yo and pull up a loop, yo, and insert hook into next ch, yo and pull up a loop, yo and draw through first 4 loops on hook, yo again and draw through 2 loops on hook, * ch 1, yo, insert hook in same ch as last st, yo and pull up a loop, yo, and insert hook into next ch, yo and pull up a loop, yo and draw through first 4 loops on hook, yo again and draw through 2 loops on hook; rep from * across, make hdc in same ch as last st.

Row 2: Ch 1, turn, sc in first hdc, sk next st, * sc into next ch 1 sp, sk the next st; rep from * across, sc in top of turning ch.

Row 3: Ch 2, turn; yo, insert hook into first sc, yo and pull loop up, yo, insert hook into next sc, yo and pull up a loop, yo and draw through first 4 loops on hook, yo and draw through 2 loops on hook, * ch 1, yo, insert hook into same sc as last st, yo again and pull up a loop, yo, insert hook into next sc, yo and pull up a loop, yo and draw through first 4 loops on hook, yo and draw through 2 loops on hook; rep from * across, hdc in same sc as last st.

Rep rows 2 and 3 until work measures 7 in.

Sweet Baby Afghan Sampler

BOX
See figure 1.

FILET HEART
See figure 2.

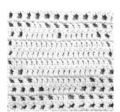

Sky Blue Squares

TALL CABLES
Ch 26.

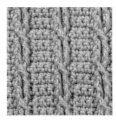

Row 1: Sc in second ch from hook, and in each ch across (25 sc).

Row 2: Ch 1, turn; sc in each sc across.

Row 3: Ch 1, turn; sc in first 2 sc, work FPdc around the post of sc *below* next sc, sk the sc behind FPdc, sc in next sc, work FPdc around post of sc *below* next sc, * sc in next 3 sc, work FPdc around post of sc *below* next sc; rep from * across to last 2 sc, sc in last 2 sc.

Row 4: Ch 1, turn; sc in st across.

Row 5: Ch 1, turn; sc in first 2 sc, work FPdc around post of 1st FPdc, sc in next sc, work FPdc around post of next FPdc, * sc in next 3 sc, work FPdc around post of next FPdc, sc in next sc, work FPdc around post of next FPdc; rep from * across to last 2 sc, sc in last 2 sc.

Row 6: Ch 1, turn; sc in st across.

Row 7: Ch 1, turn; sc in first 2 sc, sk first FPdc, work FPdc around post of next FPdc, sc in next sc, work FPdc around post of skipped FPdc, * sc in next 3 sc, sk next FPdc, work FPdc around post of next FPdc, sc in next sc, work FPdc around post of skipped FPdc; rep from * across to last 2 sc, sc in last 2 sc.

Row 8: Ch 1, turn; sc across.

Row 9: Ch 1, turn; sc in first 2 sc, work FPdc around post of first FPdc, sc in next sc, work FPdc around post of next FPdc, * sc in next 3 sc, work FPdc around post of next FPdc, sc in next sc, work FPdc around post of next FPdc; rep from * across to last 2 sc, sc in last 2 sc.

Rep Rows 4–9 until work measures approximately 7 in.

ALTERNATE
Ch 27.

Row 1: Sc in second ch from hook and in each ch across (26 sc).

Row 2: Ch 1, turn; sk first sc, (sc,dc) in next sc, * sk next sc, (sc,dc) in next sc; rep from * across.

Row 3: Ch 1, turn; (sc, dc) in each dc across.

Rep row 3 until work measures 7 in.

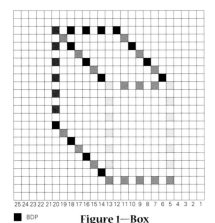

Figure 1—Box

- ■ BDP
- ▨ BDC
- ▨ FDP
- ▨ FDC

Ch 26; sc across, except as noted.

Ch 1 at the end of each row, turn.

Note: FDP and BDP are the same, except one is created from the front of the work and the other from the back. FDC and BDC are basically the same thing, but they are created around a previous FDP or BDP.

BDP: Yo, insert hook from back to front to back again around the post of the st from the previous row, complete dc.

BDC: Yo, insert hook around the stem of the dc from the previous row (back side) and complete dc.

FDP: Yo, insert hook front to back and to front again around the post of the st from the previous row, complete dc.

FDC: Yo, insert hook around the stem of dc from the previous row (front side) and complete dc.

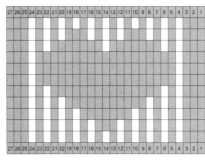

- ☐ ch 1
- ▨ dc

Figure 2—Filet Heart

Ch 29, dc in third ch from hook and across. (27 dc). Ch 3, turn.

Follow chart (color is dc, white is ch 1). For turns, do not go into first st.

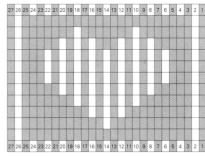

- ☐ ch 1
- ▨ dc

Figure 3—Reverse Filet Heart

*Ch 29, dc in fifth ch from hook, ch 1, sk ch, * dc, sk ch, ch 1, rep from * across. (13 sps). Ch 4, turn.*

Follow chart (color is dc, white is ch 1). For turns, do not go into first st.

REVERSE FILET HEART

See figure 3.

DEEZER

Ch 29 loosely.

Row 1: Sc in 2nd ch from hook and in each ch across (28 sc).

Row 2: Ch 2, turn; in first st * hdc in front loop, in next st hdc in back loop, rep from * across (28 hdc).

Row 3: Ch 2, turn; alternating from crocheting in the back loop to front loop only, make 28 hdc.

Rep rows 2 and 3 until work measures 7 in.

BOW TIES

Ch 27 loosely.

Row 1: Sc in second ch from hook and in each ch across (26 sc).

Row 2: Ch 1, turn; sc in first 3 sc, ch 8, sk next 7 sc, sc in next 6 sc, ch 8, sk next 7 sc, sc in last 3 sc.

Rows 3–4: Ch 1, turn; sc in first 3 sc, ch 8, sc in next 6 sc, ch 8, sc in last 3 sc.

Row 5: Ch 1, turn; sc in first 3 sc, ch 3, sl st around all 3 chain loops below, ch 3, sc in next 7 sc, ch 3, sl st around all 3 chain loops below, ch 3, sc in last 3 sc.

Row 6: Ch 1, turn; sc in first 3 sc, ch 8, sc in next 6 sc, ch 8, sc in last 3 sc.

Rows 7–25: Rep rows 3–6 four times; then rep rows 3–5 once more.

Row 26: Ch 1, turn; sc in first 3 sc, ch 7 *loosely*, sc in next 6 sc, ch 7 *loosely*, sc in last 3 sc.

Row 27: Ch 1, turn; sc in each sc and in each ch across (26 sc).

Pink Squares

SPIKE

Ch 28 loosely.

Row 1: Sc in second ch from hook and in each ch across (27 sc).

Row 2: Ch 1, turn; sc in each sc across.

Row 3–5: Ch 1, turn; sc in each sc across.

Row 6: Ch 1, turn; sc in 3 sc, * work long sc in sc 3 rows below next sc, sk sc behind long sc (now & throughout), sc in next 3 sc; rep from * across (6 spikes).

Row 7–9: Ch 1, turn; sc in each sc across.

Row 10: Ch 1, turn; sc in first sc, work long sc in sc 3 rows below next sc, * sc in next 3 sc, work long sc in sc 3 rows below next sc; rep from * across to last sc, sc in last sc (7 spikes).

Rep rows 3–10 until work measures approximately 7 in.

TULIPS

Note: For Tulip loops only, work ch sts very tightly or use smaller size hook.

Ch 26.

Row 1: Sc in second ch from hook, sc in each ch across, ch 1, turn (25 sc).

Row 2: Sc in first 6 sts. (Ch 9, sc, ch 10, sc, ch 9) in next sc—Tulip loops made. Sc in next 11 sts. Work Tulip loops again in next sc. Sc in last 6 sts, ch 1, turn.

Row 3: Sc in first 6 sts. * Hold Tulip loops toward front side. Sk first sc at the base of the loops; sc in next 2 sc as one (work a dec), sk last sc at the base of loops *, sc in next 11 sts. Rep between * once. Sc in last 6 sts. Ch 1, turn.

Row 4: Sc across, ch 1, turn (25 sc).

Row 5: Sc in first 3 sts; * insert hook through first loop of Tulip as you work, sc in next st. Sk center loop, sc in next 5 sts inserting hook through last loop of same Tulip. Sc in next st, sc in next 5 sts; rep from * once. Ch 1, turn.

Row 6: Sc across, ch 1, turn (25 sc).

Sweet Baby Afghan Sampler

Row 7: Sc in first 6 sts, * insert hook through center loop of Tulip, work 6 dc in next st—top of Tulip completed; sc in next 13 sts; rep from * across ending last rep with sc in last 6 sc. Ch 1, turn.

Row 8: Sc in first 6 sts. In next st of previous row * (yo insert hook through st, yo and pull through—should have 3 loops on hook—yo and pull through 2 loops) sc in last st of top of Tulip pulling through all loops on hook. Sc in next 11 sts. Rep from * once, sc in next 6 sts. Ch 1, turn.

Row 9: Sc across, ch 1, turn (25 sc).

Row 10: Sc in first 12 sts across, make Tulip loops in next sc, sc in remaining 12 sts. Ch 1, turn.

Row 11: Sc in first 12 sts, work dec st in back of Tulip, sc in rem 12 sts, ch 1, turn.

Row 12: Sc in first 9 sts, insert hook through first loop of Tulip as you work, sc in next st, sk center loop, sc in next 5 sts; insert hook in last loop of Tulip, sc in next st. Sc in rem 9 sts, ch 1, turn.

Row 13: Sc across, ch 1, turn (25 sts).

Row 14: Sc 12, 6 dc in middle Tulip loop, 13 sc.

Row 15: Sc 12, do a double-single dec, sc in remaining 12 sts, ch 1, turn.

Row 16: Sc across, ch 1, turn (25 sts).

Rows 17–24: Rep rows 2–9.

POPCORN HEART

See figure 4.

SEDGE

Ch 26.

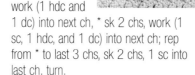

Row 1: Sk 2 chs (counts as a sc), work (1 hdc and 1 dc) into next ch, * sk 2 chs, work (1 sc, 1 hdc, and 1 dc) into next ch; rep from * to last 3 chs, sk 2 chs, 1 sc into last ch, turn.

Row 2: Ch 1 (counts as a sc), work (1 hdc, 1 dc) into first st, * sk (1 dc and 1 hdc), work (1 sc, 1 hdc, and 1 dc) into next sc; rep from * to last 3 sts, sk (1 dc and 1 hdc), 1 sc into top of turning ch, turn.

Rep row 2 until work measures 7 in.

SWEETPEA

Ch 28 loosely.

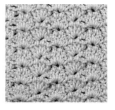

Row 1: Dc in fourth ch from hook, *sk next 2 chs, 5 dc in next ch (5-dc group), sk next 2 chs, dc in next 2 chs (2-dc group); rep from * across to last 3 chs, sk next 2 chs, 3 dc in last ch.

Row 2: Ch 3, turn; dc in sp between first 2 dc, * 5 dc in sp between dc of next 2-dc group, dc in sp between second and third dc of next 5-dc group and in next sp (between third and fourth dc); rep from * across to last 4 sts, 3 dc in sp between last dc and turning ch.

Rep row 2 until work measures 7 in.

Yellow Squares

WATTLE

Ch 27.

Row 1: Sk 2 ch (counts as a sc),

* work (1 sc, 1 ch, and 1 dc) into next ch, sk 2 ch; rep from * ending with 1 sc into last ch. Turn.

Row 2: Ch 1 (counts as a sc), sk first sc and next dc, * work (1 sc, 1 ch, and 1 dc) into next ch sp, sk 1 sc and 1 dc; rep from * ending with (1 sc, 1 ch, and 1 dc) into last ch sp, sk next sc, 1 sc into top of turning ch, turn.

Rep row 2 until work measures 7 in.

HERRINGBONE

Ch 28 loosely.

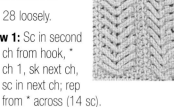

Row 1: Sc in second ch from hook, * ch 1, sk next ch, sc in next ch; rep from * across (14 sc).

Row 2: Ch 1, turn; sc in next sc, * ch 1, sc in next sc: rep from * across.

Row 3: Ch 1, turn; sc in first sc, ch 1, sc in next sc, * ch 6, sk next 2 ch-1 sp, sl st in sk ch of beg ch below next ch-1 sp, ch 6, sk next 2 ch-1 sp, sc in next sc, ch 1, sc in next sc; rep from * across.

Row 4: Ch 1, turn; sc in first sc; ch 1, sc in next sc, * (ch 1, dc in next sc) 4 times, (ch 1, sc in next sc) twice; rep from * across.

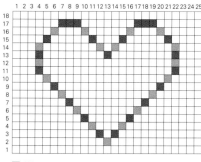

Figure 4—Popcorn Heart

☐ Hdc
▨ Back Popcorn
▬ Front Popcorn

Ch 27 loosely.

Follow chart, using hdc and stitches below:

Back popcorn—5 hdc in st, drop loop from hook, insert hook from back into first hdc of 5-hdc group, hook dropped loop and draw through, ch 1 to close.

Front popcorn—5 hdc in st, drop loop from hook, insert hook from back into first hdc of 5-hdc group, hook dropped loop and draw through, ch 1 to close.

Row 5: Ch 1, turn; sc in first sc, ch 1, sc in next sc, * ch 6, sl st in skipped ch-1 row *above* previous slip st, ch 6, sc in next sc, ch 1, sc in next sc; rep from * across.

Row 6: Ch 1, turn; sc in first sc, ch 1, sc in next sc, * (ch 1, dc in next dc) 4 times, (ch 1, sc in next sc) twice; rep from * across.

Rep rows 5–6 until work measures approximately 6¼ in., ending by working row 5.

LEAF

Ch 31 loosely.

Row 1: Sc in second ch from hook and in each ch across (30 sc).

Row 2 (right side): Ch 1, turn; sk first sc, 2 sc in next sc, * sk next sc, 2 sc in next sc; rep from * across.

Rep row 2 until work measures 7 in.

STEPS

Ch 28 loosely.

Row 1: Dc in fourth ch from hook and in each ch across (25 dc).

Row 2: Ch 2, turn; * work FPdc around next 4 dc, work BPdc around next 4 dc; rep from * 2 more times, hdc in top of turning ch.

Row 3: Ch 2, turn; 1 BPdc, 4 FPdc, * 4 BPdc, 4 FPdc; rep from * once more, 3 BPdc, hdc in turning ch.

Row 4: Ch 2, turn; 2 FPdc, 4 BPdc, * 4 FPdc, 4 BPdc; rep between * once more, 2 BPdc, hdc in turning ch.

Row 5: Ch 2, turn; 3 BPdc, 4 FPdc, * 4 BPdc, 4 FPdc; rep from * once, work 1 BPdc, hdc in turning ch.

Row 6: Ch 2, turn; * 4 BPdc, 4 FPdc, rep 2 more times; hdc in turning ch.

Row 7: Ch 2, turn; 1 FPdc, 4 BPdc, * 4 FPdc, 4 BPdc; rep from * once more, 3 FPdc, hdc in turning ch.

Row 8: Ch 2, turn; 2 BPdc, 4 FPdc, * 4

BPdc, 4 FPdc; rep from * once, work 2 BPdc, hdc in turning ch.

Row 9: Ch 2, turn; 3 FPdc, 4 BPdc, * 4 FPdc, 4 BPdc; rep from * once, work FPdc, hdc in turning ch.

Rep rows 2–9 until work measures 7 in.

HUGS & KISSES

Ch 26 loosely.

Row 1: Sc in second ch from hook and across (25 sc).

Row 2–3: Ch 1, sc across (25 sc).

Row 4: Ch 3 (counts as first dc), turn; dc in next 2 sts, * sk next 2 sts, tr in next 2 sts, working *behind* 2 tr just made, tr in 2 skipped sts, sk next 2 sts, tr in next 2 st, working in *front* of 2 tr just made, tr in 2 skipped sts, dc in next 3 sts; rep from * across.

Row 5: Rep row 4.

Row 6–7: Ch 1, sc across; 25 sc.

Row 8: Ch 3 (counts as first dc), turn; dc in next 2 sts, * sk next 2 sts, tr in next 2 sts, working in *front* of 2 tr just made, tr in 2 skipped sts, sk next 2 sts, tr in next 2 sts, working *behind* 2 tr just made, tr in 2 skipped sts, dc in next 3 sts; rep from * across.

Row 9–10: Ch 1, sc across (25 sc).

Row 11–12: Rep rows 4–5.

Row 13–15: Ch 1, sc across 25 sc.

Green Squares

PICOT

Ch 26 loosely.

Row 1: Sc in second ch from hook and in each ch across (25 sc).

Row 2: (right side): Ch 1, turn; sc in first sc, * (insert hook in next st and pull up a loop on hook, [yo and draw through 1 loop on hook] 3 times, yo and draw through both loops on hook—picot st made) in next sc, sc in next sc; rep from * across.

Sweet Baby Afghan Sampler

Row 3: Ch 1, turn, sc in first sc and in each sc across.

Row 4: Ch 1, turn; sc in first 2 sc, work Picot st in next sc, (sc in next sc, work Picot st in next sc) across to last 2 sc, sc in last 2 sc.

Row 5: Ch 1, turn; sc in first sc and in each sc across.

Rep rows 2–5 until work measures approximately 7 in., ending by working a *wrong side row*.

LACY V

Ch 29.

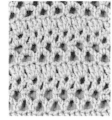

Row 1: Dc in fifth ch from hook, * sk the next 2 chs, (dc, ch 1, dc) into the next ch; rep from * across. Ch 3, turn.

Row 2: Make 2 dc in first ch-1 sp, 3 dc in each ch-1 sp across. Ch 1, turn.

Row 3: Sc in first 2 dc, * ch 3, sk next 2 dc, sc in next dc, rep from * across to the last st, sc in top of turn ch. Ch 1, turn.

Row 4: Sc into first sc, ch 3, (sc in next ch-3 sp, ch 3) across, sk the next sc, sc in last sc. Ch 4, turn.

Row 5: Make a dc in first ch-3 sp, (3 dc) in each ch-3 sp across.

Rep rows 4–5 until work measures 7 in.

HALF-DOUBLE PUFFS

Ch 27.

Row 1: In fifth ch from hook, † (* yo, insert hook into stitch, yo and pull up a loop; rep from * 2 more times, yo and draw through all 7 loops on hook)—puff made, ch 1, sk next ch. Rep from † across. Ch 3, turn (12 puffs).

Row 2: Work Puff in first ch-1 sp of previous row, ch 1, work Puff and ch 1 in each ch-1 sp across, work Puff in sp of turning ch.

Rep row 2 until work measures 7 in.

EXCHANGE

Ch 28 loosely.

Row 1: Sc in second ch from hook and into each ch across.

Row 2: Ch 1, turn; sc in first sc, * sk next sc, sc in next sc, working around sc just created, sc in sk sc; rep from * across.

Rep row 2 until work measures 7 in.

CRUNCH

Ch 27 loosely.

Row 1: Sl st loosely in third ch from hook, * hdc in next ch, sl st loosely in next ch, rep from * across.

Row 2 (right side): Ch 2, turn; hdc into first sl st, slip st loosely into next hdc, * hdc into next sl st, rep from * across to last st.

Note: While creating this pat, notice that the sl st bends the hdc downward, causing a slant. Do not crochet into the slant—crochet into the top two loops of st only.

Rep row 2 until piece measures 7 in.

FINISHING SQUARES

Each sampler square is finished off with two rounds of sc, one in the same color as the square and one in white, as follows.

FINISHING EDGE

Rnd 1: Join yarn with right side facing in any corner, ch 1, * make 3 sc in corner, work 25 sc *evenly spaced* across to next corner, rep from * 3 times more, join with sl st to first sc (112 sc).

Rnd 2 (crochet in back loops only): Ch 1, sc in same st, * 3 sc in next sc (corner), sc in next 27 sc, rep from * 3 times more, join with sl st to first sc, finish off (120 sc around).

ASSEMBLY

Squares are joined together in vertical strips of 5 blocks, and then the strips are joined together. See figure 1 for placement.

Hold wrong sides together and whipstitch into the back loops only of both squares.

AFGHAN BORDER

Note: Joining sc is worked as follows—insert hook into noted stitch, yo and pull up a loop, insert hook into next noted stitch and pull up a loop, yo and draw through all loops on hook.

Rnd 1: With white, right side facing, join yarn with sl st in any corner, ch 1, 3 sc in the same corner, (* sc in next 29 sc, create joining sc between squares, rep from * 3 more times, sc in next 29 sts, 3 sc in corner), rep between ( ) 2 more times, † sc in next 29 sc, create joining sc between squares, repeat from † 3 more times, sc in next 29 sts, join with sl st to beginning sc (608 sts).

Rnd 2: Ch 1, * 3 sc in corner, sc across to next corner, 3 sc in corner, rep from * around. Join with sl st to beginning sc (620 sts).

Rnd 3: Rep rnd 2 (632 sts)

Rnd 4: Rep rnd 2. (644 sts)

Rnd 5: Note: This row entails a lot of color changing. Carry the colors not in use along the wrong side of the work and crochet over them when not in use. While crocheting, keep the tension of all strands taut, but not so tight that puckering occurs. This technique is similar to tapestry crochet, where the colors are carried along (cocheted over) until needed.

How to color change: prior to creating last yo of required stitch, drop the current color, yo with new color and pull through stitch loops on hook.

Ch 1, 3 sc in corner, lay end of *pink* over work to crochet over while creating sc with *white* in next 4 sts, changing over to *pink* on last sc.

Continuing with *pink*, fdp (see figure 2) around sc made in row 3, changing back to color *white* in last yo.

Lay end of *yellow* over work along with the *pink* and sc over with *white* in next 3 sts, changing over to *yellow* on last sc.

Continuing with *yellow*, fdp around sc made in row 3, changing back to color *white* in last yo.

Lay end of *green* over work along with the *pink* and *yellow* and sc over with *white* in next 3 sts, changing over to *green* on last sc.

Continuing with *green*, fdp around sc made in row 3, changing back to color *white* in last yo.

Lay end of *blue* over work along with the *pink, yellow,* and *green* and sc over with *white* in next 3 sts, changing over to *blue* on last sc.

1	2	3	4	5
6	7	8	9	10
11	12	13	14	15
16	17	18	19	20
21	22	23	24	25

Placement Chart

1. Tall Cables, 2. Lattice, 3. Picot, 4. Spike, 5. Wattle, 6. Lacy V, 7. Tulips, 8. Herringbone, 9. Alternate, 10. Tall Fans, 11. Leaf, 12. Reverse Filet Heart, 13. Cluster, 14. Half-Double Puffs, 15. Popcorn Heart, 16. Box, 17. Exchange, 18. Sedge, 19. Steps, 20. Deezer, 21. Sweetpea, 22. Hugs & Kisses 23. Bow Ties, 24. Filet Heart, 25. Crunch

Continuing with *blue*, fdp around sc made in Row 3, changing back to color *white* in last yo.

Sc with *white* in next 3 sts, (* fdp with color, sc in next 3 sts with white, rep from * across to corner, 3 sc in corner, sc in next 4 sts), rep between ( ) 2 more times, 3 sc in corner, sc in next 4 sts, † fdp with color, sc in next 3 sts with white, rep from † across to first corner. (Note: after working last pink fdp, end off pink after next 3 white sc are made, do the same for the yellow, green and blue.) Join with sl st.

Rnd 6–9: Ch 1, 3 sc in corner, * sc across to next corner, 3 sc in corner, rep from * 2 more times, sc to beg corner, join with sl st to beginning sc. Finish off.

Variation: To make row 5 less complicated, variegated yarn may be substituted for the four colors. Use the following directions if using variegated yarn.

Rnd 5 (variation): Ch 1, 3 sc in corner, lay end of variegated yarn over work to crochet over while creating sc with white in next 4 sts, change over to variegated yarn and fdp around sc made in rnd 3, changing back to white in last yo, sc with white in next 3 sts, * fdp with variegated, sc in next 3 sts with white across to corner, 3 sc in corner, sc in next 4 sts, rep from * two more times, † fdp with variegated, sc in next 3 sts with white, rep from † across to first corner, join with sl st.

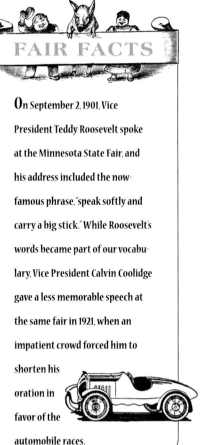

FAIR FACTS

On September 2, 1901, Vice President Teddy Roosevelt spoke at the Minnesota State Fair, and his address included the now-famous phrase, "speak softly and carry a big stick." While Roosevelt's words became part of our vocabulary, Vice President Calvin Coolidge gave a less memorable speech at the same fair in 1921, when an impatient crowd forced him to shorten his oration in favor of the automobile races.

Original Design

Classic Crocheted Ripple Afghan

Kathleen M. Smith

Kathleen substituted variegated yarn in warm, inviting shades to create this timeless ripple afghan.

Materials & Tools

Worsted-weight yarn, approximately:
  16 oz. dark rust
  8 oz. each of dark orange, medium orange, light orange, and yellow

Crochet hook size I, or size to match gauge

Tapestry needle

Gauge

To test gauge, ch 32 and work in pat st for 12 rows (foundation row counts as a row). Piece should measure 7 in. wide and 4½ in. long, measured across the width of three complete ripples.

Finished size

Approximately 45 x 72 in.

PATTERN STITCH
(Multiple of 11 plus 10)

Foundation Row: Ch desired number, loosely. (It is especially important to start with a loose chain on an afghan; otherwise, the bottom will be tight, and as you work, the afghan will start spreading out but a tight bottom chain will never stretch.) Sc in second ch from hook, 1 sc in each of next 3 chs, * 3 sc in next ch, 1 sc in each of next 4 chs, sk 2 chs, 1 sc in each of next 4 chs; rep from * across, ending 3 sc in next ch, 1 sc in each of last 4 chs, turn.

Ripple Pattern Row

*Note: On this row, unless otherwise specified, work through **back loop only** on each sc. This creates an attractive ridge effect.*

Ch 1, sk 1 sc. (Now remember to work in back loops only.) * 1 sc in each of next 4 sc, 3 sc in next sc, 1 sc in each of next 4 sc, sk 2 sc, rep from * across to within last 5 sts, end 1 sc in each of next 3 sc, sk 1 sc, 1 sc through *both loops* of last sc, turn. Repeat Ripple Pattern Row until piece reaches desired length.

INSTRUCTIONS FOR ONE-PIECE AFGHAN

Ch 230 loosely. Following Pattern Stitch instructions, work 4 rows (foundation row counts as a row) dark rust; 2 rows dark orange; 2 rows medium orange; 2 rows light orange; 2 rows yellow. Rep this 12-row color sequence until piece measures approx. 72 in. long, ending with 4 rows of dark rust.

To change colors at the end of a row, complete row and turn, cut yarn, leaving about a 4-in. tail. Then make starting ch-1 of next row with the new color, and continue working with new color. The tails can be woven in later with a tapestry needle, or you can work over them as you go, if you prefer.

INSTRUCTIONS FOR STRIP AFGHAN

Ch 76 loosely. Follow instructions for One-Piece Afghan as above. Make two more strips the same. Place two strips, right sides facing, together and join loosely with sl st or sew with back stitch, taking care to match stripes. Join third strip in same manner.

Alterations: Kathleen added a decorative edging and used variegated yarn only.

Compliments of Leisure Arts, Inc., USA. For a complete line of products, call Leisure Arts, Inc. @ 800-526-5111 or log on to www.leisurearts.com.

Sweet Hearts

Beverley Hite Young

Beverley must have had a boy in mind for her version of this adorable design, for she worked it in the perfect shade of blue.

Materials & Tools
Sport-weight yarn, approximately:
25 oz. light blue

Crochet hook size F, or size
to match gauge

Gauge
In pat, 16 sts = 4 in.;
15 rows = 4 in.

Finished size
Approximately 37 x 41 in.,
excluding fringe

INSTRUCTIONS
Leaving a 3-in. tail of yarn, ch 165. Fasten off, leaving a 3-in. tail of yarn.

Note: All rows are worked beg with a slip knot (as if you were going to start a ch) and then worked across the right side of the fabric only, then fastened off. Leave a 3-in. tail of yarn at beg and end of each row for side fringe.

Row 1: Sc in each ch across (165 sc).

Note: Beg with row 2 work first 2 sc and last 2 sc in **both loops** *and all other sc in the* **back loop** *only.*

Row 2: Sc in each st across.

Row 3: Sc in first 7 sc; {yo, with hook at front of work insert hook from below into the rem (front) loop below next sc (skip the sc behind this st), yo and draw loop through, [yo, and through 2 loops] twice}—dcb made; [sc in next 9 sc, dcb] 15 times, sc in last 7 sc.

Row 4: Sc in first 6 sc, [dcb, sc in next st, dcb, sc in next 7 sc] 15 times, dcb, sc in next st, dcb, sc in last 6 sc.

Row 5: Sc in first 5 sc, [dcb, sc in next 3 sts, dcb, sc in next 5 sc] 16 times.

Row 6: Sc in first 4 sc, [dcb, sc in next 5 sts, dcb, sc in next 3 sts] 16 times, sc in last sc.

Row 7: Sc in first 3 sc, [dcb, sc in next 7 sts, dcb, sc in next st] 16 times, sc in last 2 sc.

Row 8: Sc in first 2 sc, [dcb, sc in next 9 sts] 16 times, dcb, sc in last 2 sc.

Row 9: Sc in first 2 sc; yo, *insert hook from the right to the left around the post of the next dcb, yo and draw loop through, [yo and through 2 loops] twice*—Fdc made; [sc in next 4 sts, dcb, sc in next 4 sts, Fdc] 16 times, sc in last 2 sc.

Row 10: Sc in first 2 sc, Fdc, [sc in next 3 sts, dcb, sc in next st, dcb, sc in next 3 sts, Fdc] 16 times, sc in last 2 sc.

Row 11: Sc in first 3 sc, [dcb, sc in next sc, dcb, sc next 3 sts, dcb, sc in next st, dcb, sc in next st] 16 times, sc in last 2 sc.

Row 12: Rep row 6.

Rows 13–16: Rep row 2.

Rep rows 3–16 eight more times, then rep rows 3–13 once more (10 rows of heart motifs).

FINISHING
Fringe: Cut 6-in. strands of yarn. Knot 1 strand in each st and row end around afghan. Trim ends.

Tip: To keep fringe from coming undone, run a row of machine stitching across fringe at the very edge of the afghan.

Pattern Courtesy of Coats & Clark

Deep South

Sweet Hearts

Andrea Murphy

Some designs are so wonderful that they deserve more than one blue ribbon, and this is the perfect example. Andrea's charming rendition was awarded the top prize in Florida.

Materials & Tools
Sport-weight yarn, approximately:
  25 oz. peach

Crochet hook size F, or size
  to match gauge

Gauge
In pat, 16 sts = 4 in.; 15 rows = 4 in.

Finished size
Approximately 37 x 41 in.,
  excluding fringe

INSTRUCTIONS
Leaving a 3-in. tail of yarn, ch 165. Fasten off, leaving a 3-in. tail of yarn.

Note: All rows are worked beg with a slip knot (as if you were going to start a ch) and then worked across the right side of the fabric only, then fastened off. Leave a 3-in. tail of yarn at beg and end of each row for side fringe.

Row 1: Sc in each ch across (165 sc).

*Note: Beg with row 2 work first 2 sc and last 2 sc in **both loops** and all other sc in the **back loop** only.*

Row 2: Sc in each st across.

Row 3: Sc in first 7 sc; {yo, with hook at front of work insert hook from below into the rem (front) loop below next sc (skip the sc behind this st), yo and draw loop through, [yo, and through 2 loops] twice}—dcb made; [sc in next 9 sc, dcb] 15 times, sc in last 7 sc.

Row 4: Sc in first 6 sc, [dcb, sc in next st, dcb, sc in next 7 sc] 15 times, dcb, sc in next st, dcb, sc in last 6 sc.

Row 5: Sc in first 5 sc, [dcb, sc in next 3 sts, dcb, sc in next 5 sc] 16 times.

Row 6: Sc in first 4 sc, [dcb, sc in next 5 sts, dcb, sc in next 3 sts] 16 times, sc in last sc.

Row 7: Sc in first 3 sc, [dcb, sc in next 7 sts, dcb, sc in next st] 16 times, sc in last 2 sc.

Row 8: Sc in first 2 sc, [dcb, sc in next 9 sts] 16 times, dcb, sc in last 2 sc.

Row 9: Sc in first 2 sc; yo, *insert hook from the right to the left around the post of the next dcb, yo and draw loop through, [yo and through 2 loops] twice*—Fdc made; [sc in next 4 sts, dcb, sc in next 4 sts, Fdc] 16 times, sc in last 2 sc.

Row 10: Sc in first 2 sc, Fdc, [sc in next 3 sts, dcb, sc in next st, dcb, sc in next 3 sts, Fdc] 16 times, sc in last 2 sc.

Row 11: Sc in first 3 sc, [dcb, sc in next sc, dcb, sc next 3 sts, dcb, sc in next st, dcb, sc in next st] 16 times, sc in last 2 sc.

Row 12: Rep row 6.

Rows 13–16: Rep row 2.

Rep rows 3–16 eight more times, then rep rows 3–13 once more (10 rows of heart motifs).

FINISHING

Fringe: Cut 6-in. strands of yarn. Knot 1 strand in each st and row end around afghan. Trim ends.

Tip: To keep fringe from coming undone, run a row of machine stitching across fringe at the very edge of the afghan.

Pattern Courtesy of Coats & Clark

FAIR FACTS

To celebrate its centennial, the Missouri State Fair featured high-wheel bicycle races, accompanied by an exhibit on the history of the bicycle.

Stars for America

Mary Johnson

Doesn't this afghan look like it belongs at the state fair? Mary's design is a clever reworking of the elements from our flag.

Materials & Tools
Worsted-weight yarn, approximately:
  16 oz. white
  24 oz. cherry red
  32 oz. blue
  3 oz. red/white/blue variegated
      yarn for fringe

Crochet hook size I, or size to
  match gauge

Gauge
3 shells = 4 in.

Finished size
Approximately 50 x 68 in.

INSTRUCTIONS
With red, ch 219.

Foundation Row: Sc in second ch from hook
  and in each ch across, turn (218 sc).

Row 1: Ch 1, sc into first sc, 3 dc in next
  sc, sk 2 sc, sc in next sc * sc in next sc,
  3 dc in next sc, sk next 2 sc, rep from *
  to last sc, dc in last sc, turn.

Row 2: Ch 1, sc in first dc, * 3 dc in next sc,
  sk 2 dc, sc in next dc, rep from * to last
  sc, dc in last sc, turn.

Rows 3–4: Rep row 2, changing to blue in
  the last st of row.

Row 5: Rep row 2, at the end of row
  change to white in the last st.

Rows 6–10: Rep row 2 with white, changing
  to blue on the last st on row 10, turn.

Row 11: Rep row 2, changing to red at the
  last st, turn.

Row 12–15: Rep row 2, changing to blue
  on the last st, turn.

Row 16–36: With blue, repeat row 2.

Repeat rows 2–36 twice more.

Repeat rows 2–15.

Weave in all ends.

FRINGE
Cut variegated yarn into 6-in. lengths for
fringe and attach at ends.

STARS (Make 50)
With white, ch 4, join with sl st, ch 1, 15 sc
in ring, join with sl st. * Ch 6, sl st in second
ch from hook, sc in next ch, hdc in next ch,
dc in next ch, tr in next ch.

Sk 2 sc, sl st in next sc, rep from * around.
Making 5 points, join with sl st. Fasten off.
Sew the stars (tacking each point) to the
three wide blue stripes.

Original Design

Baby Rings

Millie Crawford

Millie chose jewel tones for this intricate afghan. Keeping the ring closures to the back, she says, was the most challenging part of this project.

Materials & Tools

Worsted-weight yarn, approximately:
- 14 oz. white
- 6 oz. variegated
- 4½ oz. each of five solid colors that match the colors in the variegated yarn

Tapestry needle

Crochet hook size G, or size to match gauge.

Gauge

4 dc = 1 in.; dc is ¾ in. tall. Panel is 4½ in. wide.

Finished size

Approximately 33½ x 38 in.

PANEL (Make 7)

Center (Make 30 rings)

Ring 1: With first solid color, ch 14, sl st in first ch to form ring, ch 2, work 28 hdc in ring, join with sl st in top of first hdc. Fasten off.

Ring 2: With second solid color, ch 14; with right side of sts on ring facing you, thread end of ch 14 through Ring 1, join with sl st in first ch (to form Ring 2), ch 2, work 28 hdc in ring, join with sl st in top of first hdc. Fasten off.

Rem rings: Using each of rem solid colors, rep Ring 2. Each new ring is interlocked with the one before it and always thread the ch 14 through ring in the same direction. When each of the colors has been used, start the color sequence over and repeat the sequence until all rings are made.

Border

Rnd 1: Hold Center with right side of work facing you and hide the joining of each ring behind the next interlocking ring as you work; working in *back loops* only, with white yarn, join with sc in a hdc on Ring 2, ch 2, dc in next 3 sts; *(working on next ring, dc in next 4 sts) down side to last ring, dc in next 6 sts, 2 dc in each of next 6 sts, dc in next 6 sts; rep from *, join with sl st in top of ch 2. Fasten off.

Rnd 2: With variegated yarn, join with sc in first st on rnd 1, ch 3, dc in side of sc just made, sk next 2 dc, *(sc in next dc, ch 3, dc in side of sc just made, sk next 2 sts) down side; in 6 end sts work (sc in next dc, ch 3, dc in side of sc, sk 1 dc) 3 times; rep from *, (sc in next dc, ch 3, dc in side of sc just made —see figure

1, sk next 2 sts) across to beg, join with sl st in first sc. Fasten off.

Rnd 3: With white yarn, join with sc in first sc on last rnd, ch 2, 2 dc in same st, work 3 dc in each sc around with 4 dc in each of the 4 sc at center of each end, join with sl st in first ch 2. Fasten off.

ASSEMBLY

Leaving 21 sts around each end free (see figure 2), whipstitch edges of panels together through *back loops* of sts only.

Pattern Courtesy of Annie's Attic

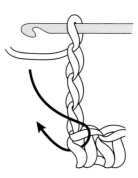

Figure 1

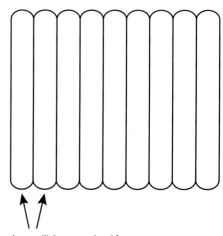

Leave stitches around end free.

Figure 2

United States Flag

Loi Tra Carter

Here's the patriotic symbol that flies at every state fair in our country. Loi has also made a smaller version to display on a wall.

Materials & Tools

Worsted-weight yarn, approximately:
28 oz. each of red, white,
and navy blue

Crochet needle size G, or size
to match gauge

Gauge
(3 dc, ch 2) 3 times = 3 in.

Finished size
Approximately 44 x 90 in.

STAR MOTIF (Make 50)

With white, ch 3, join to form a ring

Row 1: Ch 1, sc 10 in ring.

Row 2: Ch 1 (2 sc in each sc) (20 sc), join.

Row 3: Ch 4, (yo twice, draw loop through next sc, yo draw through 2 loops [twice]). Rep ( ) 3 more times, yo, draw through all 6 loops on hook—first point of star complete. Rep ( ) 5 times for second point, starting in last sc of first point. Make 3 more points with ch 9 between each. Join last ch 9 to top of first point, finish off.

Join blue.

Row 4: 12 sc in each ch-9 sp. Join to first sc.

Row 5: Ch 5, tr in next 2 sc, (dc in next 6 sc, tr in next 2 sc, ch 3, tr same sc, tr next 2 sc), ch 6 dc, ch 3. Rep ( ) around, ending dc in 6 sc, ch 3. Join to top of first ch 5. Finish off.

HALF STAR MOTIF
(Make 10)

Row 1: With blue, make a loop, ch 1, 5 sc in loop.

Row 2: Ch 1, turn, 2 sc in each sc (10 sc).

Row 3: Ch 8, turn. Make 3 points on star, separated by ch 9. Ch 4 and tr in last sc.

Row 4: Ch 1, turn, 5 sc in ch-4 (loop). 12 sc in next two 9 chs (loops). 5 sc in last loop, sc in fifth ch of ch 9.

Row 5: Ch 6 (count as tr and ch 3) * tr in same sc. Tr next sc, dc in next 7 sc, tr next 2 sc, ch 3 *, tr in same sc, tr in the next sc, dc in next 7 sc. Tr in next sc, ch 30. Rep from * to *. Finish off. Whipstitch motifs together, using half motif to fill in long side.

Using blue yarn, fill in uneven edge with stitches of appropriate length.

Tr at left hand corner, tr in next 2 tr, dc in next 3 dc, sk 1 ch. Dc in next 2 dc, sc next 2 tr, sk 3 chs. Sc next 2 tr, dc next 2 tr, sk 1, dc next 3 tr, tr next 2 dc, tr in last tr. Sk next 3-ch loop. 1 tr in the whipstitch joining motifs. Sk 3-ch loop chs. Tr next 2 tr, dc next 3 dc, sk ch-1 loop. Dc in next 2 sts, sc next 3 sts, sk 3-ch loop, sc next 3 sts. Rep to the end.

Crochet other side the same.

Edge all 4 sides of star field.

Start sc at any sc and sc in each st to the corner. Ch 3 in each corner. Join. Finish off.

Star field = 24 x 46 in.

STRIPES

With red, ch 403.

Row 1: Dc in fourth ch from hook, dc next ch. Sk 1 ch and ch 1, dc next 3 ch. Rep to end (100 of 3-dc group).

Row 2: Ch 4 (count 1 dc and 1 ch). 3 dc in next ch-1 sp. Continue as row 1. End ch 1, dc in last dc.

Row 3: Ch 3, turn, (count as 1 dc), 2 dc in ch-1 sp. Continue. Rep rows 2 and 3 to row 6 for bottom red stripe. Change to white, make 6 stripes total (3 red, 3 white).

For 7 short stripes, start at edge of star field. Lay out star field. Being sure it's even on the left edge, join red yarn to white stripe at the bottom right of field.

Ch 4 (count as dc and 1 ch), 3-dc group in ch-1 sp. Rep pat for 7 more alternating stripes, starting and ending with red stripes, and finish off.

Whipstitch star field together with 13 stripes. Edge around whole flag with reverse sc.

Original Design

Baby ABC's Afghan

Kathy Antus

Here is the first of two versions of this adorable baby afghan; Kathy chose a mint green yarn for her prize-winning coverlet decorated with the letters of the alphabet.

Materials & Tools

Sport-weight yarn, approximately:
 35 oz. mint

Crochet hook size G, or size
 to match gauge

Gauge
18 sc = 4 in.

Finished size
Approximately 33 x 36 in.

CHART STITCHES: □ = sc,

● = puff stitch (ps). For puff st, yo, pull up
loop 4 times, (9 loops on hook), yo, pull
through 8 loops, yo, pull through 2 loops,
push puff to front of work, work next st.

INSTRUCTIONS

Ch 140, follow chart working first sc in second ch from hook, 139 sc.

FINISHING

Ch 1, turn, (sc, ps, sc) in first sc—corner
made, ps, sc across, working corner as
before, working down side, ps in first row, sc
in next row, rep around, sl st in first sc, ch 1,
sc in each sc and ps around all sides, working 3 sc in each corner ps, sl st in first sc,
finish off. Weave in all ends.

Pattern Courtesy of Coats & Clark

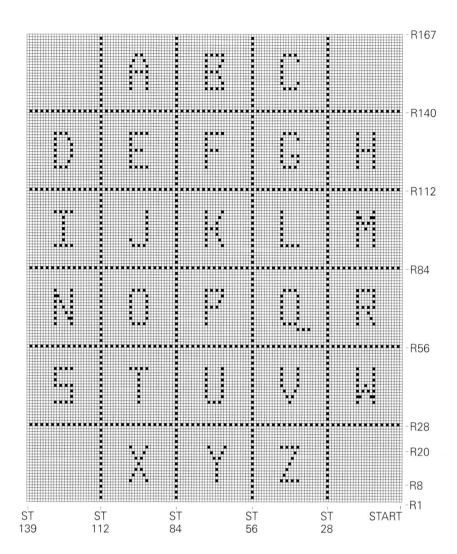

Baby ABC's Afghan

Beverley Hite Young

Beverley chose a soft white sport weight for her blue ribbon winner. The blend in the yarn gives this afghan a bit of a sparkle.

Materials & Tools
Sport-weight yarn, approximately:
    35 oz. soft white

Crochet hook size G, or size
    to match gauge

Gauge
16 sc = 4 in.

Finished size
Approximately 36 x 46 in.

SEE CHART PAGE 59

CHART STITCHES:
□ = sc, ● = puff stitch (ps). For puff st, yo, pull up loop 4 times, (9 loops on hook), yo, pull through 8 loops, yo, pull through 2 loops, push puff to front of work, work next st.

INSTRUCTIONS
Ch 140, follow chart working first sc in second ch from hook, 139 sc.

FINISHING
Ch 1, turn, (sc, ps, sc) in first sc—corner made, ps, sc across, working corner as before, working down side, ps in first row, sc in next row, rep around, sl st in first sc, ch 1, sc in each sc and ps around all sides, working 3 sc in each corner ps, sl st in first sc, finish off. Weave in all ends.

Pattern Courtesy of Coats & Clark

FAIR FACTS

Over the past two decades, pig racing has become a major fair event. Vietnamese pot-bellies and standard Yorkshires are the swine of choice for these contests. How do you convince a pig to run in the first place? Tempt it with a prize, of course. Cheese puffs and cookies seem to work especially well.

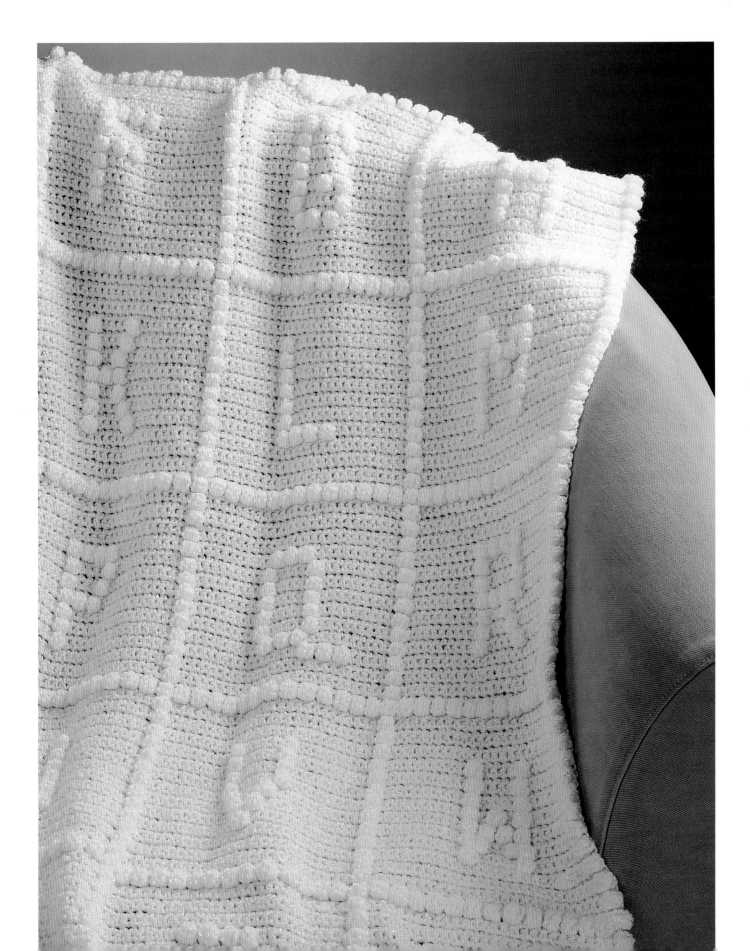

Red, White & Blue

Charliene B. Smith

Charliene's ribbon is a perfect match for the blue in this adaptation of the granny square. She made this award winner for a friend in military service.

Materials & Tools
Worsted-weight yarn, approximately:
20 oz. each red, white, and blue
28 oz. variegated red, white, and blue

Crochet hook size G, or size to match gauge

Gauge
3 dc cluster = 3 in.

Finished size
Approximately 72 x 72 in.

GRANNY SQUARE
With red, ch 4, join with sl st to form ring.

Rnd 1: Ch 3 (counts as 1 dc), 2 dc into ring, ch 2 (for corner), * 3 dc into ring, ch 2, rep from * twice, join with sl st in last ch of beg ch 3. Sl st back to beg of ch-2 corner sp.

Rnd 2: Ch 3, 2 dc into corner sp, ch 2, 3 dc into same corner sp, * ch 1, (3 dc into ch-2 sp, ch 2, 3 dc into same ch-2 sp—corner made, rep from * twice, ch 1, sl st into top of beg ch 3. Sl st forward to corner ch-2 sp.

Rnd 3: Ch 3, 2 dc into corner sp, ch 2, 3 dc into same corner sp, * ch 1, 3 dc into ch-1 sp, ch 1, make corner, rep from * twice, ch 1, 3 dc into ch-1 sp, ch 1, sl st into top of beg ch 3. Sl st forward to corner ch-2 sp.

Rnd 4 and rem rnds: As rnd 3, but with one more group of 3 dc between corners on each rnd. Side groups of 3 dc are separated by ch 1, corner pair by ch 2. Join new yarn in corner ch-2 sp when changing colors.

First 5 rnds red, then 4 rnds each of white, blue, and red, with solid colors each separated by 2 rnds in variegated yarn, until afghan is desired size.

Original Design

FAIR FACTS

The first air mail delivery in the country was made at the 1918 Maryland State Fair.

Rodeo Afghan

Lois W. McLeod

The cowboy on this afghan could have been a contestant in most any state fair! Lois brings the spirit of competition alive in this unique project.

Materials & Tools
Chunky-weight yarn, approximately:
    33 oz. blue
    14 oz. dark rust

Crochet hook size J, or size to
    match gauge

Tapestry needle

Gauge
5 sc sts = 2 in., 11 sc rows = 4 in.

Finished size
Approximately 44 x 57 in,
    excluding fringe

AFGHAN

Note: When changing colors, always drop second color to same side of work. Do not carry dropped color across to next section of same color. Use a separate skein of yarn for each color section.

Row 1: With blue, ch 109, sc in second ch from hook, sc in each ch across, turn (108 sc).

Rows 2–8: Ch 1, sc in each st across, turn.

Row 9: Ch 1, sc in first 45 sts changing to dark rust in last st made, sc in each of next 2 sts changing to blue in last st made, sc in each st across, turn.

Rows 10–154: Ch 1, sc in each st across changing colors according to chart at right. Fasten off dark rust when no longer needed.

Rnd 155: Working around entire outer edge, ch 1, sc in end of each row and in each st around with 3 sc in each corner, join with sl st in first sc, fasten off.

FRINGE

For each fringe, cut 2 strands each blue and dark rust 12 in. long. With all 4 strands held together, fold in half, insert hook in st, draw fold through, draw all loose ends through fold, tighten, trim.

Fringe in first st and in every following third st across short ends of afghan.

Alteration: Lois substituted black yarn for the dark rust.

Pattern Courtesy of Annie's Attic

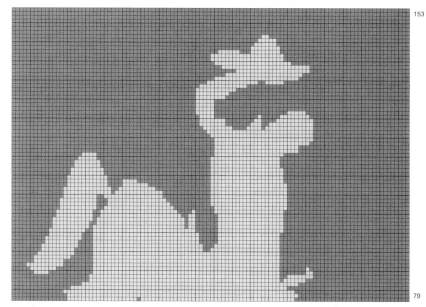

☐ Dark Rust　■ Blue

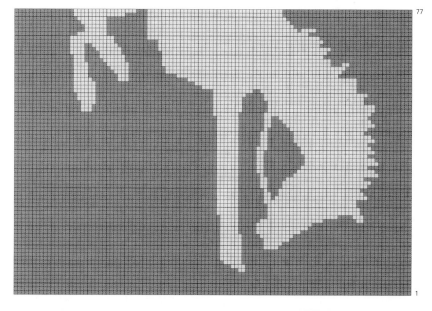

Irish Afghan

Nancy Sheck

Nancy's determination to master the stitches in this pattern paid off when she received the top honor for this excellent piece of work.

Materials & Tools

Worsted-weight yarn, approximately:
68 oz. natural

Crochet hook sizes I and J, or
sizes to match gauge

Gauge
19 sc = 5 in.; 1 panel = 4 in.;
24 rows = 5 in. (size I hook)

Finished size
Approximately 45 x 61 in.,
excluding fringe

STITCH PATTERNS

Note: Do not work in st directly behind raised dc or double raised dc, or in eye of a cluster.

Cluster—(Yo hook, draw up a loop in st) 4 times, yo and draw through all 9 loops on hook. Ch 1 tightly to form eye. (Cluster is worked from wrong side but appears on right side.)

Raised Dc—Dc around upright bar of dc 1 row below, inserting hook behind dc from front to back to front, for ridge on right side.

Double Raised Dc—Holding back last loop of each dc on hook, make 2 dc around upright bar of st 1 row below, yo and through all 3 loops on hook.

Popcorn—4 dc in st, drop loop off hook, insert hook in top of first dc, pick up dropped loop and pull through.

Note: This afghan is difficult to start. Once you have completed row 3 and "set" your sts correctly, the work becomes relatively easy. Before starting afghan, make a swatch of one pat to familiarize yourself with the sts. Ch 28.

Row 1: Sc in second ch from hook and in each ch across (27 sc).

Row 2: Sc in each of first 5 sts, cluster in next st, sc in each of next 15 sts, cluster in next st, sc in each of last 5 sts.

Row 3: Sc in each of first 3 sc; count off 3 sts on row 1 and work dc around next post (raised dc), sk the sc on row 2 behind the dc just made and make 1 sc in each of next 3 sts (be sure to work in the cluster st only once; do not work in the eye of the cluster), sk 3 sc on row 1 from last raised dc and work a raised dc around next st, sk the sc on row 2 behind the dc just made, sc in each of next 4 sc; sk 4 sc on row 1 from last raised dc and make double raised dc around next sc, sk the sc behind it and work 1 sc, sk 1 sc on row 1 and make another double raised dc, sk the sc behind it and work 4 sc; sk 4 sc on row 1 and work a raised dc around the next sc, sk the sc behind it, work 3 sc (the cluster st is the center st of these 3 sc), sk 3 sc on row 1 and work another raised dc around the next sc, sk the sc behind it, work sc in each of last 3 sts.

Beginning with row 4 of the afghan, work pat without reps on 27 sts. On all right-side rows from row 3 on, the raised dcs are worked around the previous raised dcs and the double raised dcs are worked around the double raised dcs.

AFGHAN

With I hook, ch 172 loosely.

Row 1: Sc in second ch from hook and in each ch across (171 sc). Ch 1, turn each row.

Row 2 (wrong side): Sc in each of first 5 sts, (cluster in next st, sc in each of next 15 sts) 10 times; end cluster in next st, sc in each of last 5 sts.

Row 3 (right side): Sc in each of first 3 sc, * work dc around post of next sc 1 row below (row 1), sk next sc on row 2 (see Stitch Patterns: Note), sc in each of next 3 sts, dc around post of next sc 1 row

Irish Afghan

below, sk next sc on row 2, sc in each of next 4 sc; holding back last loop of each dc on hook, make 2 dc around next sc 1 row below, yo and through 3 loops on hook, sk next sc on row 2, sc in next sc, sk 1 sc on row 1, make 2 dc around next sc as before, sk next sc on row 2, sc in each of next 4 sc, rep from * across, end dc around post of next sc 1 row below, sc in each of next 3 sts, dc around post of next sc 1 row below, sc in each of last 3 sc.

Row 4: Sc in each of first 4 sts, (cluster in next sc, sc in next sc, cluster in next sc, sc in each of next 13 sts) 10 times, end cluster in next sc, sc in next sc, cluster in next sc, sc in each of last 4 sts.

FAIR FACTS

Wouldn't'cha figure? The Eastern Idaho State Fair features a Best Dressed Potato contest.

Row 5: Sc in each of first 3 sc, * (raised dc in raised dc, sc in each of next 3 sts) twice, (double raised dc in double raised dc, sc in each of next 3 sc) twice, rep from * across, end (raised dc in raised dc, sc in each of next 3 sts) twice.

Row 6: Rep row 2.

Row 7: Sc in each of first 3 sc, * raised dc in raised dc, sc in each of next 3 sts, raised dc in raised dc, sc in each of next 2 sc, double raised dc in double raised dc, sc in each of next 5 sc, double raised dc in double raised dc, sc in each of next 2 sc, rep from * across, end raised dc in raised dc, sc in each of next 3 sts, raised dc in raised dc, sc in each of last 3 sc.

Row 8: Rep row 4.

Row 9: Sc in each of first 3 sc, * raised dc in raised dc, sc in each of next 3 sts, raised dc in raised dc, sc in next sc, double raised dc in double raised dc, sc in each of next 3 sc, popcorn in next sc, sc in each of next 3 sc, double raised dc in double raised dc, sc in next sc, rep from * across, end raised dc in raised dc, sc in each of next 3 sts, raised dc in raised dc, sc in each of last 3 sc.

Row 10: Rep row 2.

Row 11: Rep row 7.

Row 12: Rep row 4.

Row 13: Rep row 5.

Row 14: Rep row 2.

Row 15: Sc in each of first 3 sc, * raised dc in raised dc, sc in next 3 sts, raiscd dc in raised dc, sc in each of next 4 sc, double raised dc in double raised dc, sc in next sc, doubled raised dc in double raised dc, sc in each of next 4 sc, rep from * across, end (raised dc in raised dc, sc in next 3 sts) twice.

Rep rows 4–15 until 24 diamond patterns have been completed. End off. From right side, work 1 row sc across last row, end 2 sc in last st. Do not end off.

Edging

Rnd 1: Working down side of afghan, from right side, * sc in end st of next 2 rows, sk 1 row, rep from * to corner, 3 sc in corner st, sc in each st across end to corner, 3 sc in corner; working up side, rep from first * to beg of rnd, sl st in first sc.

Rnd 2: Join another strand of yarn. Using double strand and J hook, working from left to right, work sc in every other sc, inc at corners to keep work flat. Join; end.

FRINGE

Cut strands 14 in. long. Hold 10 strands together, fold in half. With hook, pull fold through edge of afghan, pull ends through loop; tighten knot. Knot a fringe in center of each diamond and cluster panel at each end and in each corner. Trim fringe.

Originally Published in McCall's Book of Afghans

Granny's Ripple

Jean M. Roush

Jean's design pays homage to the classic granny square, but she adds her own flourish by adding ripples to create this octagonal afghan.

Granny's Ripple

Materials & Tools
Worsted-weight yarn, approximately:
- 8 oz. white (color A)
- 20 oz. light blue (color B)
- 28 oz. dark blue (color C)

Crochet hook size N, or size to match gauge

Gauge
In ripple pat, 6 dc = 3 in.

Finished size
Diameter = 72 in.

Note: The light blue and dark blue squares attached to the center square aren't the same distance from the center square, which means the ripple sections based on them are a different size (color C sections are slightly larger).

STEP 1
Center granny square: With color A, ch 4, join with sl st to form a ring.

Rnd 1: Ch 3, 2 dc in ring (ch 2, 3 dc) 3 times more in ring, hdc in top of beg ch 3 to join. (Counts as last ch-2 sp.)

Rnd 2: Ch 3, 2 dc in sp just made (ch 1, 3 dc, ch 2, 3 dc in next ch-2 sp) 3 times. Ch 1, work 3 dc in same sp as beg ch 3, ch 2, join with sl st to beg ch 3. Fasten off.

STEP 2
Make four basic granny squares that will be joined to ch-2 sps of center granny square. With color B, work same as center granny square through rnd 1.

Rnd 2: Ch 3, 2 dc in same sp, ch 1, 3 dc in next sp, (holding wrong sides of squares together) ch 1, sl st in a corner sp of center granny square, ch 1, (counts as a ch-2 sp). Continue around working the rest same as the center granny square.

Rep this granny square 3 times, joining one in each rem corner sp on center granny square.

STEP 3
Make 4 more granny squares to place between the ones made with color B. With color C, work same as center granny square through rnd 1.

Rnd 2: Ch 3, 2 dc in sp just made. Ch 1, 3 dc in next sp, ch 2, 2 dc in same sp, with wrong side facing sl st in corner sp of granny square to your right (made with color B), continuing around working granny square, dc in same sp last 2 dc worked. Ch 1, 3 dc in next sp, ch 4, sl st in ch-1 sp side of center granny square, ch 4, 3 dc in same sp last 3 dc worked, ch 1, 1 dc in next ch-2 sp of working granny square, sl st in corner sp of granny square to left of working granny square, 2 dc ch 2 3dc in same sp last dc made in working granny square. Ch 1, 3 dc, ch 2 in next sp join with sl st to beg ch 3. Fasten off.

Rep this granny square 3 times, joining between rem granny squares worked in step 2.

STEP 4
Work a rnd of sc around the granny squares.

Rnd 1: With color A, join with a sc in second available dc of any granny square added in step 2. Work sc in each dc and in each ch up to last dc available outside that granny square, sk that dc. Ch 1, in next granny square work (sc in second ch of ch-2 sp and each st around to last available ch-2 sp. Sc only in first ch of that space, ch 1 *. In next granny square

work sc in second available dc and each dc and ch up to last dc. Sk that dc, ch 1). Then rep from ( ) 2 times more, then between (to * once more. Join with sl st to beg sc.

STEP 5

Work 19 rows of dc ripple pattern, ripple rnds worked in back loops only, changing colors as needed for pat: one row white, two rows light blue, three rows dark blue. Rep three times, finish with one row white. To change colors, fasten off, change to new color and join with sl st in second dc of any section. Then work ch 3 (counts as first dc) then continue working same as rnd 2 below.

Rnd 1: Sl st to next sc, ch 3 (counts as first dc). Dc in next 4 sc, 2 dc in next sc, ch 2, 2 dc in next sc, dc in next 5 sc (sk next 3 sts, dc in next 7 sc, 2 dc in next sc, ch 2, 2 dc in next sc, dc in next 7 sc. Sk next 3 sts * dc in next 5 sc, 2 dc in next sc, ch 2, 2 dc in next sc, dc in next 5 sc, sk next 3 sts.) Rep from ( ) 3 times, then between (and * once more, join with sl st to beg ch 3. Fasten off.

Rnd 2: With color B, join with sl st to second dc of any section, ch 3 (counts as first dc) * Dc in each remaining dc across to ch-2 sp at top of section. 2 dc in first ch, ch 2, 2 dc in next ch, dc in each rem dc up to the last dc in that section, sk that dc and first dc in next section. Rep from * around.

Rnds 3–19: Rep row 2 following pattern for color changes.

STEP 6

Surround the ripple rnds with small granny squares. Work around the afghan as follows:

Join first granny square in third dc of any large section. Sk 4 dc, join next granny square, rep 3 more times. Sk 4 dc, join next granny square in ch-2 sp. Sk 4 dc, join next granny square. Rep 7 times. Continuing up side of smaller section sk next 3 dc, join next granny square, sk next 4 dc, join next granny square. Sk next 3 dc, join next granny in ch-2 sp at top of smaller section, sk next 3 dc, join granny square, sk 4 dc join granny square, sk 3 dc join granny square, sk 4 dc join granny square twice; continue around afghan following this pat.

First granny square: Ch 4, join with sl st to form a ring. Ch 3, 2 dc in ring, ch 2, 3 dc in ring, ch 1, then hold wrong sides together join with sl st in third dc of any section, ch 1, 3 dc in ring, ch 2, 3 dc in ring, join with sl st in top of beg ch 3. Fasten off. Working around to the right, sk the required number of dc, then work the next granny square.

Second through next-to-last granny square: Ch 4, join with sl st to form ring. Ch 3, 2 dc in ring, ch 2, 3 dc in ring, ch 1, join with sl st in dc (or ch-2 sp of afghan), ch 1, 3 dc in ring, ch 1, sl st in side ch-2 sp of previous granny square, ch 1, 3 dc in working granny square, ch 2, join with sl st in top of beg ch 3. Fasten off.

Last granny square: Ch 4, join with sl st to form ring. Ch 3, 2 dc in ring, ch 1. Join with sl st in rem side ch-2 sp of first granny, ch 1, 3 dc in ring, ch 1, sl st in dc on blanket, ch 1, 3 dc in ring, ch 1, sl st in side ch-2 sp of previous granny square. Ch 1 work 3 dc in ring, ch 2, join with sl st to top of beg ch 3. Fasten off.

STEP 7

Surround the small granny squares with a row of sc and sc decreases. Work sc dec as follows: insert hook in st and pull up a loop, insert hook in next st and pull up a loop, yo and draw through all loops on hook.

Edging rnd: With right side facing, join with sc in any ch-2 sp, ch 1, sc in same sp, sc in next 2 dc, sc dec in next 2 dc, sc in next 2 dc * sc, ch 1, sc in next ch-2 sp, sc in next 2 dc, sc dec in next 2 dc, sc in next 2 dc. Rep from * around, join to beg sc. Fasten off and hide threads.

Original Design

FAIR FACTS

Some of the early fairs in the frontier states were wild and wooly affairs. In New Mexico, the county sheriff was enlisted to umpire the baseball games, which were apparently quite, ah, competitive; he was forced to wear his badge to keep the game civil. Prior to the 1881 fair, the local newspaper published a notice that warned "those creating a disturbance are liable to be shot on sight."

IOWA
Throw Afghan

Frances Burgess

The design for this award-winner was passed down through Frances's family; it's a simply elegant stitch that is also elegantly simple.

Materials & Tools
Worsted-weight yarn, approximately:
  80 oz. variegated

Crochet hook size J, or size to
  match gauge

Gauge
12 dc = 4 in.

Finished size
Approximately 42 x 54 in.

INSTRUCTIONS
Ch 137.

Row 1: Dc in fourth ch from hook, then dc in every ch, turn (134 dc).

Row 2: Ch 3, dc in dc, * FPdc around each of next 2 dc, then dc in next 2 dc. Rep from * across.

Row 3: Ch 3, FPdc in dc, * dc in next 2 FPdc, FPdc in ech of nest 2 dc. Rep from * across.

Row 4–129: Rep rows 2 and 3.

Row 130: Dc in every st.

BORDER
First side: Join yarn at corner, ch 3, 4 dc in first sp, sl st in next sp, * 5 dc in next sp, sl st in next sp. Rep from * down side.

Bottom: Ch 3, 4 dc in first sp, * sk 2 sps, sl st in next sp, sk 2 sps, 5 dc in next sp. Rep from * across, ending sk 2 sps, sl st in next sp.

Second side: As first side.

Top: As bottom; join with last sl st, fasten off.

Tip: Add more stitches in groups of 4 or rows if you want a bigger afghan.

Original Design

FAIR FACTS

Befitting its location in the West, Colorado's fair offers professional rodeo, but also includes competitions for amateur cowpokes, like World Champion Mutton Bustin' (sheep riding). You can also box with three-foot inflatable gloves or compete in the jousting ring— with a padded pole, of course.

Wine Ripple

Anne R. Scharf

Anne makes afghans only as gifts for family and friends. Who wouldn't want this rich burgundy prizewinner?

Materials & Tools

Worsted-weight yarn, approximately:
   54 oz. burgundy

Crochet hook size G, or size to
   match gauge

Gauge

Approximately 3¾ in. from peak
   to peak of ripple

Finished size

Approximately 48 x 60 in.

INSTRUCTIONS

Ch 252.

Row 1: Sc in second ch from hook, sc in next 8 chs, (3 sc in next ch, sc in next 9 chs, sk next 2 chs, sc in next 9 chs) 11 times, 3 sc in next ch, sc in rem 10 chs. Ch 1, turn.

Row 2: Pick up back loop only of each sc throughout. Sk first sc, (sc in next 9 sc, 3 sc in next sc, sc in next 9 sc, sk 2 sc) 11 times, ending, sc in next 9 sc, 3 sc in next sc, sc in rem 10 sc. Ch 1, turn.

Rep row 2 for rest of afghan.

EDGING

Row 1: With right side facing, sc closely along one long edge. Turn.

Row 2: With wrong side facing, sl st in each sc of previous row. Tie off and fasten.

Work edging along opposite side.

Original Design

FAIR FACTS

A fire threatened to cancel Oregon's fair in 1967, as the inferno destroyed two huge exhibit buildings just as preparations for the fair were underway. Undaunted, state officials agreed to stage the fair and borrowed tents for the festivities, which lent an air of nostalgia from fairs gone by.

Irish Soft Mist

Ravon L. Noble

Ravon created this beautiful afghan by adding her own touches to the original design. She created this project as one piece, rather than in panels, and alternated the stitch patterns as she worked.

Materials & Tools
Worsted-weight yarn, approximately:
60 oz. ecru

Crochet hook sizes J and K, or
sizes to match gauge

Gauge
With smaller size hook in each
pat st, 3 sts = 1 in.

Finished size
Approximately 45 x 66 in.,
excluding fringe

Special note: Before starting your afghan, practice the Fisherman Pattern Stitches. Work several repeats of each pattern until you become familiar with the stitch and can obtain gauge (3 sts = 1 in.).

FISHERMAN PATTERN STITCHES
Note: Use smaller size hook for working each pat st.

Cable (worked over 2 sts)
Rows 1–4: Sc in each sc across.

Row 5 (cable row): Sc in next sc; work cable [To work cable: Ch 4, sl st around post of sc 4 rows below sc just made (figure 1); turn work slightly so wrong side of ch-4 is facing you; sc in top loop only in each of the 4 chs (figure 2)—cable made]; return to working row, sc in next sc (behind cable).

Row 6: Sc in next sc, sk cable, sc in next sc.

Rep rows 3 through 6 for pat.

Note: On each following cable row (row 5), work sl st (following ch-4) around post of first sc in previous cable row (figure 3).

Front Post (worked over 1 st)
Rows 1 and 2: Sc in next sc.

Row 3: Work FP (front post) around post of next sc in second row below. [To work FP: yo, insert hook around st from front to back to front; yo and draw loop through (3 loops now on hook); then complete st as a regular dc—(yo and draw through 2 loops on hook) twice—FP made]; return to working row, sk sc behind FP just made.

Row 4: Sc in top of FP.

Row 5: Work FP around post of FP in second row below.

Rep Rows 4 and 5 for pat.

Diamond (worked over 9 sts)
Row 1: Sc each of next 4 sc, ch 1 *loosely* (now and throughout Diamond Pat); sk 1 sc, sc in each of next 4 sc.

Row 2: Sc in each of next 3 sc; ch 1, sk 1 sc, sc in ch-1 sp; ch 1, sk 1 sc, sc in each of next 3 sc.

Row 3: Sc in each of next 3 sc; (ch 1, sk ch-1 sp, sc in next sc) twice; sc in each of next 2 sc.

Row 4: Sc in each of next 2 sc; ch 1, sk 1 sc, sc in ch-1 sp; sc in next sc, sc in ch-1 sp; ch 1, sk 1 sc, sc in each of next 2 sc.

Row 5: Sc in each of next 2 sc; ch 1, sk ch-1 sp, sc in each of next 3 sc; ch 1, sk ch-1 sp, sc in each of next 2 sc.

Row 6 (popcorn row): Sc in next sc; ch 1, sk 1 sc, sc in ch-1 sp; sc in next sc, popcorn in next sc. [To work popcorn: Work 5 sc in st; remove hook and insert hook in first sc of 5-sc group just made;

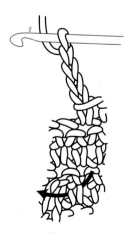

Figure 1

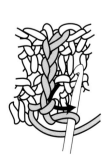

Figure 2

Figure 3

Irish Soft Mist

hook dropped loop and pull through st, ch 1—popcorn made]; sc in next sc, sc in ch-1 sp; ch 1, sk 1 sc, sc in next sc.

Row 7: Sc in next sc; ch 1, sk ch-1 sp, sc in each of next 2 sc; sc in popcorn (work in sc where dropped loop was pulled through), sc in each of next 2 sc; ch 1, sk ch-1 sp, sc in next sc.

Row 8: Sc in next sc, sc in ch-1 sp; ch 1, sk 1 sc, sc in each of next 3 sc; ch 1, sk 1 sc, sc in ch-1 sp, sc in next sc.

Row 9: Rep row 5.

Row 10: Sc in each of next 2 sc, sc in ch-1 sp; ch 1, sk 1 sc, sc in next sc; ch 1, sk 1 sc, sc in ch-1 sp, sc in each of next 2 sc.

Row 11: Rep row 3.

Row 12: Sc in each of next 3 sc, sc in ch-1 sp; ch 1, sk 1 sc, sc in ch-1 sp, sc in each of next 3 sc.

Note: Your work should now resemble graph in figure 4.

Row 13: Sc in each of next 4 sc, ch 1, sk ch-1 sp, sc in each of next 4 sc.

Rep rows 2–13 for pat. When all pat repeats are completed, work outline of diamonds as follows.

Diamond Outline

Note: Outline is worked on right side, using larger size hook and 2 strands of yarn (yarn is held at back of work).

First Half: Insert larger size hook in ch-1 sp at bottom of first diamond pat (at beg edge) from front to back, hook 2 strands of yarn and pull up a loop, leaving 4-in. ends for weaving in later. Working diagonally to the left, sl st in each of next 5 ch-1 sps (see figure 5). (To work sl st: Insert hook in ch-1 sp, hook yarn from beneath work and draw through work and loop on hook—sl st made); sl st in next ch-1 sp (above prev sl st). Now working diagonally to the right, sl st in each of next 12 sps (figure 6). Continue working in this manner (diagonally to the left and then to the right) through all rows of Diamond Pat. Finish off; weave in all ends. Then work Second Half as follows.

Second Half: Reversing direction (diagonally to the right and then diagonally to the left, etc.), work in same manner as First Half.

Note: On rows 12 and 13 of each diamond repeat, you will be working into same ch-1 sps where sl sts were worked in First Half of outline (crossing over prev sl st).

Blackberry (worked over an uneven number of sts)

Row 1: Sc in each st across.

Row 2 (blackberry row): Sc in first sc; * blackberry st in next sc [To work blackberry st: Insert hook in st and draw up a loop; (yo and draw through last loop on hook) 3 times; yo and draw through both loops on hook (figure 7), keeping ch-3 to front of work —blackberry made], sc in next sc; rep from * across.

Row 3: Rep row 1.

Row 4 (blackberry row): Sc in each of first 2 sc; * blackberry in next sc, sc in next sc; rep from * to last sc, sc in last sc.

Rep rows 1–4 for pat.

Note: Blackberry sts will be alternating every other row.

AFGHAN INSTRUCTIONS
Panel A (Make 3)
With smaller size hook, ch 30 *loosely*.

Row 1 (right side): Sc in second ch from hook and in each rem ch across (29 sc).

Row 2: Ch 1, turn; sc in each of first 10 sc, work row 1 of Diamond Pat over next 9 sc; sc in each of last 10 sc.

Row 3: Ch 1, turn; sc in first sc; * *work (row 3 of FP Pat) twice, sc in each of next 2 sc [remember to sk 1 sc behind each FP]; work row 3 of FP Pat once [you will be skipping 2 sc from last FP in 2nd row below] sc in each of next 2 sc; work (row 3 of FP Pat) twice* ;*

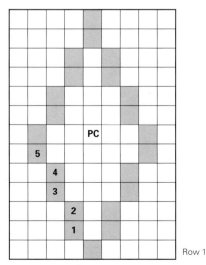

Figure 4

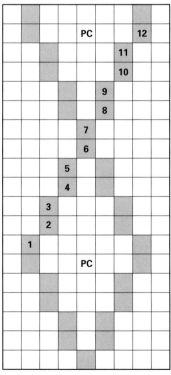

Figure 6

sc

ch-1 sp

work row 2 of Diamond Pat; rep from * to * once; sc in last sc.

Row 4: Ch 1, turn; sc in each of first 10 sts, work row 3 of Diamond Pat; sc in each of last 10 sts.

Row 5: Ch 1, turn; sc in first sc, * work (row 5 of FP Pat) twice, work row 5 of Cable Pat over next 2 sts; work row 5 of FP Pat once, work row 5 of Cable Pat over next 2 sts; work (row 5 of FP pat) twice *; work Row 4 of Diamond Pat; rep from * to * once; sc in last sc.

Row 6: Ch 1, turn; sc in each of first 4 sts, (sk cable, sc in each of next 3 sts) twice; work row 5 of Diamond Pat; (sc in each of next 3 sts, sk cable) twice; sc in each of last 4 sts.

Row 7: Ch 1, turn; sc in first sc; * work (row 5 of FP Pat) twice, sc in each of next 2 sc; work (row 5 of FP Pat) once, sc in each of next 2 sc; work (row 5 of FP pat) twice *; work row 6 of Diamond Pat; rep from * to * once; sc in last sc.

Row 8: Ch 1, turn; sc in each of first 10 sts, work row 7 of Diamond Pat; sc in each of last 10 sts.

Row 9: Ch 1, turn; sc in first sc; rep from * to * in row 5 of Panel A, once; work row 8 of Diamond Pat; rep from * to * in row 5 of Panel A, once; sc in last sc.

Row 10: Rep row 6.

Row 11: Ch 1, turn; sc in first sc, rep from * to * in row 7 of Panel A, once, work row 10 of Diamond Pat; rep from * to * in Row 7 of Panel A, once; sc in last sc.

Row 12: Rep row 4.

Row 13: Ch 1, turn; sc in first sc, rep from * to * in row 5 of Panel A, once; work row 12 of diamond pat; rep from * to * in row 5 of panel A, once; sc in last sc.

Figure 7

Row 14: Ch 1, turn; sc in each of first 4 sts, (sk cable, sc in each of next 3 sts) twice; work row 13 of Diamond Pat; (sc in each of next 3 sts, sk cable) twice; sc in each of last 4 sts.

Row 15: Ch 1, turn; sc in first sc, rep from * to * in row 7 of Panel A, once; work row 2 of Diamond Pat; rep from * to * in row 7 of Panel A, once; sc in last sc.

Rep rows 4 through 15 until work measures approx. 66 in. long, ending by working row 13.

Last Row (wrong side): Ch 1, turn; sc in each of first 4 sts, (sk cable, sc in each of next 3 sts) twice; sc in each of next 4 sc, sc in ch-1 sp, sc in each of next 7 sts; (sk cable, sc in each of next 3 sts) twice, sc in last sc. Finish off.

Work Diamond Outline on center diamond pat. Weave in all ends.

Panel B (Make 2)

With smaller size hook, ch 26 loosely.

Row 1 (wrong side): Sc in second ch from hook and in each rem ch across (25 sc).

Note: At beg of each following row, ch 1 and turn.

Following instructions for Blackberry Pat, beg with row 2 and work in pat until panel measures same length as Panel A, ending by working row 3. Finish off; weave in all ends.

Assembling

Alternating panels, place panels side by side with right side facing you and beg edge of each panel at same end of afghan. To join 2 panels, hold yarn at back of work and work sl st on right side, alternating from edge to edge as follows. Use smaller size hook and join yarn with a sl st in st at bottom edge of right panel. Insert hook in corresponding st at bottom edge of left panel, hook yarn from beneath work and draw up through work and loop on hook—sl st made. Sl st in next st on right panel, then sl st in corresponding st on left panel. Continue working in this manner (alternating sl sts from edge to edge) until panels are joined; finish off. Join rem panels in same manner.

Edging

With right side facing and working from *left to right*, use smaller size hook and work 1 row in reverse sc, evenly spaced (approximately every other row) across each long edge of afghan.

Fringe

Make triple knot of fringe. Cut 24-in. strands of yarn; use 8 strands for each knot of fringe. Tie knots evenly spaced (approximately every third st) across each short end of afghan. Then work double and triple knots; trim ends evenly.

Alterations: Ravon used light yellow yarn and worked this afghan as one piece, rather than in panels. She alternated stitches as stated above, and also used an original edging rather than the fringe called for in the instructions.

Pattern Courtesy of American School of Needlework

Take-Along Sampler Afghan

Ruth Ellen Klug

This glorious riot of color is an obvious prizewinner! Ruth Ellen says this afghan is fun to do and, as the name suggests, is easy to carry along so you can work on the go.

Materials & Tools

Worsted-weight yarn, approximately:
- 16 oz. black
- 2 oz. each of light green, violet, rose, natural, blue, marine blue, pink, gold, medium olive, brown, dark gold, copper, yellow, red, dark green, light brown, cranberry, beige, baby blue, olive, orange, white, and scarlet.

Afghan hook size H , or size to match gauge

Crochet hook size G, or size to match gauge

Tapestry needle

Gauge

4 sts = 1 in.; 3 rows = 1 in.

Finished size

Approximately 56 x 70 in., excluding fringe

INSTRUCTIONS

Block 1: With light green and afghan hook, ch 29. Work in plain afghan st on 29 sts for 21 rows. Change to crochet hook, sl st in each vertical bar across top of block.

EDGING

Rnd 1: Sc, ch 1, sc in corner; working down side of block, sc in each row to next corner, sc, ch 1, sc in corner; sc in each of next 3 ch, * sk 1 ch, sc in each of next 3 ch, rep from * across, sc, ch 1, sc in corner; sc in each row to next corner, sc, ch 1, sc in corner; working across top, sc in each of next 3 sts, * sk 1 st, sc in each of next 3 sts, rep from * across, sl st in first sc. End off.

Rnd 2: With black, sc in each sc around block, 3 sc in each corner ch-1 sp. Join; end off.

Following chart, embroider block in cross-stitch.

Block 2: With violet, work as for block 1.

Block 3: With rose, work as for block 1.

Block 4: With natural, work as for block 1 for 2 rows. Work off last 2 loops on hook with blue. Cut natural. With blue, work 1 row, work off last 2 loops on hook with gold. Cut blue. Always changing colors in this way, work 1 row gold, 1 row yellow, 1 row blue, 1 row pink, 1 row rose, 1 row blue, 3 rows marine blue, 1 row blue, 1 row rose, 1 row pink, 1 row blue, 1 row yellow, 1 row gold, 1 row blue, 2 rows natural. Finish as for block 1, working rnd 1 of edging with natural.

Block 5: With medium olive, work as for block 1.

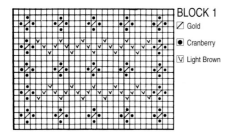

BLOCK 1
- ⊿ Gold
- ● Cranberry
- Ⅴ Light Brown

Note: Charts may be enlarged if necessary.

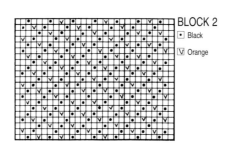

BLOCK 2
- • Black
- Ⅴ Orange

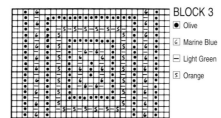

BLOCK 3
- ● Olive
- Ɠ Marine Blue
- — Light Green
- S Orange

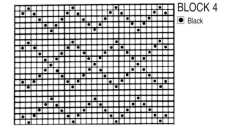

BLOCK 4
- ● Black

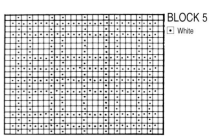

BLOCK 5
- • White

Take-Along Sampler Afghan

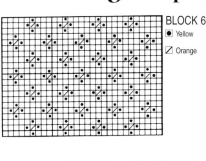

BLOCK 6
- ● Yellow
- ⧄ Orange

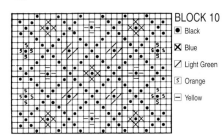

BLOCK 10
- ● Black
- ✕ Blue
- ⧄ Light Green
- Ⓢ Orange
- ▬ Yellow

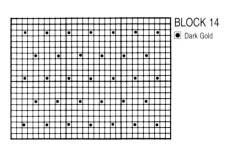

BLOCK 14
- ● Dark Gold

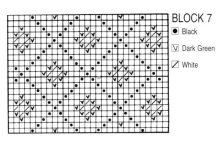

BLOCK 7
- ● Black
- Ⓥ Dark Green
- ⧄ White

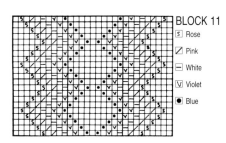

BLOCK 11
- Ⓢ Rose
- ⧄ Pink
- ▬ White
- Ⓥ Violet
- ● Blue

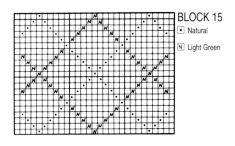

BLOCK 15
- · Natural
- Ⓝ Light Green

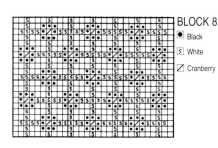

BLOCK 8
- ● Black
- Ⓢ White
- ⧄ Cranberry

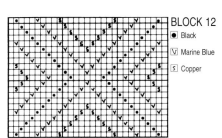

BLOCK 12
- ● Black
- Ⓥ Marine Blue
- Ⓢ Copper

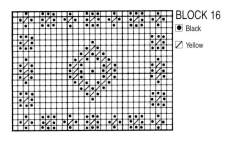

BLOCK 16
- ● Black
- ⧄ Yellow

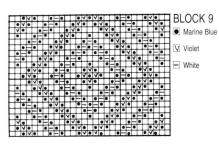

BLOCK 9
- ● Marine Blue
- Ⓥ Violet
- ▬ White

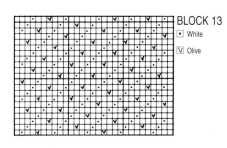

BLOCK 13
- · White
- Ⓥ Olive

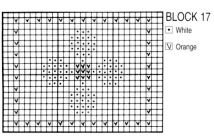

BLOCK 17
- · White
- Ⓥ Orange

Block 6: With brown, work as for block 1.

Block 7: With dark gold, work as for block 1.

Block 8: With gold, work as for block 1.

Block 9: With blue, work as for block 1.

Block 10: With copper, work as for block 1.

Block 11: With black, work as for block 1.

Block 12: With yellow, work as for block 1.

Block 13: With red, work as for block 1.

Block 14: With dark green, work as for block 1.

Block 15: With light brown, work as for block 1.

Block 16: With cranberry, work as for block 1.

Block 17: With marine blue, work as for block 1.

Block 18: With light green, work as for block 1.

Block 19: With beige, work as for block 1.

Block 20: With marine blue, work as for block 1.

Block 21: With black, work as for block 1.

Block 22: With pink, work as for block 1.

Block 23: With brown, work as for block 1 for 3 rows. Changing colors as for block 4, work 3 rows copper, 3 rows beige, 3 rows light green, 3 rows beige, 3 rows copper, 3 rows brown. Finish as for block 1, working rnd 1 of edging with brown.

Block 24: With baby blue, work as for block 1.

Block 25: With black, work as for block 1.

Block 26: With dark green, work as for block 1 for 2 rows. Changing colors as for block 4, work 2 rows black, 2 rows baby blue, 2 rows black, 5 rows cranberry, 2 rows black, 2 rows baby blue, 2 rows black, 2 rows dark green. Finish as for block 1, working both rnds of edging with black.

Block 27: With natural, work as for block 1.

Block 28: With olive, work as for block 1.

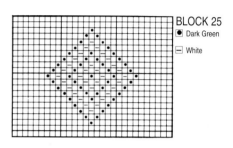

BLOCK 24
- ⊟ Dark Gold
- Ⅴ Olive
- · Rose
- ☒ Blue

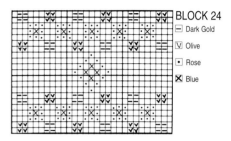

BLOCK 25
- ● Dark Green
- ⊟ White

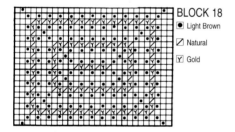

BLOCK 18
- ● Light Brown
- ⧄ Natural
- Ⲩ Gold

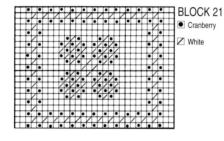

BLOCK 21
- ● Cranberry
- ⧄ White

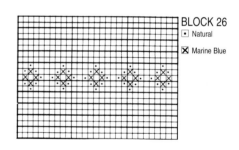

BLOCK 26
- · Natural
- ☒ Marine Blue

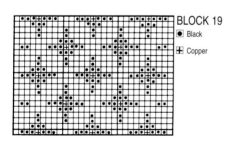

BLOCK 19
- ● Black
- ➕ Copper

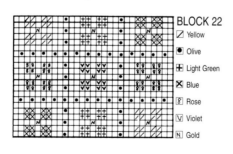

BLOCK 22
- ⧄ Yellow
- ● Olive
- ➕ Light Green
- ☒ Blue
- ⊗ Rose
- Ⅴ Violet
- Ⲛ Gold

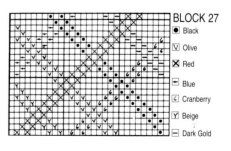

BLOCK 27
- ● Black
- Ⅴ Olive
- ☒ Red
- ⊟ Blue
- ⧏ Cranberry
- Ⲩ Beige
- ⊟ Dark Gold

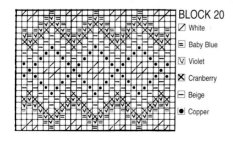

BLOCK 20
- ⧄ White
- ⊟ Baby Blue
- Ⅴ Violet
- ☒ Cranberry
- ⊟ Beige
- ● Copper

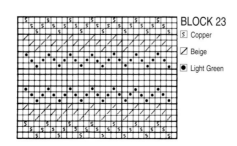

BLOCK 23
- �Ꙅ Copper
- ⧄ Beige
- ● Light Green

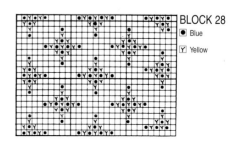

BLOCK 28
- ● Blue
- Ⲩ Yellow

Take-Along Sampler Afghan

Block 29: With orange, work as for block 1.

Block 30: With white, work as for block 1.

Block 31: With scarlet, work as for block 1.

Block 32: With light green, work as for block 1 for 3 rows. Changing colors as for block 4, work 3 rows light brown, 2 rows olive, 2 rows red, 1 row olive, 2 rows red, 2 rows olive, 3 rows light brown, 3 rows light green. Finish as for block 1, working 1 rnd of edging with light green.

Finishing

Sew blocks together with black, picking up back loops of sts on edge; see placement chart at right. With black, work 1 rnd sc around entire afghan, working 3 sc in each corner.

Fringe

Cut black in 10-in. lengths. Using 5 strands together for each fringe, knot a fringe in every fourth st across short ends of afghan.

Alterations: This is a pattern you can really have a lot of fun with, as did Ruth Ellen. She altered some of the cross-stitched blocks, changed the colors, created her own placement chart, omitted the fringe and made the afghan larger.

Originally Published in McCall's Book of Afghans

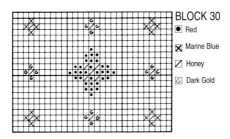

BLOCK 29
- Ⅴ Copper
- ● Black
- G Medium Olive
- ∕ Natural

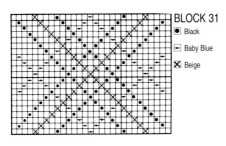

BLOCK 30
- ● Red
- ✕ Marine Blue
- ∕ Honey
- G Dark Gold

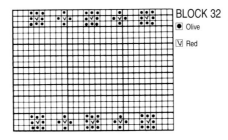

BLOCK 31
- ● Black
- ⊟ Baby Blue
- ✕ Beige

BLOCK 32
- ● Olive
- Ⅴ Red

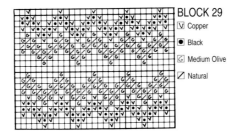

FAIR FACTS

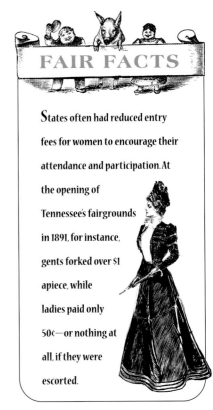

States often had reduced entry fees for women to encourage their attendance and participation. At the opening of Tennessee's fairgrounds in 1891, for instance, gents forked over $1 apiece, while ladies paid only 50¢—or nothing at all, if they were escorted.

PLACEMENT CHART

1	2	3	4	5	6	7
8	9	10	11	12	13	9
14	12	15	16	17	18	19
20	21	22	23	24	25	26
27	28	29	30	29	28	31
31	25	24	23	22	21	32
17	26	8	16	15	27	2
32	13	18	11	14	10	1
7	6	5	4	3	19	20

Popcorn Stitch Afghan

Sara Janzen

Sara's skillful rendering of this pattern won the top prize for an afghan she made for her granddaughter, Hannah—it's perfect for a special little girl's room.

Popcorn Stitch Afghan

Materials & Tools
Worsted-weight yarn, approximately:
- 72 oz. white
- 12 oz. variegated

Crochet hook size H, or size to match gauge

Tapestry needle

Gauge
7 dc = 2 in.; 4 dc rows and 4 sc rows = 3 in.; 1 fan = 1 in.; 2 dc rows = 1 in.

Finished size
Approximately 56½ x 65½ in.

Note: Use white unless otherwise stated.

SPECIAL STITCHES
Front post stitch (fp) and back post stitch (bp): Yo, insert hook from right to left around post of st on previous row, complete as dc.

HEART PANEL (Make 3)
Row 1: Starting at *bottom*, ch 31, dc in fourth ch from hook, dc in each ch across, turn (29 dc).

Row 2: Ch 1, sc in each st across, turn (29 sc).

Row 3: Ch 3, dc in next 13 sts; *for popcorn st, 4 dc in next st, drop loop from hook, insert hook in top of first dc of group, pull dropped loop through st;* dc in last 14 sts, turn (1 popcorn st, 28 dc). Ch 3 at beginning of row is counted as first dc. Front of row 3 is right side of work.

Row 4: Rep row 2.

Row 5: Ch 3, dc in next 11 sts, popcorn st in next st, dc in each of next 3 sts, popcorn st, dc in last 12 sts, turn (2 popcorn st, 27 dc).

Row 6: Rep row 2.

Row 7: Ch 3, dc in next 9 sts, popcorn st, dc in next 7 sts, popcorn st, dc in last 10 sts, turn.

Row 8: Rep row 2.

Row 9: Ch 3, dc in next 7 sts, popcorn st, dc in next 11 sts, popcorn st, dc in last 8 sts, turn.

Row 10: Rep row 2.

Row 11: Ch 3, dc in next 5 sts, popcorn st, dc in next 15 sts, popcorn st, dc in last 6 sts, turn.

Row 12: Rep row 2.

Row 13: Ch 3, dc in each of next 3 sts, popcorn st, dc in next 19 sts, popcorn st, dc in last 4 sts, turn.

Row 14: Rep row 2.

Row 15: Ch 3, dc in each of next 3 sts, popcorn st, (dc in next 9 sts, popcorn st) 2 times, dc in last 4 sts, turn (3 popcorn st, 26 dc).

Row 16: Rep row 2.

Row 17: Ch 3, (dc in next 5 sts, popcorn st) 2 times, dc in each of next 3 sts, popcorn st; rep between ( ), dc in last 6 sts, turn (4 popcorn st, 25 dc).

Row 18: Rep row 2.

Row 19: Ch 3, (dc in next 7 sts, popcorn st, dc in next st, popcorn st) 2 times, dc in last 8 sts, turn.

Row 20: Rep row 2.

Row 21: Ch 3, dc in each st across, turn.

Rows 22–161: Rep rows 2–21 consecutively. At end of last row, do not turn.

Row 162: Working in ends of rows on side, sc in end of each sc row and 2 sc in end of each dc row across (242 sc). Fasten off.

Row 163: With right side facing you, working in ends of rows on opposite side, join with sc in first row, sc in end of each sc row and 2 sc in end of each dc row across (242 sc). Fasten off.

SHELL PANEL (Make 2)
Row 1: Starting at *bottom*, ch 39, dc in fourth ch from hook, dc in next ch, * sk next 3 chs; *for shell, 5 dc in next ch or st;* ch 2, sk next 3 chs, dc in each of next 2 chs, popcorn st in next ch, dc in each of next 2 chs; rep from *, sk next 3 chs, shell, ch 2, sk next 3 chs, dc in each of last 3 sts, turn (2 popcorn st, 3 shells, 14 dc).

Row 2: Ch 3 dc in each of next 2 sts, * [sk next ch sp, shell in first dc of next shell, ch 2, sk next 4 dc], back post (bp) around next st, dc in each of next 3 sts, bp around next st; rep from *; rep between [ ], dc in each of last 3 sts, turn (3 shells, 4 bp, 12 dc).

Row 3: Ch 3, dc in each of next 2 sts, * [sk next ch sp, shell in first dc of next shell, ch 2, sk next 4 dc], front post (fp) around next post st, dc in next st, popcorn st in next st, dc in next st, fp around next post st; rep from *; rep between [ ], dc in each of last 3 sts, turn.

Rows 4–121: Rep rows 2 and 3 alternately. At end of last row, *do not turn.*

Row 122: Working in ends of rows on side, 2 sc in end of each row across (242 sc). Fasten off.

Row 123: With right side of work facing you, working in ends of rows on opposite side, join with sc in end of first row, sc in same row, 2 sc in end of each row across, turn (242 sc). Fasten off.

PANEL EDGING
Row 1: For Heart Panel 1, with right facing you, working on long edge, starting at *bottom*, join variegated with sc in first st, sc in each st across, turn.

Row 2: Working this row in *back loops*, sl st in each st across, turn.

Row 3: Working this row in unworked *front loops* of row 1, sc in each st across. Fasten off.

For Heart Panel 2, work same as Heart Panel 1. Starting at *top*, rep on opposite side.

For Heart Panel 3, starting at *top*, work same as Heart Panel 1.

For each Shell Panel, work same as Heart Panel 1. Starting at *top*, rep on opposite side.

ASSEMBLY
Sew Heart Panels and Shell Panels together as in photo on page 85.

BORDER
Rnd 1: With right side facing you, working around outer edge, join white with sc in any st, sc in each st and in end of each row around with 3 sc in each corner st, *do not join* (910 sc).

Rnd 2: Working this rnd in *front loops*, sl st in each st around.

Rnd 3: Working in unworked *back loops* of rnd 1, sc in each st around with 3 sc in each center corner st (918 sc). Fasten off.

Rnd 4: Join variegated with sl st in any center corner st, (ch 3, popcorn st, dc) in same st, * (dc in next st, popcorn st, dc in next st) around to next center corner st, (dc, popcorn st, dc) in corner st; rep from * 2 more times, (dc in next st, popcorn st, dc in next st) across, join with sl st in top of ch 3 (926 sts). Fasten off.

Rnd 5: Join white with sc in corner st on first Heart Panel, 2 sc in same st, sc in each st around with 3 sc in each center corner st, join with sl st in first sc (934 sc).

Rnd 6: Rep rnd 2, join with sl st in first sl st.

Rnd 7: Ch 1, * 3 sc in next st, (sc in next 62 st, 2 sc in next st) 3 times, sc in each st across to next center corner st, 3 sc in next st, sc in each st across * to center corner st; rep between first *, join with sl st in first sc (948 sc).

Rnd 8: Sl st in next st, ch 5, (dc, ch 2, dc) in same st, sk next 3 st, *(dc, ch 2, dc, ch 2 dc) in next st, sk next 3 sts; rep from * around, join with sl st in 3rd ch of ch 5.

Rnd 9: Sl st in first ch sp, *(ch 3, sc, ch 3, sc, ch 3) in next st, sc in each of next 2 ch sps; rep from * around to last ch sp, ch 3, sc in last ch sp, join with sl st in first sc. Fasten off.

Pattern Courtesy of Annie's Attic

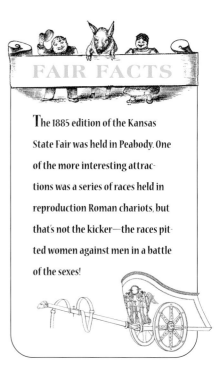

FAIR FACTS
The 1885 edition of the Kansas State Fair was held in Peabody. One of the more interesting attractions was a series of races held in reproduction Roman chariots, but that's not the kicker—the races pitted women against men in a battle of the sexes!

Pine Tree

Viola M. Heaton

Viola took an old pattern and gave it new life when she changed the color scheme to create this prizewinner: the instructions called for browns, but Viola substituted hues from the forest and meadow.

Materials & Tools
Worsted-weight yarn, approximately:
- 28 oz. dark green (color A)
- 8 oz. beige (color B)
- 12 oz. each of light blue (color C), light rose (color D), and dark rose (color E)

Afghan hook size F, or size to match gauge

Crochet hook size F, or size to match gauge

Tapestry needle

Gauge
Afghan st—9 sts = 2 in., 4 rows = 1 in.; shaded pattern— 4 sts = 1 in., 4 rows = 1 in.

Finished size
Approximately 50 x 72 in.

AFGHAN STITCH PANEL (Make 5)

Rows 1–5: Using afghan hook, with color A, ch 20 and work in afghan st for 5 rows.

† Row 6: (Bead-st pat): Draw up a loop as before through each bar (20 loops on hook), work off first 10 loops on hook as for afghan st then ch 4, yo and through both ch loop and next loop on hook— Bead-st made, work off rem loops as for afghan st.

Row 7: Draw up a loop through each bar of previous row, keeping Bead-st to front (right side) of work (20 loops on hook), work off first 9 loops, * ch 4, yo and through both ch loop and next loop on hook—Bead-st made, yo, draw through

2 loops on hook * ; rep between * once, work off rem loops on hook.

Row 8: Draw up a loop through each bar of previous row, keeping Bead-st to front (right side) of work (20 loops on hook), work off first 8 loops; rep between * of row 7 three times, work off rem loops.

Row 9: Draw up a loop through each bar (20 loops), work off 7 loops; rep between * of row 7 four times, work off rem loops.

Row 10: Draw up a loop through each bar (20 loops), work off 6 loops; rep between * of row 7 five times, work off rem loops. Then rep rows 9, 8, 7, 6. Work 7 rows in afghan st. Rep from † for pattern 15 times ending last rep with only 5 rows in afghan st (16 diamond pats), finish off with a row of sl sts. Fasten off.

SHADED PATTERN
Note: Work all rows from right side

Row 1: With color E, make a loop on size F crochet hook, working along long side of Panel, work 1 sc in end st of each of first 3 rows, * work a tr under bar of fourth st in next row, sk row in back of tr, sc in each of next 3 rows; rep from * across, fasten off.

Row 2: *Hereafter always work in back loop of sts.* With color E, sc in each of first 4 sts, * work a tr in third st of next afghan st row, *hereafter always sk st back of tr,* sc in each of next 3 sts; rep from * across, end with 2 sc, fasten off.

Row 3: With color E, sc in each of first 5 sts, * work a tr in second st of next afghan st row, sc in each of next 3 sts; rep from * across, end with 1 sc, fasten off.

Row 4: With color D, sc in each of first 2 sts, * work a tr in first st of next afghan st row, sc in each of next 3 sts; rep from * across, end with 4 sc, fasten off.

Row 5: With color D, sc in each of first 3 sts, work a tr in free loop above first tr of row 1, sc in each of next 3 sts, * a tr in free loop above next tr, sc in each of next 3 sts; rep from * across, fasten off.

Row 6: With color D, sc in each of first 4 sts, * a tr in free loop above next tr of row 2, sc in each of next 3 sts; rep from * across, end with 2 sc, fasten off.

Row 7: With color C, sc in first st, a tr in free loop of second st of row 3, sc in each of 3 sts; continue in pat across, end with 1 sc, fasten off.

Row 8: With color C, sc in each of first 2 sts, a tr in free loop above next tr of row 4 below, sc in each of 3 sts; continue in pat across, end with 4 sc, fasten off.

Row 9: With color C, sc in each of first 3 sts, a tr in free loop above next tr of row 5 below, sc in each of 3 sts; continue in pat across, fasten off.

Row 10: With color B, sc in each of first 4 sts, a tr in free loop above next tr of row 6 below, sc in each of next 3 sts; continue in pat across, fasten off.

Row 11: With color B, sc in first st, a tr in free loop of second st of row 7, sc in each of 3 sts; continue in pat across, fasten off. Work same Shaded Pattern on opposite side of Panel to correspond.

FINISHING
Lay 2 strips together with Shaded Pattern sloping in same direction on both strips as shown. From right side, sew strips together. Join all strips in same way.

BORDER
Work all rnds from right side, with color E, work 1 sc in each st along long sides and about 1 sc in each row along short sides and 3 sc in each corner, join (with sl st) in first sc, fasten off.

Rnd 2: With color E, work 3 dc in any corner st, * ch 1, sk next 3 sts, 3 dc in next st; rep from * to next corner, ch 1, 3 dc in corner st; continue in same way around, join in first dc, fasten off.

Rnd 3: With color D, work 3 dc in center dc of corner 3-dc group, * ch 1, 3 dc in next ch-1 sp; rep from * to next corner, ch 1, 3 dc in center dc of corner group; continue in same way around, join, fasten off.

Rnd 4: With color C, rep rnd 3.

Rnd 5: With color B, work [2 dc, ch 1, 2 dc] in center dc of a corner group, * ch 1, [2 dc, ch 1, 2 dc] in next ch-1 sp; rep from * to next corner, ch 1, [2 dc, ch 1, 2 dc] in corner dc; continue in same way around, join, fasten off.

Rnd 6: With color A, work [2 sc, ch 1, 2 sc] in ch-1 sp of any corner Shell, sc in next ch-1 sp (between Shells), [2 sc, ch 1, 2 sc] in ch-1 sp of next Shell; continue in same way around, join, fasten off.

Alterations: Viola's afghan is sized for a queen-sized bed; she also changed the colors.

Originally Published by Bernhard Co.

Blue Granny Square Afghan

Laura Bareuther

Laura makes wonderful use of color in her granny square design. This lovely afghan—her first—was also awarded a championship ribbon.

Materials & Tools

Worsted-weight yarn, approximately:
16 oz. each of white and light blue
24 oz. medium blue

Crochet hook size H, or size to match gauge

Tapestry needle

1 piece of cardboard, approximately 5 in. wide

Gauge
One square = 6½ in.

Finished size
Approximately 49 x 62 in.

BLUE GRANNY SQUARES (Make 43)

With white ch 6, join with sl st to form ring.

Rnd 1: Ch 3, 2 dc in ring, ch 3, * 3 dc in ring, ch 3. Rep from * 2 times, end with sl st in top of beg ch-3.

Rnd 2: Ch 3, in same sp work 2 dc, ch 3, 3 dc. * Ch 2, in next sp work (3 dc, ch 3, 3 dc) ch 2, rep from * around, ending with ch 2, sl st to the top of the beg ch-3. Fasten off.

Rnd 3: Attach light blue yarn in any corner sp, ch 3, in same sp work 2 dc, ch 3, 3 dc. * Ch 2, in next sp work 3 dc, ch 2, in the corner sp work (3 dc, ch 3, 3 dc), rep from * around, ending with ch 2, sl st in the top of the beg ch-3.

Rnd 4: Ch 3, in same sp work 2 dc, ch 3, 3 dc. * Ch 1, (in next ch-2 sp work 3 dc, ch 1) twice; in corner sp work (3 dc, ch 3, 3 dc), rep from * around, ending with ch 1, sl st to the top of the ch-3 at beg of round. Fasten off.

Rnd 5: With medium blue, work as for rnd 4, except rep between ( ) 3 times.

Rnd 6: Work as for rnd 4, except rep between ( ) 4 times. Fasten off.

WHITE GRANNY SQUARES (Make 20)

Reverse the colors (medium blue, light blue, white) and repeat the instructions above for a total of 63 squares.

ASSEMBLY

Block each square to approximately 6½ x 6½ in.

Next, arrange the squares in seven rows, with nine squares in each row. The edge rows, 1 and 7, are each nine blue granny squares. Rows 2 and 6 are each seven white squares, with one blue square at either end. Rows 3, 4, and 5 begin with a blue square, then one white square, five blue squares, one white square, and end with one blue square. Stitch squares together using yarn and tapestry needle, making invisible stitches with medium blue or white yarn to match the squares. Arrange rows and stitch together with needle and yarn.

BORDER

Attach white yarn in any ch-3 corner sp, ch 3, in the same sp work 2 dc, ch 3, 3 dc. * Ch 1, in the next ch-2 sp work 3 dc, ch 1 rep from * to the corner; in the corner work (3 dc, ch 3, 3 dc). Rep for all sides and corners, end with sl st to the top of the beg ch-3. Fasten off. Rep with light blue yarn, then rep with medium blue yarn to form 3 rows of dc border. Block the border.

TASSELS

Make four large multi-colored yarn tassels, 4 in. long, by winding all three colors of yarn 12 complete times around a 5-in. wide piece of cardboard. Tie tassel at edge of cardboard with a square knot, using a piece of medium blue yarn about 12 in. long. Slide yarn from cardboard. Tie all tassel strands about 1 in. from previous tie with another piece of yarn. Cut loops at end opposite the tie; trim ends even. Repeat to make three more tassels. Tie onto each corner.

Original Design

Blue & Yellow Plaid Afghan

Kenneth B. Allen

This unique afghan is Ken's own design; he developed this technique of creating plaids in the afghan stitch. He made this prizewinner for his daughter-in-law, Tara.

Materials & Tools
Worsted-weight yarn, approximately:
  42 oz. off-white (OW)
  28 oz. yellow (BY)
  17½ oz. light blue (LB)
  7 oz. dark blue (DB)

Afghan hook size I, 14 in., modified to a length of approximately 35 in.

Crochet hook sizes F and H, or size to match gauge

Gauge
12 afghan sts = 3 in.

Finished size
Approximately 50 x 87 in.

STITCH PATTERN
Vertical stripes: 15+ OW, 10 LB, 16 OW, 12 BY, 4 DB, 12 BY, 16 OW, 10 LB (this being the center stripe), reverse this pat (+ only at end, else 16).

Horizontal stripes: 13 ++ OW, 9 LB, 14 OW, 11 BY, 3 DB, 11 BY, rep three more times with all OW stripes 14, then finish with 14 OW, 9 LB, 13++ OW. (++only at end, else 14).

Border: 4 LB, 3 OW, 2 BY, 2 DB, 2 BY, 2 OW.

FIELD
Afghan st, 180 sts wide and 295 rows high.

Sixteen yarns are worked all at the same time, one for each of the vertical colors and one for the horizontal color in use, this one changing yarn color at either the left or right side depending on the horizontal stripe being an even or odd number of rows.

Begin with OW ch 181, then put 180 bars on the hook in each row, not counting the left-most loop on the hook, it being the 181st st. Return yo and draw through 1 loop, * yo and draw through 2 loops. Rep from * across. Introduce a yarn color for the vertical stripe as per the Stitch Pattern above. (Next row use the vertical yarns for the bars and return with the horizontal yarn.) Continue working the row pat, alternating the horizontal yarn with the vertical yarns as the bars/return of the afghan st. Changing of vertical yarn color across the row is done by looping the new color behind the last st of the old color.

BORDER
Sc in each outside st/row, using size H crochet hook against the rows and size F crochet hook against the st. Sc, ch, sc, at each corner. Subsequent rows sc in the back of the previous row sc.

Tips: Here's how Ken modified his afghan hook; he added monofilament line by cutting off the stop end of the afghan hook and drilling a hole in the shaft. Then, he heated the end of the monofilament line and pressed it to make a bulb on the end. He inserted this end in the hole, hammered the shaft end tight around the line, and filed it down to the diameter of the monofilament line. Ken then added a stop on the end of the line. He cautions that you must be careful to file the hook smooth so it won't cut the yarn. He also reports that extension hooks are available commercially.

Because of the looping of yarns at the color change, stop every ten or so rows and untwist the skeins.

Original Design

Ripple Afghan

Loretta Coulson

Soothing shades of teal and turquoise make for a beautiful piece of work. Loretta adapted a stitch pattern to create this ripple afghan.

Materials & Tools

Worsted-weight yarn, approximately:
    16 oz. each of dark teal (color A), light teal (color B), turquoise (color C), and white (color D)

Crochet hook size I, or size to match gauge

Gauge

10 st = 3 in.

Finished size

Approximately 62 x 70 in.

INSTRUCTIONS

Foundation ch with color A: multiple of 21 + 20

Row 1 (right side): Sc in second ch from hook and in next 8 chs, 3 sc in next ch; sc in next 9 chs; * sk next 2 chs, sc in next 9 chs, 3 sc in next ch; sc in next 9 chs; rep from * across. Ch 1, turn.

Note: Rows 2 through 6 are worked in back loops only.

Row 2: Sc in first sc, sk next sc, sc in next 8 sc, 3 sc in next sc; * sc in next 9 sc, sk next 2 sc, sc in next 9 sc, 3 sc in next sc; rep from * to last 10 sts; sc in next 8 sc, sk next sc, sc in last sc. Change to color B by drawing loop through; cut color A. Ch 1, turn.

Rows 3–4: Rep row 2. At end of row 4, change to color C by drawing loop through; cut color B. Ch 1, turn.

Rows 5–6: Rep row 2. At end of row 6, change to color D by drawing loop through; cut color C. Ch 2, turn.

Note: Rows 7–10 are worked through both loops.

Row 7: Dc in next sc, sk next 2 sc, in next sc work (dc, ch 1, dc)—V-st made; sk next 2 sc, V-st in next sc, sk next sc, dc in next sc, ch 1, V-st in next sc; ch 1, dc in next sc, sk next sc, V-st in next sc, sk next 2 sc, V-st in next sc; * sk next 2 sc, dec over next 4 sc (to work dec: yo, draw up loop in next sc, yo, draw through 2 loops on hook, sk next 2 sc, yo, draw up loop in next sc, yo, draw through 2 loops on hook, yo and draw through all 3 loops on hook—dec made); (sk next 2 sc, V-st in next sc) twice; sk next sc, dc in next sc, ch 1, V-st in next sc; ch 1, dc in next sc, sk next sc, (V-st in next sc; sk next 2 sc) twice; rep from * to last 2 sc; dec over next 2 sc [to work dec: (yo, draw up loop in next sc, yo, draw through 2 loops on hook) twice; yo and draw through all 3 loops on hook—dec made]. Ch 2, turn.

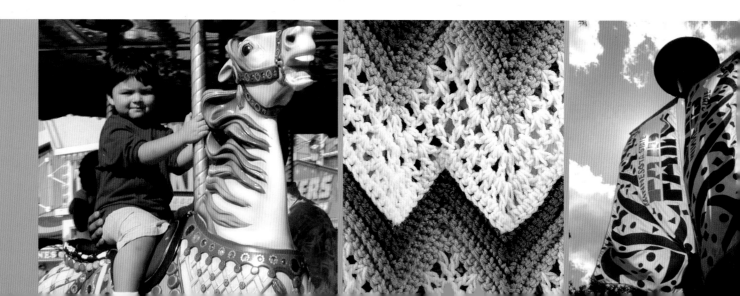

Row 8: Dc in ch-1 sp of next V-st; V-st in ch-1 sp of next V-st and in next ch-1 sp; dc in next dc, ch 1, V-st in next ch-1 sp; ch 1, dc in next dc, V-st in next ch-1 sp and in ch-1 sp of next V-st; * dec over next 2 ch-1 sps [to work dec: (yo, draw up loop in next ch-1 sp, yo, draw through 2 loops on hook) twice; yo and draw through all 3 loops on hook—dec made]; V-st in ch-1 sp of next V-st and in next ch-1 sp; dc in next dc, ch 1, V-st in next ch-1 sp, ch 1, dc in next dc, V-st in next ch-1 sp and in ch-1 sp of next V-st; rep from * to last V-st; dec over ch-1 sp of last V-st and turning ch-2 (to work dec: yo, draw up loop in ch-1 sp of last V-st, yo, draw through 2 loops on hook, yo, draw up loop in second ch of turning ch-2, yo, draw through 2 loops on hook, yo and draw through all 3 loops on hook—dec made). Ch 2, turn.

Row 9: Dc in ch-1 sp of next V-st; V-st in ch-1 sp of next V-st and in next ch-1 sp; dc in next dc, ch 1, V-st in next ch-1 sp; ch 1, dc in next dc, V-st in next ch-1 sp and in ch-1 sp of next V-st; * dec over next 2 ch-1 sps; V-st in ch-1 sp of next V-st and in next ch-1 sp; dc in next dc, ch 1, V-st in next ch-1 sp, ch 1, dc in next dc, V-st in next ch-1 sp and in ch-1 sp of next V-st; rep from * to last V-st; dec over ch-1 sp of last V-st and turning ch-2. Ch 1, turn.

Row 10: Sc in first st, sk next dc, working in each dc and in each ch, sc in next 8 sts, 3 sc in next ch-1 sp; * sc in next 9 sts, sk next st, sc in next 9 sts, 3 sc in next ch-1 sp; rep from * to last 10 sts; sc in next 8 sts, sk next 2 dc, sc in second ch of turning ch-2. Change to color A by drawing loop through; cut color D. Ch 1, turn.

Row 11: Working in back loops only, sc in first sc, sk next sc, sc in next 8 sc, 3 sc in next sc; * sc in next 9 sc, sk next 2 sc, sc in next 9 sc, 3 sc in next sc; rep from * to last 10 sts; sc in next 8 sc, sk next sc, sc in last sc. Ch 1, turn.

Rep rows 2–11 for desired length, ending with row 6.

Stitch Pattern Courtesy of American School of Needlework

Kaleidoscope

Lisa Donald

This glorious explosion of color perfectly captures the excitement of the state fair. Lisa used bits of leftover yarn to create the hexagons in this design, so each is unique.

Version A

Materials & Tools
Worsted-weight yarn, approximately:
  30 oz. medium yellow
  18 oz. orange
  11 oz. dark rust

Crochet hook size H, or size to
  match gauge

Tapestry needle

1 piece of cardboard, 6 x 10 in.

Gauge
In dc, 4 sts = 1 in.; 2 rows = 1 in.;
rnds 1–6, hexagon = 6¼ x 8-in.

Finished size
Approximately 45 x 65 in.,
  excluding tassels

INSTRUCTIONS

Pattern Stitch

Front Post Double Triple Crochet (FPdtr):
Yo 3 times, insert hook from front to back and out to front again around post of dc 2 rows below (figure 1), hook yarn and pull up a loop (5 loops on hook as shown in figure 2), (yo and draw through 2 loops) 4 times, sk dc behind FPdtr—FPdtr made.

Hexagon Motif (make 72)

With dark rust ch 6; join with sl st in beg ch to form a ring.

Rnd 1: Ch 3 (counts as first dc), 2 dcs in ring, ch 1, (3 dcs in ring, ch 1) 5 times; join with sl st in third ch of beg ch-3 (now and throughout unless otherwise specified): 6, 3-dc groups.

Rnd 2: Work beg inc as follows: ch 3, dc in same st as joining—beg inc made, dc in next dc, inc as follows: 2 dc in next dc—inc made, ch 1, sk next ch-1 space, (inc in next dc, dc in next dc, inc in next dc, ch 1, sk next ch-1 space) 5 times; finish off.

Rnd 3: Join orange with sl st in first dc to left of any ch-1 sp, work beg inc, dc in next dc, work FPdtr around post of center dc in 3-dc group 2 rows below, dc in next dc, inc in next dc, ch 1, sk next ch-1 sp, (inc in next dc, dc in next dc, work FPdtr as before, dc in next dc, inc in next dc, ch 1, sk next ch-1 sp) 5 times.

Rnd 4: Work beg inc, dc in next 5 sts (working in top of FPdtr same as in each dc), inc in next dc, ch 1, sk next ch-1 space, (inc in next dc, dc in next 5 sts, inc in next dc, ch-1, sk next ch-1 sp) 5 times; finish off.

Rnd 5: Join yellow same as orange, work beg inc, dc in next dc, work FPdtr around post of second dc of inc 2 rows below, dc in next 3 dcs, work FPdtr around post of first dc of next inc 2 rows below, dc in next dc, inc in next dc, ch 1, sk next ch-1 sp, (inc in next dc, dc in next dc, work FPdtr as before, dc in next 3 dc, work FPdtr, dc in next dc, inc in next dc, ch 1, sk next ch-1 sp) 5 times.

Rnd 6: Work beg inc, dc in next 9 sts, inc in next dc, ch 1, sk next ch-1 sp, (inc in next dc, dc in next 9 sts, inc in next dc, ch 1, sk next ch-1 sp) 5 times; finish off. Weave in yarn ends.

Half Motif (Make 10)

Note: All rows are worked on right side with yarn finished off at end of each row.

Row 1: With dark rust ch 4, (2 dc, ch 1, 3 dc, ch 1, 3 dc) in fourth ch from hook; finish off.

Row 2: Join dark rust with sl st in last ch of ch-4 on previous row, work beg inc as follows: ch 3, dc in same ch as joining—beg inc made, dc in next dc, inc as follows: 2 dcs in next dc—inc made, ch 1, sk next ch-1 sp, inc in next dc, dc in next dc, inc in next dc, ch 1, sk next ch-1 sp, inc in next dc, dc in next dc, inc in rem dc; finish off.

Row 3: Join orange with sl st in third ch of beg ch-3 on previous row, work beg inc, (dc in next dc, work FPdtr around post of center dc in 3-dc group 2 rows below, dc in next dc, inc in next dc, ch 1, sk next ch-1 sp, inc in next dc) twice, dc in next dc, work FPdtr as before, dc in next dc, inc in remaining dc; finish off.

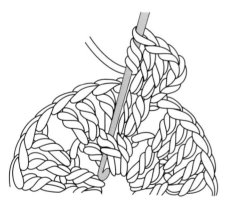

Figure 1

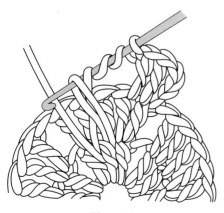

Figure 2

Kaleidoscope

Row 4: Join orange as before, work beg inc, [dc in next 5 sts (working in top of FPdtr same as in each dc), inc in next dc, ch 1, sk next ch-1 sp, inc in next dc] twice, dc in next 5 sts, inc in rem dc; finish off.

Row 5: Join medium yellow same as orange, work beg inc, (dc in next dc, work FPdtr around post of 2nd dc of inc 2 rows below, dc in next 3 dc, work FPdtr around post of first dc of next inc 2 rows below, dc in next dc, inc in next dc, ch 1, sk next ch-1 sp, inc in next dc) twice, dc in next dc, work FPdtr, dc in next 3 dc, work FPdtr, dc in next dc, inc in rem dc; finish off.

Row 6: Join medium yellow as before, work beg inc, (dc in next 9 sts, inc in next dc, ch 1, sk next ch-1 sp, inc in next dc) twice, dc in next 9 sts, inc in remaining dc; finish off. Weave in yarn ends.

Finishing

With 2 motifs wrong sides together, thread tapestry or yarn needle with medium yellow and join in first dc to left of any ch-1 sp. Sew edges together carefully matching st to next ch-1 sp; finish off. Join 42 motifs to form six strips of seven motifs each. Join 30 motifs to form five strips of six motifs with one half motif at each end. Join strips in same manner as motifs, working through all three ch-1 sps where three motifs meet. Piece should look like figure 3.

Edging

With piece right side facing, join medium yellow with sl st in first dc to left of ch-1 sp marked A in figure 3.

Rnd 1: Working around entire afghan, beg with top edge, work beg inc, dc in next 11 dcs, inc in next dc, ch 1, † * inc in next dc, dc in next 12 dc, dec in inside corner as follows: yo, (pull up a loop in next ch-1 sp) twice, (yo and draw through 2 loops) 3 times—dec made, dc in next 12 dc, inc in next dc, ch 1; rep from * 5 times, inc in next dc, dc in next 11 dc, inc in next dc, ch 1, inc in next dc, dc in next 12 dc, ch 1, dc in next dc,

(2 dc around post of last dc at end of next row on half motif) 5 times, dc in center sp of half motif, (2 dc around post of last dc at end of next row on half motif) 5 times, dc in next dc, ch 1, dc in next 13 dcs on next motif, ch 1, continue to work each motif and each half motif in same manner to last motif on long side of afghan, dc in next 12 dc on side of last motif, inc in next dc, ch 1 †, inc in next dc, dc in next 11 dc, inc in next dc, ch 1; rep from † to † once; join with sl st in third ch of beg ch-3; finish off.

Tassels (Make 14)

Cut a piece of cardboard 10 in. long and 6 in. wide. For each tassel, wind yarn loosely 30 times around 10 in. length. Cut a piece of yarn 20 in. long, double it and thread into tapestry needle. Thread under all strands at top of cardboard and pull up tightly; knot securely. Cut at opposite side of cardboard. Cut another strand of yarn 10 in. long and wrap tightly twice around tassel 1½ in. below top knot. Knot; let excess fall in as part of tassel. Tie one tassel in ch-1 sp at center of each point on top and bottom edges of afghan.

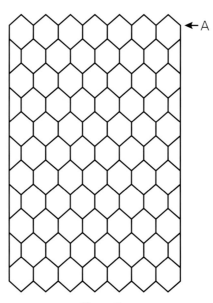

Figure 3

Version B
Materials & Tools
Worsted weight yarn, approximately:
16 oz. ecru
42 oz. in assorted colors

Crochet hook size H, or size to match gauge

Gauge
In dc, 4 sts = 1 in.; 2 rows = 1 in.; rnds 1–6, hexagon = 6¼ x 8 in.

Finished size
Approximately 45 x 65 in., excluding tassels

INSTRUCTIONS

Hexagon Motif (Make 72)

Rnd 1: With desired center color, follow instructions for Version A hexagon motif rnd 1; at end of rnd, finish off.

Rnd 2: Join second color in first dc to left of any ch-1 sp, work same as Version A rnd 2.

Rnds 3–6: Joining new color each rnd and using ecru for rnd 6, work same as Version A rnds 3–6.

Half Motif (Make 10)

Using a different color for each row and ecru for row 6, work same as Version A half motif.

Finishing

Following Version A finishing instructions, join motifs and work edging with ecru.

For basic fringe, cut 14-in. strands of ecru. Using three strands for each knot, tie one knot in each ch-1 sp and in every other dc across each short end.

Alterations: Lisa made Version B, substituting dark brown yarn for the ecru. She used odds and ends from her collection of yarn for the assorted colors, incorporating both acrylic and wool.

Compliments of Leisure Arts, Inc., USA. For a complete line of products, call Leisure Arts, Inc. @ 800-526-5111 or log on to www.leisurearts.com.

Victorian Elegance

LeAnn Hill

This afghan was a wedding gift—what a lucky bride and groom! The romantic design is embellished with satin flowers and ribbon.

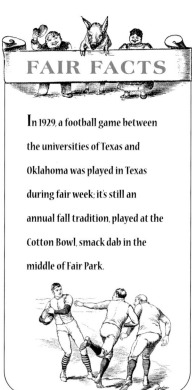

FAIR FACTS

In 1929, a football game between the universities of Texas and Oklahoma was played in Texas during fair week; it's still an annual fall tradition, played at the Cotton Bowl, smack dab in the middle of Fair Park.

Victorian Elegance

Materials & Tools
Cotton worsted-weight yarn,
approximately:
  37 oz. natural
  10 yds. of ⅜-in. satin
    ribbon—natural

Crochet hook size G, or size to match
gauge

Tapestry needle

Gauge
In pat, 3 crown sts = 6½ in.,
  12 rows = 5¼ in.

Finished size
Approximately 46 x 58 in.

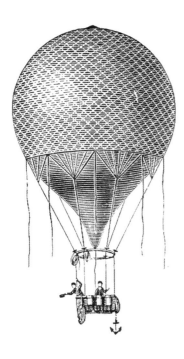

PATTERN STITCHES

Crown St: Sc in st indicated, (ch 7, sc) 3
times in same st.

Cluster: * Yo, insert hook in sp indicated, yo
and pull up a loop, yo and draw through
2 loops on hook; rep from * 2 times
more, yo and draw through all 4 loops
on hook.

Decrease: (uses next 2 dc) * Yo, insert hook
in *next* dc, yo and pull up a loop, yo and
draw through 2 loops on hook; rep from
* once *more*, yo and draw through all 3
loops on hook.

BODY
Ch 157 loosely.

Row 1: Work Crown St in twelfth ch from
hook, ch 4, sk next 4 chs, dc in next ch,
* ch 4, sk next 4 chs, work Crown St in
next ch, ch 4, sk next 4 chs, dc in next
ch; rep from * across (15 Crown Sts).

Row 2 (right side): Ch 1, turn; sc in first
dc, ch 1, sk next ch-4 sp, sc in next
loop, (ch 3, sc in next loop) twice, ch 1,
* sk next ch-4 sp, sc in next dc, ch 1,
sk next ch-4 sp, sc in next loop, (ch 3,
sc in next loop) twice, ch 1; rep from *
across to last loop, sk next 4 chs, sc in
next ch (61 sc).

*Note: Loop a short piece of yarn around any
stitch to mark last row as **right** side.*

Row 3: Ch 8, turn; (sc, ch 7, sc) in first sc,
ch 4, sk next ch-3 sp, dc in next sc, ch
4, * sk next sc, work Crown St in next sc,
ch 4, sk next ch-3 sp, dc in next sc, ch
4; rep from * across to last 2 sc, sk next
sc, (sc, ch 7, sc, ch 3, tr) in last sc (14
Crown Sts).

Row 4: Ch 1, turn; sc in first tr, ch 3, sc in
next loop, ch 1, sk next ch-4 sp, sc in
next dc, ch 1, * sk next ch-4 sp, sc in
next loop, (ch 3, sc in next loop) twice,
ch 1, sk next ch-4 sp, sc in next dc, ch
1; rep from * across to last ch-4 sp, sk
next ch-4 sp, sc in next loop, ch 3, sc in
last loop (61 sc).

Row 5: Ch 7, turn; sk next sc, work Crown
St in next sc, ch 4, sk next ch-3 sp, dc
in next sc, * ch 4, sk next sc, work
Crown St in next sc, ch 4, sk next ch-3
sp, dc in next sc; rep from * across (15
Crown Sts).

Rep rows 2-5 until afghan measures
approximately 46 in. from beg ch, ending by
working row 4; do *not* finish off.

EDGING

Rnd 1: Ch 1, work 205 sc evenly spaced
across end of rows to next corner loop,
work 6 sc in corner loop; working in free
loops of beg ch and in ch-4 sps, work
148 sc evenly spaced across to next
corner loop, work 6 sc in corner loop;
work 205 sc evenly spaced across end
of rows to next corner; working across
last row, work 156 sc evenly spaced
across; join with sl st to first sc (726 sc).

Rnd 2 (Eyelet rnd): Turn; sl st in front loop
only of next 2 sc, ch 5, turn; sk next 2
sc, (dc in back loop only of next sc, ch 2,
sk next 2 sc) around; join with sl st to
third ch of beg ch-5 (242 ch-2 sps).

Rnd 3: Ch 1, sc in back loop only of each
ch and in each dc around; join with sl st
to first sc (726 sc).

Rnd 4: Working in both loops, sl st in next
sc, ch 3 (counts as first dc, now and
throughout), dc in next sc, ch 5, sk next
3 sc, sc in next sc, (ch 3, sk next 2 sc,
sc in next sc) 5 times, ch 5, * sk next 4
sc, dc in next 2 sc, ch 5, sk next 4 sc, sc
in next sc, (ch 3, sk next 2 sc, sc in next
sc) 5 times, ch 5; rep from * around to
last 3 sc, sk last 3 sc; join with sl st to
first dc (196 sps).

Rnd 5: Sl st in next dc, ch 3, dc in same st,
ch 7, sk next loop, sc in next ch-3 sp,
(ch 3, sc in next ch-3 sp) 4 times, ch 7,
2 dc in next dc, ch 1, * 2 dc in next dc,
ch 7, sk next loop, sc in next ch-3 sp,
(ch 3, sc in next ch-3 sp) 4 times, ch 7,
2 dc in next dc, ch 1; rep from * around;
join with sl st to first dc.

Rnd 6: Ch 3, dc in next dc, ch 7, sc in next ch-3 sp, (ch 3, sc in next ch-3 sp) 3 times, ch 7, dc in next 2 dc, ch 2, * dc in next 2 dc, ch 7, sc in next ch-3 sp, (ch 3, sc in next ch-3 sp) 3 times, ch 7, dc in next 2 dc, ch 2; rep from * around; join with sl st to first dc.

Rnd 7: Ch 3, dc in next dc, ch 7, sc in next ch-3 sp, (ch 3, sc in next ch-3 sp) twice, ch 7, dc in next 2 dc, † ch 2, work Cluster in next ch-2 sp, ch 2, dc in next 2 dc, ch 7, sc in next ch-3 sp, (ch 3, sc in next ch-3 sp) twice, ch 7, dc in next 2 dc †, rep from † to † across to next corner ch-2 sp, ch 5, work Cluster in corner ch-2 sp, ch 5, * dc in next 2 dc, ch 7, sc in next ch-3 sp, (ch 3, sc in next ch-3 sp) twice, ch 7, dc in next 2 dc, rep from † to † across to next corner ch-2 sp, ch 5, work Cluster in corner ch-2 sp, ch 5; rep from * around; join with sl st to first dc.

Rnd 8: Ch 3, dc in next dc, ch 7, sc in next ch-3 sp, ch 3, sc in next ch-3 sp, ch 7, dc in next 2 dc, † ch 3, (work Cluster in next ch-2 sp, ch 3) twice, dc in next 2 dc, ch 7, sc in next ch-3 sp, ch 3, sc in next ch-3 sp, ch 7, dc in next 2 dc †, rep from † to † across to next corner loop, ch 7, (work Cluster in next loop, ch 7) twice, * dc in next 2 dc, ch 7, sc in next ch-3 sp, ch 3, sc in next ch-3 sp,

ch 7, dc in next 2 dc, rep from † to † across to next corner loop, ch 7, (work Cluster in next loop, ch 7) twice; rep from * around; join with sl st to first dc.

Rnd 9: Ch 3, dc in next dc, ch 7, sc in next ch-3 sp, ch 7, dc in next 2 dc, † ch 3, (work Cluster in next ch-3 sp, ch 3) 3 times, dc in next 2 dc, ch 7, sc in next ch-3 sp, ch 7, dc in next 2 dc †, rep from † to † across to next corner loop, ch 5, (work Cluster, ch 5) twice in each of next 3 loops, * dc in next 2 dc, ch 7, sc in next ch-3 sp, ch 7, dc in next 2 dc, rep from † to † across to next corner loop, ch 5, (work Cluster, ch 5) twice in each of next 3 loops; rep from * around; join with sl st to first dc.

Rnd 10: Ch 3, dc in next dc, ch 1, dtr in next sc, ch 1, dc in next 2 dc, † ch 5, (work Cluster in next ch-3 sp, ch 5) 4 times, dc in next 2 dc, ch 1, dtr in next sc, ch 1, dc in next 2 dc †, rep from † to † across to next corner loop, ch 5, (work Cluster in next loop, ch 5) 7 times, * dc in next 2 dc, ch 1, dtr in next sc, ch 1, dc in next 2 dc, rep from † to † across to next corner loop, ch 5, (work Cluster in next loop, ch 5) 7 times; rep from * around; join with sl st to first dc.

Rnd 11: Ch 2, dc in next dc, dc in next dtr, dec, † (4 dc hdc) in next loop, sc in next Cluster, [(hdc, 4 dc, hdc) in next loop, sc

in next Cluster] 3 times, (hdc, 4 dc) in next loop, dec, dc in next dtr, dec †, rep from † to † across to next corner loop, (4 dc, hdc) in next loop, sc in next Cluster [(hdc, 4 dc, hdc) in next loop, sc in next Cluster] 6 times, (hdc, 4 dc) in next loop, *dec, dc in next dtr, dec, rep from † to † across to next corner loop, (4 dc, hdc) in next loop, sc in next Cluster, [(hdc, 4 dc, hdc) in next loop, sc in next Cluster] 6 times, (hdc, 4 dc) in next loop; rep from * around; sk beg ch-2 and join with sl st to first dc, finish off.

FINISHING
Weave ribbon through Eyelet rnd along one side, leaving 25 in. at each end. Rep for rem three sides. Tie ends in a bow at each corner.

Alteration: LeAnn added satin roses at each corner.

Compliments of Leisure Arts, Inc., USA. For a complete line of products, call Leisure Arts, Inc. @ 800-526-5111 or log on to www.leisurearts.com.

Pretty in Purple

Julie Roberts

Inspired by her aunt, Julie now makes afghans as gifts, based on the recipient's favorite color—this one's obviously for a purple lover!

Materials & Tools

Worsted-weight yarn, approximately:
32 oz. each white, lavender, and purple

Size Q crochet hook, or size to match gauge

1 piece of cardboard, approximately 5 in. wide

Gauge

4 rows = 3 in.; 5 st = 3 in.

Finished size

Approximately 57 x 72 in.

INSTRUCTIONS

Note: Rows are lengthwise.

Use two strands of the same color together as one.

Ch 81, turn.

Row 1: Sc in second ch from hook. Continue sc in each chain to end (80 sts).

Row 2: Ch 1 turn, sc in the first sc. Continue to sc in each sc to end. Repeat second row for pat.

While continuing pat above, alternate colors as follows:

8 rows white; 24 rows purple; 4 rows white; 24 rows lavender; 16 rows white; 24 rows lavender; 4 rows white; 24 rows purple; 8 rows white

TASSELS

Use white yarn and wrap the yarn around the cardboard about 25 times. Take an 11-in. piece of white yarn and tie the bundle securely at the top of the cardboard. (Use this 11-in. piece of yarn to fasten the completed tassel in place.) Cut the yarn at the bottom of the cardboard.

Make a total of 22 white tassels, 24 purple tassels, and 24 lavender tassels. Take the yarn used to tie the bundles together and tie the tassels onto the afghan every 4 rows, starting in the corners. Change colors as indicated: attach 2 white; 6 purple; 1 white; 6 lavender; 5 white; 6 lavender; 1 white; 6 purple; and 2 white. Repeat on other side of the afghan.

After all tassels are on, start at the corners and tie half of the first tassel with an 11-in. piece of yarn. Then, take another 11-in. piece of yarn and tie the remaining half of the first tassel to half of the second tassel. Repeat this process on both sides of the afghan. Use the same color of yarn as tassel. When you have a tassel that contains two colors, use either color yarn you prefer.

Original Design

Afghan Fisherman Stitch

Shirley's elegant afghan demonstrates her love of modifying challenging patterns; she added additional panels and used her own joining stitch in this prizewinner.

Materials & Tools

Worsted-weight yarn, approximately:
    42 oz. off-white

Size I afghan hook, or size to
    match gauge

Size I crochet hook, or size to
    match gauge

Gauge

4 afghan sts = 1 in.; 10 rows = 3 in.

Finished size

Approximately 44 x 60 in.

Note: Mark starting ch of each panel for lower edge of afghan.

WIDE PANEL (Make 2)

Starting at narrow edge, ch 38 having 4 ch sts to 1 in. Work in afghan st until First Half of row 2 is completed—38 loops on hook. *Second Half of Row 2:* Yo and draw through 1 loop, (yo and draw through 2 loops) 18 times; ch 4 to be formed into a picot on First Half of next row; (yo and draw through 2 loops) 19 times.

Row 3: *First Half Of Row:* Holding each ch-4 loop toward front of work to form picot, work as for First Half of previous row—38 loops on hook. *Second half of row:* Following row 3 on figure 1, yo and draw through 1 loop, (yo and draw through 2 loops) 17 times; ch 4, (yo and draw through 2 loops) twice; ch 4, (yo and draw through 2 loops) 18 times.

Row 4: *First Half Of Row:* Holding ch-4 loops in front, work as for First Half of previous row.

Note: Figure 1 shows the Second Half of each row. Follow each row on figure 1 from A to B.

Starting with row 4 on figure 1 and working First Half of each row as established, follow figure 1 until Second Half of row 33 is completed.

Next Row: *First Half of Row:* Work as before. Then starting with Second Half of row 32, follow figure 1 back until Second Half of row 1 is completed. Starting with row 2, rep last 64 rows worked 2 more times.

Last Row: Sl st in each vertical bar across. Fasten off.

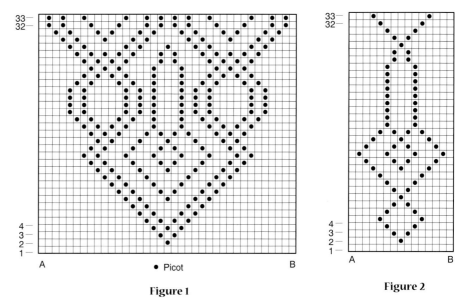

Figure 1

• Picot

Figure 2

Figures 1 and 2 show Second Half of Rows only. Each vertical line on each row represents a vertical bar of an afghan stitch. Each dot represents a picot.

Afghan Fisherman Stitch

NARROW PANEL (Make 3)

Starting at narrow edge, ch 16 to measure 4 in. Work as for Wide Panel until First Half of row 2 is completed—16 loops. Starting with Second Half of row 2 on figure 2, follow figure 2 in same way as figure 1.

SIDE BORDERS OF PANEL

With right side facing, attach yarn to lower right-hand corner of any panel.

Row 1: Working along end sts of rows; *ch 3, drawing up each loop to same height, draw up a loop in second ch from hook, draw up a loop in third ch from hook, draw up a loop in end st on first row, draw up a loop in end st of next row, yo and draw through 5 loops on hook, ch 1 for eye—starting star st made; * draw up a loop in eye of star st, draw up a loop in back of last drawn up loop, draw up a loop in end st of each of next 2 rows, yo and draw through 5 loops on hook, ch 1 for eye—star st made. Rep from * across long edge to next corner (97 star sts). Ch 2, turn.*

Row 2: Hdc in eye of first star st, make 2 hdc in eye of each star st across, then sl st in top of last st. Fasten off.

Attaching yarn at upper left-hand corner, work border along other long edge in same way. Work borders on each remaining panel.

Having marked edge of each panel at same end, with wrong side of panels together and matching rows, sc panels together in the following order: Narrow Panel, (Wide Panel, Narrow Panel) twice.

TOP BORDER

With right side facing, attach yarn to upper right-hand corner. Working into sts instead of end sts of rows, work as for Side Borders.

LOWER BORDER

Attaching yarn to lower left-hand corner, work to correspond with Top Border, do not break off at end of last row. Ch 1, turn.

OUTER EDGING

Keeping work flat and making 3 sc, in each of the four corners, sc around entire outer edge of afghan.

Alterations: Shirley enlarged this afghan by adding one motif to each panel, and also added additional panels. She used left to right sc edging; a joining stitch; an additional sc row to each end; and two sc rows between each motif.

Pattern Courtesy of Coats & Clark

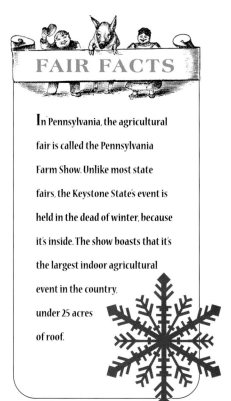

FAIR FACTS

In Pennsylvania, the agricultural fair is called the Pennsylvania Farm Show. Unlike most state fairs, the Keystone State's event is held in the dead of winter, because it's inside. The show boasts that it's the largest indoor agricultural event in the country, under 25 acres of roof.

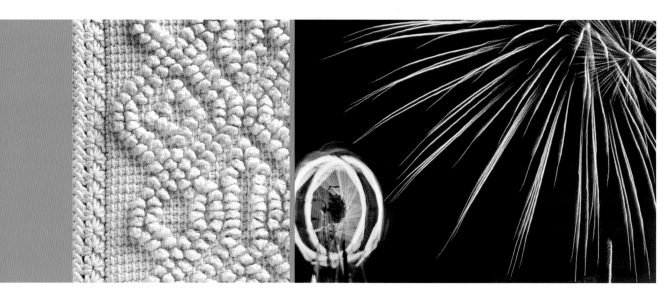

Halloween Afghan

Sadie H. Sanchez

This not-too-spooky afghan features a border of friendly ghosts and bats surrounding one big witch. This seasonal afghan is sure to be a prizewinner at home, too.

Figure 1

Materials & Tools

Worsted-weight yarn, approximately:
- 35 oz. orange
- 35 oz. black
- 5 oz. white

Crochet hook size G, or size to match gauge

Gauge

4 sc = 1 in.; 4 sc rows = 1 in.

Finished size

Approximately 53½ x 66½

RIGHT SIDE

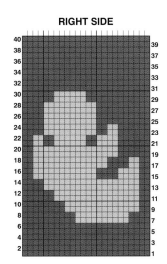

Figure 2

LEFT SIDE

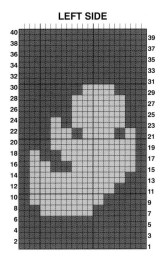

Figure 3

- ☐ Orange
- ■ Black
- ▨ White

Halloween Afghan

SPECIAL STITCHES

Cluster—yo, insert hook in corner ch sp, yo, pull loop through, yo, pull through 2 loops on hook, (yo, insert hook in same ch sp, yo, pull through, yo, pull through 2 loops on hook) 2 times, yo, pull through all loops on hook.

Joining—ch 1, sc in corresponding ch sp on adjacent piece, ch 1.

*Notes: For **color change**, always change color in last st made, drop unused color to wrong side of work, pick up when needed.*

Each square on graph(s) = 1 sc

AFGHAN

Center

Row 1: With orange, ch 127, sc in second ch from hook, sc in each ch across, turn. (126 sc made)

Rows 2–20: Ch 1, sc in each st across, turn.

Rows 21–172: Ch 1, sc in each st across changing colors according to figure 1 on page 108, turn. At end of last row, fasten off.

Rnd 173: Working around entire outer edge, join black with sc in first st, sc in each st across, ch 2, evenly space 174 sc across ends of rows, ch 2; working in starting ch on opposite of row 1, sc in each ch across, ch 2, evenly space 174 sc across ends of rows, ch 2, join with sl st in first sc. (600 sc, 4 ch sps)

Rnds 174–176: Ch 1, sc in each st around with (sc, ch 2, sc) in each corner ch sp, join. At end of last rnd, fasten off. (624)

Rnd 177: Join white with sl st in any corner ch sp, ch 3, (yo, insert hook in same ch sp as sl st, yo, pull loop through, yo, pull through 2 loops on hook) 2 times, yo, pull through all loops on hook (cluster made), ch 3, (yo, insert hook in same ch sp as sl st, yo, pull loop through, yo, pull through 2 loops on hook) 3 times, yo, pull through all loops on hook (cluster made), (ch 3, dc next 3 sts together)

across to next corner ch sp, ch 3; *(cluster—see Special Stitches, ch 3, cluster) in corner ch sp, (ch 3, dc next 3 sts together) across to next corner ch sp, ch 3; rep from * around, join with sl st in top of first cluster. Fasten off.

Right Side

Row 1: With black, ch 25, sc in second ch from hook, sc in each ch across, turn. (24 sc made)

Rows 2–6: Ch 1, sc in each st across, turn.

Rows 7–40: Ch 1, sc in each st across changing colors according to figure 2, turn.

Rows 41–142: Rep rows 7–40 consecutively.

Rows 143–172: Rep rows 7–36.

Rnd 173: Working around entire outer edge, ch 1, sc in each st across, ch 2, evenly space 174 sc across ends of rows, ch 2; working in starting ch on opposite of row 1, sc in each ch across, ch 2, evenly space 174 sc across ends of rows, ch 2, join with sl st in first sc. (396 sc)

Rnds 174–176: Ch 1, sc in each st around with (sc, ch 2, sc) in each corner ch sp, join. At end of last rnd, fasten off. (420)

Rnd 177: Join white with sl st in lower right-hand corner ch sp, ch 3, (yo, insert hook in same ch sp as sl st, yo, pull loop through, yo, pull through 2 loops on hook) 2 times, yo, pull through all loops on hook, (ch 3, cluster) in same ch sp as first cluster, (ch 3, dc next 3 sts together) across to next corner ch sp, ch 3, (cluster, ch 3, cluster) in corner ch sp, (ch 3, dc next 3 sts together) across to next corner ch sp, ch 3, (cluster, *joining*—see Special Stitches, cluster) in next corner ch sp, joining, (dc next 3 sts together, joining) across to corner ch sp, (cluster, joining, cluster) in corner ch sp, ch 3, (dc next 3 sts together, ch 3) across, join with sl st in top of first cluster. Fasten off.

Left Side

Row 1–Rnd 176: Using Left Side graph (figure 3), work same as Right Side.

Rnd 177: Join white with sl st in upper left-hand corner ch sp, ch 3, (yo, insert hook in same ch sp as sl st, yo, pull loop

Halloween Afghan

through, yo, pull through 2 loops on hook) 2 times, yo, pull through all loops on hook, (ch 3, cluster) in same ch sp as first cluster, (ch 3, dc next 3 sts together) across to next corner ch sp, ch 3, (cluster, ch 3, cluster) in corner ch sp, (ch 3, dc next 3 sts together) across to next corner ch sp, ch 3, (cluster, joining, cluster) in next corner ch sp, joining, (dc next 3 sts together, joining) across to corner ch sp, (cluster, joining, cluster) in corner ch sp, ch 3, (dc next 3 sts together, ch 3) across, join with sl st in top of first cluster. Fasten off.

Top

Row 1: With black, ch 127, sc in second ch from hook, sc in each ch across, turn. (126 sc made)

Rows 2–6: Ch 1, sc in each st across, turn.

Rows 7–36: Ch 1, sc in each st across changing colors according to figure 4, turn.

Rnd 37: Working around entire outer edge, ch 1, sc in each st across, ch 2, sc in end of each row across, ch 2; working in starting ch on opposite side of row 1, sc in each ch across, ch 2, sc in end of each row across, ch 2, join with sl st in first sc. (324)

Rnds 38–40: Ch 1, sc in each st around with (sc, ch 2, sc) in each corner ch sp, join. At end of last rnd, fasten off. (348)

Rnd 41: Join white with sl st in upper right-hand corner ch sp, ch 3, (yo, insert hook in same ch sp as sl st, yo, pull loop through, yo, pull through 2 loops on hook) 2 times, yo, pull through all loops on hook, (ch 3, cluster) in same ch sp as first cluster, (ch 3, dc next 3 sts together) across to next corner ch sp, ch 3, (cluster, ch 3, cluster) in corner ch sp, (ch 3, dc next 3 sts together) across to next corner ch sp, ch 3, (cluster, joining, cluster) in next corner ch sp, joining, (dc next 3 sts together, joining) across to corner ch sp, (cluster, joining, cluster) in corner ch sp, ch 3, (dc next 3 sts together, ch 3) across, join with sl st in top of first cluster. Fasten off.

Bottom

Row 1–Rnd 40: Work same rows and rnds of Top.

Rnd 41: Join white with sl st in lower left-hand corner ch sp, ch 3, (yo, insert hook in same ch sp as sl st, yo, pull loop through, yo, pull through 2 loops on hook) 2 times, yo, pull through all loops on hook, (ch 3, cluster) in same ch sp as first cluster, (ch 3, dc next 3 sts together) across to next corner ch sp, ch 3, (cluster, ch 3, cluster) in corner ch sp, (ch 3, dc next 3 sts together) across to next corner ch sp, ch 3, (cluster, joining, cluster) in next corner ch sp, joining, (dc next 3 sts together, joining) across to corner ch sp, (cluster, joining, cluster) in corner ch sp, ch 3, (dc next 3 sts together, ch 3) across, join with sl st in top of first cluster. Fasten off.

Bat A
UPPER RIGHT CORNER

Row 1: With orange, ch 25, sc in second ch from hook, sc in each ch across, turn. (24 sc made)

Rows 2–6: Ch 1, sc in each st across, turn.

Rows 7–36: Ch 1, sc in each st across changing colors according to Bat A graph (figure 5) on page 111, turn. At end of last rnd, fasten off.

Rnd 37: Join black with sc in first st, sc in each st across, ch 2, sc in end of each row across, ch 2; working in starting ch on opposite side of row 1, sc in each ch across, ch 2, sc in end of each row across, join with sl st in first sc. (120)

Rnds 38–40: Ch 1, sc in each st around with (sc, ch 2, sc) in each corner ch sp, join. At end of last rnd, fasten off. (144)

Rnd 41: Join white with sl st in upper right-hand corner ch sp, ch 3, (yo, insert hook in same ch sp as sl st, yo, pull loop through, yo, pull through 2 loops on hook) 2 times, yo, pull through all loops on hook, (ch 3, cluster) in same ch sp as first cluster, (ch 3, dc next 3 sts together) across to next corner ch sp, ch 3; join to *Top* and *Right Side*, *(cluster, joining, cluster) in next corner ch sp, joining, (dc next 3 sts together, joining) across to corner ch sp; rep from *, (cluster, joining, cluster) in corner ch sp, ch 3, (dc next 3 sts together, ch 3) across, join with sl st in top of first cluster. Fasten off.

TOP/BOTTOM

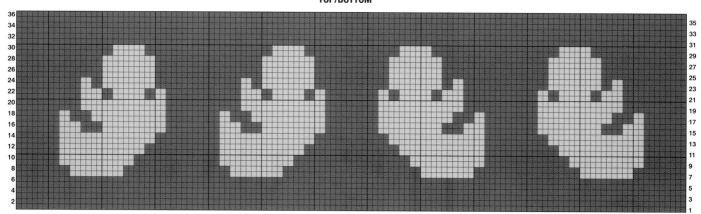

Figure 4

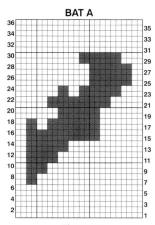

BAT A

Figure 5

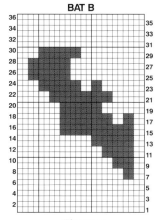

BAT B

Figure 6

LOWER RIGHT CORNER

Row 1–Rnd 40: Work same rows and rnds as Upper Right Corner on Bat A.

Rnd 41: Join white with sl st in lower right-hand corner ch sp, ch 3, (yo, insert hook in same ch sp as sl st, yo, pull loop through, yo, pull through 2 loops on hook) 2 times, yo, pull through all loops on hook, (ch 3, cluster) in same ch sp as first cluster, (ch 3, dc next 3 sts together) across to next corner ch sp, ch 3; join to *Right Side* and *Bottom*, *(cluster, joining, cluster) in next corner ch sp, joining, (dc next 3 sts together, joining) across to corner ch sp; rep from *, (cluster, joining, cluster) in corner ch sp, ch 3, (dc next 3 sts together, ch 3) across, join with sl st in top of first cluster. Fasten off.

Bat B
UPPER LEFT CORNER

Row 1–Rnd 40: Using Bat B graph (figure 6), work same rows and rnds as Bat A.

Rnd 41: Join white with sl st in upper left-hand corner ch sp, ch 3, (yo, insert hook in same ch sp as sl st, yo, pull loop through, yo, pull through 2 loops on hook) 2 times, yo, pull through all loops on hook, (ch 3, cluster) in same ch sp as first cluster, (ch 3, dc next 3 sts together) across to next corner ch sp, ch 3; join to *Left Side* and *Top*, *(cluster, joining, cluster) in next corner ch sp, joining, (dc next 3 sts together, joining) across to corner ch sp; rep from *, (cluster, joining, cluster) in corner ch sp, ch 3, (dc next 3 sts together, ch 3) across, join with sl st in top of first cluster. Fasten off.

LOWER LEFT CORNER

Row 1–Rnd 40: Work same rows and rnds as Upper Left Corner on Bat B.

Rnd 41: Join white with sl st in lower left-hand corner ch sp, ch 3, (yo, insert hook in same ch sp as sl st, yo, pull loop through, yo, pull through 2 loops on hook) 2 times, yo, pull through all loops on hook, (ch 3, cluster) in same ch sp as first cluster, (ch 3, dc next 3 sts together) across to next corner ch sp, ch 3; join to *Bottom* and *Left Side*, *(cluster, joining, cluster) in next corner ch sp, joining, (dc next 3 sts together, joining) across to corner ch sp; rep from *, (cluster, joining, cluster) in corner ch sp, ch 3, (dc next 3 sts together, ch 3) across, join with sl st in top of first cluster. Fasten off.

Alteration: This must be the Wicked Witch of the East, because she's flying home to the right instead of the left!

Pattern Courtesy of Annie's Attic

Zig Zag Afghan

Such an elegant piece of work deserves a special place in the home. Jeanney made a few alterations to this pattern when she created this lovely afghan.

Materials & Tools

Worsted-weight yarn, approximately:
7 oz. each of navy (color A), blue (color B), aqua (color C), and white (color D)

Crochet hook size J, or size to match gauge

1 piece of cardboard, approximately 3 in. wide

Gauge

3 sts = 1 in.

Finished size

Approximately 45 x 60 in., with 3 in. fringe

PATTERN STITCH

Multiple of 25 ch, plus 22 ch; measures 4 in. point to point

Row 1: 1 sc in second ch from hook, 1 sc in each of next 9 ch, * 5 sc in next ch, 1 sc in each of next 10 ch. Sk 4 ch, 1 sc in each of next 10 ch, rep from * across, ch 1, turn.

Row 2: Sk 2 sts, * sc in back loop of each of 10 sts, 5 sc in back loop of next st, 1 sc in back loop of next 10 sts, sk 4 sts, rep from * across, ending with 1 sc in back loop of each of 10 sts (omitting last 2 sts), ch 1, turn.

Repeat row 2 for Pattern Stitch.

AFGHAN

With color A, ch 222. Work in Pattern Stitch with stripes as follows (always draw new color through last loop on hook):

* 2 rows each, colors A, B, C and D; 6 rows with color A; 2 rows each, colors B, C, D and A; 6 rows with color B; 2 rows each, colors C, D, A, and B; 4 rows with color C.

Rep from *. Fasten off.

FRINGE

Wind yarn around 3 in. cardboard, cut loops at one side. Using one strand, fold and knot 1 fringe in each st across ends as follows:

* 4 each, colors A, B and C; 2 each color D. Rep across. Matching color of stripes, knot 2 strands in the end of each row, 2 in turn st and 2 in each omitted st.

Finished afghan should have 9 points only.

Alterations: Jeanney used only three colors, blue, cream, and dark blue, to create this lovely ripple afghan. She also omitted the fringe.

Originally Published by Malina Company Inc.

Rainbow Waves Afghan

Janice Trautman Cook

Did Janice find a pot of gold at the end of this afghan? Probably not, but its colorful stripes did earn a blue ribbon for excellence.

Materials & Tools

Worsted-weight yarn, approximately:
 7 oz. each of medium blue,
  light blue, lilac, light lilac,
  rose, light rose, peach,
  light peach, yellow,
  light aqua, and aqua

Crochet hook size K, or size to
 match gauge

Gauge

In sc, 5 sts = 2 in., 4 rows = 1 in.

Finished size

Approximately 48 x 63 in.,
 excluding fringe

INSTRUCTIONS

Afghan is worked across long edge. Use colors in sequence as listed above.

With first color, ch 158.

Foundation Row: Sc in second ch from hook and in each ch across (157 sc). Ch 1, turn.

Rows 1–3: Sc in first sc and in each sc across. Ch 1, turn. At end of row 3, work color change in last sc as follows: insert hook in last st and draw up a loop, drop color in use and cut yarn leaving 6-in. tail; with next color, yo and draw through loops on hook. Ch 1, turn.

Row 4: Sc in first sc, * sc in next sc 1 row below, sc in next sc 2 rows below, sc in next sc 3 rows below, sc in next sc 2 rows below, sc in next sc 1 row below, sc in next sc. Rep from * across. Ch 1, turn.

Rep rows 1–4 in each color listed, then rep total color sequence 3 more times, end with changing color to first color and working rows 4, 1 and 2.

FRINGE

Cut nine strands of first color each 17 in. long. Insert hook from back to front in end of first stripe. Double strands over hook and draw loop through, then draw ends through loop. Pull to form knot. Work knot in both ends of each stripe, matching colors. Trim evenly.

Pattern Courtesy of the Craft Yarn Council of America, Gastonia, NC
www.knitandcrochet.com

Noah's Ark

Sadie H. Sanchez

An ancient tale comes to life in this delightful rendering of Noah and his ark full of animals. Sadie says that this afghan always receives compliments.

Materials & Tools

Worsted-weight yarn, approximately:
- 19½ oz. green
- 13 oz. blue
- 9 oz. dark blue
- 4 oz. brown
- 3½ oz. gold
- 1½ oz. each of white and grey
- 1 oz. each of rose and purple
- ¼ oz. tan

Crochet hook size H, or size to match gauge

¾-in. buttons for giraffes' spots—12

1-in. buttons for stars—4

6 mm round black beads for eyes—16

Sewing needle and thread

Safety pins

Tapestry needle

Gauge

On Panels, in pattern, 3 Shells and 8 rows = 4 in.; (sc, dc) 6 times and 12 rows = 4 in. On all other pieces, 7 sc and 7 rows = 2 in..

Finished size

Approximately 45 x 61 in.

STITCH GUIDE

Treble Crochet (tr): Yo twice, insert hook in st indicated, yo and pull up a loop (4 loops on hook), (yo and draw through 2 loops on hook) 3 times.

Shell (uses one st): Dc in st indicated, (ch 1, dc in same st) twice.

Beginning Decrease (beg dec): Pull up a loop in first 2 sc, yo and draw through all 3 loops on hook (*counts as one sc*).

Decrease (dec): Pull up a loop in next 2 sc, yo and draw through all 3 loops on hook (*counts as one sc*).

Bobble (uses one ch): * Yo, insert hook in ch indicated, yo and pull up a loop, yo and draw through 2 loops on hook; rep from * 2 times *more*, yo and draw through all 4 loops on hook.

AFGHAN BODY

Center Panel

With dark blue, ch 78 *loosely*.

Row 1: Sc in second ch from hook, * sk next ch, work Shell in next ch, sk next ch, sc in next ch; rep from * across: 19 Shells and 20 sc.

Row 2 (right side): Ch 4 (*counts as first dc plus ch 1, now and throughout*), turn; working in Back Loops Only, dc in same st, sk next dc, sc in next dc, * sk next dc, work Shell in next sc, sk next dc, sc in next dc; rep from * across to last 3 sts, sk next ch and next dc, (dc, ch 1, dc) in last sc: 18 Shells and 19 sc.

*Note: Loop a short piece of yarn around any stitch to mark row 2 as **right** side.*

Row 3: Ch 1, turn; working in both loops, sc in first dc, * sk next dc, work Shell in next sc, sk next dc, sc in next dc; rep from * across: 19 Shells and 20 sc.

Row 4: Ch 4, turn; working in Back Loops Only, dc in same st, sk next dc, sc in next dc, * sk next dc, work Shell in next sc, sk next dc, sc in next dc; rep from * across to last 3 sts, sk next ch and next dc, (dc, ch 1, dc) in last sc: 18 Shells and 19 sc.

Rows 5–34: Rep Rows 3 and 4, 15 times.

Row 35: Ch 1, turn; working in both loops, sc in first dc, * sk next dc, work Shell in next sc, sk next dc, sc in next dc; rep from * across changing to blue in last sc: 19 Shells and 20 sc.

Row 36: Ch 1, turn; working in Back Loops Only, sc in first sc, place marker around sc just made for Edging placement, dc in same st, * sc in next dc, sk next ch, dc in next dc, sk next ch, sc in next dc, dc in next sc; rep from * across: 78 sts.

Rows 37–110: Ch 1, turn; working in both loops, sc in first dc, dc in next sc, (sc in next dc, dc in next sc) across.

Finish off.

EDGING

Rnd 1: With *right* side facing and working in end of rows, join blue with sc in marked row; sc in each row across; working across sts on Row 110, 3 sc in first sc, sc in each st across to last dc, 3 sc in last dc; sc in end of first 75 rows changing to dark blue in last sc, work 50 sc evenly spaced across end of rows; working in free loops of beg ch, 3 sc in ch at base of first sc, work 76 sc evenly spaced across to last ch, 3 sc in last ch;

Noah's Ark

work 50 sc evenly spaced across end of rows; join with sl st to first sc, finish off: 414 sc.

Rnd 2: With *right* side facing, join tan with sc in any sc; sc in each sc around working 3 sc in center sc of each corner 3-sc group; join with sl st to first sc, finish off: 422 sc.

Side Panel (Make 2)

With green, ch 23 *loosely*.

Row 1 (right side): Sc in second ch from hook, dc in next ch, (sc in next ch, dc in next ch) across: 22 sts.

*Note: Mark row 1 as **right** side.*

Rows 2–125: Ch 1, turn; sc in first dc, dc in next sc, (sc in next dc, dc in next sc) across; do *not* finish off.

Edging

Rnd 1: Ch 1, do *not* turn; sc in end of each row across; working in free loops of beg ch, 3 sc in first ch, sc in next 20 chs, 3 sc in next ch; sc in end of each row across; working across sts on Row 125,

3 sc in first sc, sc in each st across to last dc, 3 sc in last dc; join with sl st to first sc, finish off: 302 sc.

Rnd 2: With *right* side facing, join tan with sc in any sc; sc in each sc around working 3 sc in center sc of each corner 3-sc group; join with sl st to first sc, finish off: 310 sc.

Bottom Panel

With green, ch 79 *loosely*.

Row 1 (right side): Sc in second ch from hook, dc in next ch, (sc in next ch, dc in next ch) across: 78 sts.

Note: Mark row 1 as right side.

Rows 2–20: Ch 1, turn; sc in first dc, dc in next sc, (sc in next dc, dc in next sc) across; at end of row 20, do *not* finish off.

Edging

Rnd 1: Ch 1, turn; 3 sc in first dc, sc in each st across to last sc, 3 sc in last sc; sc in end of each row across; working in free loops of beg ch, 3 sc in first ch, sc in next 76 chs, 3 sc in next ch; sc in end of each row across; join with sl st to first sc, finish off: 204 sc.

Rnd 2: With *right* side facing, join tan with sc in any sc; sc in each sc around working 3 sc

in center sc of each corner 3-sc group; join with sl st to first sc, finish off: 212 sc.

Top Panel

Work same as Bottom Panel.

Corner Panel (Make 4)

Note: Make 2 each of dark blue and blue.

With color indicated, ch 23 *loosely*.

Row 1 (right side): Sc in second ch from hook, dc in next ch, (sc in next ch, dc in next ch) across: 22 sts.

*Note: Mark row 1 as **right** side.*

Rows 2–20: Ch 1, turn; sc in first dc, dc in next sc, (sc in next dc, dc in next sc) across; at end of row 20, do *not* finish off.

Edging

Rnd 1: Ch 1, turn; 3 sc in first dc, sc in each st across to last sc, 3 sc in last sc; sc in end of each row across; working in free loops of beg ch, 3 sc in first ch, sc in next 20 chs, 3 sc in next ch; sc in end of each row across; join with sl st to first sc, finish off: 92 sc.

Rnd 2: With *right* side facing, join tan with sc in any sc; sc in each sc around working 3 sc in center sc of each corner 3-sc group; join with sl st to first sc, finish off: 100 sc.

Assembly

Using photo at left as a guide for placement, join Panels in the following order: Side Panels to Center Panel, dark blue Corner Panels to Top Panel, blue Corner Panels to Bottom Panel, Top Panel section to Center Panel section, and Bottom Panel section to Center Panel section.

To join first two Panels, place Panels with *wrong* sides together. Working through *inside* loop of each stitch on *both* pieces, join tan with sl st in center sc of first corner 3-sc group; (ch 1, sl st in next sc) across ending in center sc of next corner 3-sc group; finish off.

Join rem Panels in same manner.

Border

With *right* side facing and working in Back Loops Only, join tan with sl st in center sc of any corner 3-sc group; ch 1, (sl st in same st, ch 1) twice, (sl st in next sc, ch 1) around

working (sl st, ch 1) 3 times in center sc of each corner 3-sc group; join with sl st to first sl st, finish off.

ADDITIONAL PIECES

Ark

BOTTOM

With brown, ch 41 *loosely.*

Row 1 (right side): Sc in back ridge of second ch from hook and each ch across: 40 sc.

*Note: Mark row 1 as **right** side.*

Rows 2–8: Ch 1, turn; 2 sc in first sc, sc in each sc across to last sc, 2 sc in last sc: 54 sc.

Row 9: Ch 1, turn; sc in each sc across.

Row 10 (increase row): Ch 1, turn; 2 sc in first sc, sc in each sc across to last sc, 2 sc in last sc: 56 sc.

Rows 11–20: Rep Rows 9 and 10, 5 times: 66 sc.

Rows 21–37: Ch 1, turn; sc in each sc across.

Finish off.

Waves: With *right* side facing and working in free loops of beg ch, join dark blue with sl st in first ch; ch 1, (sc, ch 3) twice in same st and in next 37 chs, [(sc, ch 3) twice, sl st] in next ch; finish off.

ROOF

With brown, ch 51 *loosely.*

Row 1: Sc in back ridge of second ch from hook and each ch across: 50 sc.

Row 2 (right side): Ch 1, turn; sc in each sc across.

*Note: Mark row 2 as **right** side.*

Row 3 (dec row): Ch 1, turn; work beg

dec, sc in each sc across to last 2 sc, dec: 48 sc.

Row 4: Ch 1, turn; sc in each sc across.

Rows 5–20: Rep rows 3 and 4, 8 times: 32 sc.

Finish off.

HOUSE

With tan and leaving a 20-in. end for sewing, ch 16 *loosely.*

Row 1 (wrong side): Sc in back ridge of second ch from hook and each ch across: 15 sc.

*Note: Mark **back** of any **stitch** on row 1 as right side.*

Rows 2–40: Ch 1, turn; sc in each sc across.

Finish off, leaving a 20-in. end for sewing.

LARGE HEART

Row 1 (right side): With rose, ch 2, 3 sc in second ch from hook: 3 sc.

*Note: Mark row 1 as **right** side.*

Row 2: Ch 1, turn; 2 sc in first sc, sc in next sc, 2 sc in last sc: 5 sc.

Row 3: Ch 1, turn; sc in each sc across.

Row 4 (increase row): Ch 1, turn; 2 sc in first sc, sc in each sc across to last sc, 2 sc in last sc: 7 sc.

Rows 5–9: Rep rows 3 and 4 twice, then rep row 3 once *more*; do *not* finish off: 11 sc.

First Side

Row 1: Ch 1, turn; work beg dec, sc in next 3 sc, leave rem 6 sc unworked: 4 sc.

Row 2: Ch 1, turn; sc in each sc across.

Row 3: Ch 1, turn; work beg dec, dec; finish off: 2 sc.

Second Side

Row 1: With *wrong* side facing, sk next sc from First Side and join rose with sc in next sc; sc in next 2 sc, dec: 4 sc.

Row 2: Ch 1, turn; sc in each sc across.

Row 3: Ch 1, turn; work beg dec, dec: 2 sc.

Edging: Ch 1, turn; sc evenly around entire Heart working 3 sc at bottom point; join with sl st to first sc, finish off leaving a long end for sewing.

Noah

BODY

With purple, ch 11 *loosely.*

Row 1: Sc in second ch from hook and in each ch across: 10 sc.

Row 2 (right side): Ch 1, turn; sc in each sc across.

*Note: Mark row 2 as **right** side.*

Row 3 (Dec row): Ch 1, turn; work beg dec, sc in each sc across to last 2 sc, dec: 8 sc.

Rows 4–6: Ch 1, turn; sc in each sc across.

Rows 7–11: Rep rows 3-6 once, then rep row 3 once *more*: 4 sc.

Row 12: Ch 1, turn; sc in each sc across.

Edging: Ch 1, do *not* turn; sc evenly across end of rows; working in free loops of beg ch, 3 sc in ch at base of first sc, sc in each ch across to last ch, 3 sc in last ch; sc evenly across end of rows; working across sts on row 12, 3 sc in first sc, sc in last 3 sc, place marker around last sc made for Head placement, 2 sc in same st; join with sl st to first sc, finish off leaving a long end for sewing.

HEAD

Row 1: With *wrong* side of Body facing, join tan with sc in marked sc; sc in next 3 sc, leave rem sc unworked: 4 sc.

Row 2: Ch 1, turn; working in Back Loops Only, 2 sc in first sc, sc in next sc, place marker around sc just made for Mustache placement, sc in next sc, 2 sc in last sc: 6 sc.

Rows 3 and 4: Ch 1, turn; sc in both loops of each sc across.

Row 5: Ch 1, turn; work beg dec, sc in next 2 sc, dec: 4 sc.

Row 6: Ch 1, turn; sc in each sc across; finish off.

Edging: With *right* side facing, join tan with sl st in right end of row 1; work 15 sc

Noah's Ark

evenly spaced around Head, sl st in opposite end of row 1; finish off leaving a long end for sewing: 17 sts.

HAIR

First Side: With *right* side facing, sk first 3 sts on Head Edging and join white with sl st in next sc; sc in same st and in next 2 sc, sl st in next sc, leave rem 10 sts unworked; finish off.

Second Side: With *right* side facing, sk next 3 sc from First Side and join white with sl st in next sc; sc in next 2 sc, (sc, sl st) in next sc, leave rem 3 sts unworked; finish off.

BEARD

Row 1: With *right* side facing, Head toward you, and working in free loops of sts on row 1 on Head, join white with sc in first sc; sc in last 3 sc: 4 sc.

Row 2: Ch 1, turn; work beg dec, dec: 2 sc.

Row 3: Ch 1, turn; sc in next 2 sc.

Row 4: Ch 1, turn; work beg dec: one sc.

Row 5: Ch 1, turn; sc in next sc; finish off leaving a long end for sewing.

Sew bottom of Beard to Body.

Mustache: With *right* side facing and Body toward you, join white with sl st in right end of Row 1 on Beard; ch 2, sl st around post of marked sc on Head, ch 2, sl st in opposite end of Row 1 on Beard; finish off.

ARM (Make 2)

Row 1 (Right side): With purple, ch 2, sc in second ch from hook: one sc.

*Note: Mark row 1 as **right** side.*

Rows 2–5: Ch 1, turn; sc in next sc.

Edging: Ch 1, do *not* turn; sc evenly around entire Arm; join with sl st to first sc, finish off leaving a long end for sewing.

Using photo as a guide for placement, page 119, sew Arms to Body.

HAND (Make 2)

With tan, ch 2, (3 sc, sl st) in second ch from hook; finish off leaving a long end for sewing.

Using photo as a guide for placement, page 119, sew Hands to Arms.

Mrs. Noah

Work same as Noah through row 1 of Head: 4 sc.

Row 2: Ch 1, turn; 2 sc in first sc, sc in next 2 sc, 2 sc in last sc: 6 sc.

Rows 3 and 4: Ch 1, turn; sc in each sc across.

Row 5: Ch 1, turn; work beg dec, sc in next 2 sc, dec: 4 sc.

Row 6: Ch 1, turn; sc in each sc across; finish off.

Edging: With *right* side facing, join tan with sl st in right end of Row 1; work 15 sc evenly spaced around Head, sl st in opposite end of row 1; finish off leaving a long end for sewing: 17 sts.

HAIR

With *right* side facing, sk first sl st on Head Edging and join white with sl st in next sc; ch 3, sc in same st, ch 3, (sc, ch 3) twice in each sc around to last 2 sts, (sc, ch 3, sl st) in next sc, leave rem sl st unworked; finish off.

ARMS AND HANDS

Work same as Noah.

SMALL HEART

Row 1 (right side): With rose, ch 2, sc in second ch from hook: one sc.

*Note: Mark row 1 as **right** side.*

Row 2: Ch 1, turn; 3 sc in next sc.

Row 3: Ch 1, turn; 2 sc in first sc, sc in next sc, 2 sc in last sc; do not finish off: 5 sc.

FIRST SIDE

Row 1: Ch 1, turn; work beg dec, leave rem 3 sc unworked: one sc.

Row 2: Ch 1, turn; sc in next sc; finish off.

SECOND SIDE

Row 1: With wrong side facing, sk next sc from First Side and join rose with sl st in next sc; ch 1, pull up a loop in same st and in last sc, yo and draw through all 3 loops on hook: one st.

Row 2: Ch 1, turn; sc in next st.

Edging: Ch 1, do not turn; sc evenly around entire Heart working 3 sc at bottom point; join with sl st to first sc, finish off leaving a long end for sewing.

With white and using photo as a guide, page 119, add straight stitches and French knots to Small Heart to form the word "by".

Right Dove

BODY

With white, ch 13 *loosely*, place marker in sixth ch from hook for Wing placement.

Row 1: Sc in back ridge of second ch from hook and each ch across: 12 sc.

Row 2 (right side): Ch 2, turn; 2 sc in first sc, (sc, sl st) in next sc, sk next sc, 2 dc in next sc, 2 tr in each of next 2 sc, 2 dc in next sc, sk next 2 sc, sc in next 2 sc, 2 sc in last sc: 17 sts.

*Note: Mark row 2 as **right** side.*

Row 3: Ch 2, turn; 2 dc in first sc, 2 tr in next sc, leave rem 15 sts unworked; finish off.

FIRST WING

Row 1: With *right* side facing and working in free loops of beg ch, join white with sc in marked ch; sc in next 2 chs, leave rem 5 chs unworked: 3 sc.

Row 2: Ch 1, turn; sc in first 2 sc, 2 sc in last sc: 4 sc.

Row 3: Ch 1, turn; 2 sc in first sc, sc in last 3 sc: 5 sc.

Row 4: Ch 1, turn; work beg dec, sc in next 2 sc, 2 sc in last sc.

Row 5: Ch 1, turn; work beg dec, sc in next sc, dec: 3 sc.

Row 6: Ch 1, turn; sc in first sc, dec: 2 sc.

Row 7: Ch 1, turn; work beg dec: one sc.

Row 8: Ch 1, turn; sc in next sc; finish off.

SECOND WING

Row 1: With *right* side facing and working in free loops of beg ch, join white with sc in next ch from First Wing; sc in next ch, leave rem 3 chs unworked: 2 sc.

Row 2: Ch 1, turn; 2 sc in first sc, sc in last sc: 3 sc.

Row 3: Ch 1, turn; sc in first 2 sc, 2 sc in last sc: 4 sc.

Row 4: Ch 1, turn; 2 sc in first sc, sc in next sc, dec.

Row 5: Ch 1, turn; work beg dec, dec: 2 sc.

Row 6: Ch 1, turn; work beg dec: one sc.

Row 7: Ch 1, turn; sc in next sc; finish off.

Left Dove
BODY

With white, ch 13 *loosely*, place marker in tenth ch from hook for Wing placement.

Row 1 (right side): Sc in back ridge of second ch from hook and each ch across: 12 sc.

*Note: Mark row 1 as **right** side.*

Row 2: Ch 2, turn; 2 sc in first sc, (sc, sl st) in next sc, sk next sc, 2 dc in next sc, 2 tr in each of next 2 sc, 2 dc in next sc, sk next 2 sc, sc in next 2 sc, 2 sc in last sc: 17 sts.

Row 3: Ch 2, turn; 2 dc in first sc, 2 tr in next sc, leave rem 15 sts unworked; finish off.

FIRST WING

Row 1: With *right* side facing and working in free loops of beg ch, join white with sc in marked ch; sc in next ch, leave rem 8 chs unworked: 2 sc.

Row 2: Ch 1, turn; sc in first sc, 2 sc in last sc: 3 sc.

Row 3: Ch 1, turn; 2 sc in first sc, sc in last 2 sc: 4 sc.

Row 4: Ch 1, turn; work beg dec, sc in next sc, 2 sc in last sc.

Row 5: Ch 1, turn; work beg dec, dec: 2 sc.

Row 6: Ch 1, turn; work beg dec: one sc.

Row 7: Ch 1, turn; sc in next sc; finish off.

SECOND WING

Row 1: With *right* side facing and working in free loops of beg ch, join white with sc in next ch from First Wing; sc in next 2 chs, leave rem chs unworked: 3 sc.

Row 2: Ch 1, turn; 2 sc in first sc, sc in last 2 sc: 4 sc.

Row 3: Ch 1, turn; sc in first 3 sc, 2 sc in last sc: 5 sc.

Row 4: Ch 1, turn; 2 sc in first sc, sc in next 2 sc, dec.

Row 5: Ch 1, turn; work beg dec, sc in next sc, dec: 3 sc.

Row 6: Ch 1, turn; work beg dec, sc in last sc: 2 sc.

Row 7: Ch 1, turn; work beg dec: one sc.

Row 8: Ch 1, turn; sc in next sc; finish off.

Elephant (Make 2)
BODY

With grey, ch 13 loosely.

Row 1 (right side): Sc in second ch from hook and in next ch, 2 sc in each of next 2 chs, sc in each ch across: 14 sc.

*Note: Mark row 1 as **right** side.*

Row 2: Ch 1, turn; 2 sc in first sc, sc in next 6 sc, sl st in next sc, leave rem 6 sc unworked: 9 sts.

Row 3: Ch 1, turn; sk first sl st, sl st in next sc, sc in next 6 sc, 2 sc in last sc: 9 sts.

Row 4: Ch 1, turn; 2 sc in first sc, sc in next 5 sc, dec, leave rem sl st unworked: 8 sc.

Row 5: Ch 1, turn; sc in first sc, sc in Back Loop Only of each sc across to last sc, sc in *both* loops of last sc.

Row 6: Ch 1, turn; sc in both loops of each sc across.

Row 7: Ch 8 *loosely*, turn; sc in second ch from hook and in next 6 chs, sc in next 6 sc, dec: 14 sc.

Row 8: Ch 1, turn; work beg dec, sc in each sc across: 13 sc.

Row 9: Ch 1, turn; sc in each sc across to last sc, 2 sc in last sc: 14 sc.

Row 10: Ch 1, turn; sc in first 11 sc, leave rem 3 sc unworked.

Row 11: Ch 1, turn; sc in each sc across to last sc, 2 sc in last sc: 12 sc.

Row 12: Ch 1, turn; sc in each sc across.

Row 13: Ch 1, turn; sc in each sc across to last sc, 2 sc in last sc: 13 sc.

Rows 14-16: Ch 1, turn; sc in each sc across.

Row 17: Ch 4 *loosely*, turn; sc in second ch from hook and in next 2 chs, sc in each sc across: 16 sc.

Row 18: Ch 1, turn; work beg dec, sc in each sc across: 15 sc.

Row 19: Ch 1, turn; sc in each sc across to last 2 sc, dec: 14 sc.

Row 20: Ch 1, turn; work beg dec, sc in next 6 sc, dec, leave rem 4 sc unworked: 8 sc.

Row 21: Ch 1, turn; work beg dec, sc in next 4 sc, dec: 6 sc.

Row 22: Ch 1, turn; work beg dec, sc in next sc, sl st in last 3 sc, ch 3; finish off leaving a 1-in. end for tail.

Unravel tail and trim ends as desired.

EAR

Row 1: With *right* side facing, head toward you, and working in free loops of sc on row 4, join grey with sc in first sc; sc in same st and in next 5 sc: 7 sc.

Row 2: Ch 1, turn; 2 sc in first sc, sc in next 5 sc, 2 sc in last sc: 9 sc.

Row 3: Ch 1, turn; 2 sc in first sc, sc in each sc across: 10 sc.

Row 4: Ch 1, turn; work beg dec, sc in each sc across: 9 sc.

Row 5: Ch 1, turn; work beg dec, sc in next 5 sc, dec: 7 sc.

Row 6: Ch 1, turn; work beg dec, sc in next 3 sc, dec; finish off: 5 sc.

Noah's Ark

Camel (Make 2)

Row 1 (right side): With gold, ch 2, 2 sc in second ch from hook: 2 sc.

*Note: Mark row 1 as **right** side.*

Row 2: Ch 1, turn; sc in next 2 sc.

Row 3: Ch 1, turn; 2 sc in first sc, leave rem sc unworked; do *not* finish off: 2 sc.

Row 4: Ch 1, turn; 2 sc in first sc, sc in next sc: 3 sc.

Row 5: Ch 3, turn; sl st in third ch from hook (ear), 2 sc in first sc, sc in next 2 sc: 4 sc.

Row 6: Ch 8 *loosely,* turn; 2 sc in second ch from hook, sc in next 6 chs and in next 2 sc, dec, leave ear unworked: 11 sc.

Row 7: Ch 1, turn; work beg dec, sc in each sc across to last sc, 2 sc in last sc: 11 sc.

Row 8: Ch 1, turn; 2 sc in first sc, sc in next 4 sc, sl st in last 6 sc: 12 sts.

Row 9: Turn; sk first sl st, working *around* sl sts on row 8 and in sc on row 7, sl st in next sc, sc in next 4 sc, sc in next 5 sc on row 8, 2 sc in last sc: 12 sts.

Row 10: Ch 1, turn; 2 sc in first sc, sc in next 3 sc, dec, leave rem 6 sts unworked: 6 sc.

Row 11: Ch 1, turn; sc in each sc across.

Row 12: Ch 9 *loosely,* turn; sc in second ch from hook and in next 7 chs, sc in next 5 sc, 2 sc in last sc: 15 sc.

Row 13: Ch 1, turn; 2 sc in first sc, sc in each sc across: 16 sc.

Row 14: Ch 1, turn; sc in each sc across to last sc, 2 sc in last sc: 17 sc.

Row 15: Ch 1, turn; 2 sc in first sc, sc in next 6 sc, dec, leave rem 8 sc unworked: 9 sc.

Row 16: Ch 1, turn; work beg dec, sc in each sc across to last sc, 2 sc in last sc: 9 sc.

Row 17: Ch 1, turn; 2 sc in first sc, sc in each sc across: 10 sc.

Row 18: Ch 1, turn; sc in each sc across.

Row 19: Ch 1, turn; work beg dec, sc in each sc across: 9 sc.

Row 20: Ch 1, turn; 2 sc in first sc, sc in next 6 sc, dec: 9 sc.

Row 21: Ch 1, turn; work beg dec, sc in each sc across to last sc, 2 sc in last sc: 9 sc.

Row 22: Ch 9 *loosely,* turn; sc in second ch from hook and in next 7 chs, sc in next 7 sc, dec: 16 sc.

Row 23: Ch 1, turn; work beg dec, sc in each sc across: 15 sc.

Row 24: Ch 1, turn; sc in each sc across to last 2 sc, dec: 14 sc.

Row 25: Ch 1, turn; work beg dec, sc in next 3 sc, dec, leave rem 7 sc unworked: 5 sc.

Row 26: Ch 1, turn; work beg dec, sc in next sc, dec: 3 sc.

Row 27: Turn; sl st in first sc, ch 3, leave rem 2 sc unworked; finish off leaving a 1-in. end for tail.

Unravel tail and trim ends as desired.

Sheep (Make 2)

BODY

With white, ch 11 *loosely,* place marker in third ch from hook for Leg placement.

Row 1: Tr in second ch from hook, sc in next ch, (tr in next ch, sc in next ch) across: 10 sts.

Row 2 (Right side): Ch 1, turn; sc in each st across.

*Note: Mark row 2 as **right** side.*

Row 3: Ch 1, turn; sc in first sc, (tr in next sc, sc in next sc) across to last sc, (tr, sl st) in last sc: 11 sts.

Row 4: Ch 1, turn; sk first sl st, sc in each st across: 10 sts.

Row 5: Ch 1, turn; tr in first sc, sc in next sc, (tr in next sc, sc in next sc) across.

Row 6: Ch 2, turn; 2 sc in second ch from hook (tail), sc in each st across Body, ch 3, 2 sc in second ch from hook (ear), fold ear down over Body, sl st in last sc made on Body (sc *before* ch-3); finish off.

FACE

Row 1: With *right* side facing and working in end of rows, join brown with sc in row 6 at ear; 2 sc in next row, leave rem 4 rows unworked: 3 sc.

Row 2: Ch 1, turn; pull up a loop in next 3 sc, yo and draw through all 4 loops on hook: one st.

Row 3: Ch 1, turn; sc in next st; finish off.

FIRST LEG

Row 1: With *right* side facing and working in free loops of beg ch, join brown with sc in marked ch; sc in next ch, leave rem 7 chs unworked: 2 sc.

Rows 2 and 3: Ch 1, turn; sc in each sc across.

Finish off.

NEXT LEG

Row 1: With *right* side facing and working in free loops of beg ch, sk next 4 chs from First Leg and join brown with sc in next ch; sc in next ch, leave rem ch unworked: 2 sc.

Rows 2 and 3: Ch 1, turn; sc in each sc across.

Finish off.

Giraffe (Make 2)

Row 1 (right side): With gold, ch 2, 3 sc in second ch from hook.

*Note: Mark row 1 as **right** side.*

Row 2: Ch 1, turn; sc in first 2 sc, 2 sc in last sc: 4 sc.

Row 3: Ch 1, turn; sc in each sc across.

Row 4: Ch 1, turn; sc in each sc across to last sc, 2 sc in last sc: 5 sc.

Row 5: Ch 2, turn; sc in second ch from hook (ear) and in each sc across: 6 sc.

Row 6: Ch 25 *loosely,* turn; sc in second ch

from hook and in each ch across, sc in next 3 sc, dec, leave ear unworked: 28 sc.

Row 7: Ch 1, turn; work beg dec, sc in each sc across: 27 sc.

Row 8: Ch 1, turn; sc in first 16 sc, sl st in each sc across.

Row 9: Turn; working *around* sl sts on row 8 and in sc on row 7, sl st in first 2 sc, sc in next 9 sc, sc in next 8 sc on row 8, leave rem 8 sc unworked: 19 sts.

Row 10: Ch 1, turn; 2 sc in first sc, sc in next 5 sc, dec, leave rem 11 sts unworked: 8 sc.

Row 11: Ch 1, turn; work beg dec, sc in next 5 sc, 2 sc in last sc: 8 sc.

Row 12: Ch 1, turn; 2 sc in first sc, sc in next 5 sc, dec: 8 sc.

Row 13: Ch 1, turn; work beg dec, sc in next 5 sc, 2 sc in last sc: 8 sc.

Row 14: Ch 7 *loosely*, turn; sc in second ch from hook and in next 5 chs, sc in next 6 sc, dec: 13 sc.

Row 15: Ch 1, turn; work beg dec, sc in each sc across: 12 sc.

Row 16: Ch 1, turn; sc in each sc across to last 2 sc, dec: 11 sc.

Row 17: Turn; sl st in first sc, ch 4, leave rem 10 sc unworked; finish off leaving a 1-in. end for tail.

Unravel tail and trim ends as desired.

Hippo (Make 2)

With grey and leaving a 1/2-in. end for tail, ch 9 *loosely*.

Row 1 (right side): Sc in second ch from hook and in next 5 chs, leave rem 2 chs unworked (tail): 6 sc.

*Note: Mark row 1 as **right** side.*

Row 2: Ch 1, turn; 2 sc in first sc, sc in next 4 sc, 2 sc in last sc: 8 sc.

Row 3: Ch 1, turn; 2 sc in first sc, sc in each sc across: 9 sc.

Row 4: Ch 4 *loosely*, turn; sc in second ch from hook and in next 2 chs, sc in next 8 sc, 2 sc in last sc: 13 sc.

Rows 5 and 6: Ch 1, turn; sc in each sc across.

Row 7: Ch 1, turn; sc in first 10 sc, leave rem 3 sc unworked.

Rows 8-12: Ch 1, turn; sc in each sc across.

Row 13: Ch 1, turn; work beg dec, sc in each sc across: 9 sc.

Row 14: Ch 4 *loosely*, turn; sc in second ch from hook and in next 2 chs, sc in next 7 sc, dec: 11 sc.

Row 15: Ch 1, turn; sc in each sc across.

Row 16: Ch 1, turn; sc in each sc across to last 2 sc, dec: 10 sc.

Row 17: Ch 3, turn; sl st in second ch from hook and in next ch (ear), sc in next 7 sc, leave rem 3 sc unworked: 7 sc.

Row 18: Ch 1, turn; 2 sc in first sc, sc in next 6 sc, leave ear unworked: 8 sc.

Row 19: Ch 1, turn; work beg dec, sc in next 5 sc, 2 sc in last sc: 8 sc.

Row 20: Ch 1, turn; 2 sc in first sc, sc in each sc across: 9 sc.

Row 21: Ch 1, turn; work beg dec, sc in next 5 sc, dec: 7 sc.

Row 22: Ch 1, turn; work beg dec, sc in each sc across: 6 sc.

Row 23: Ch 1, turn; work beg dec, sc in next 2 sc, dec: 4 sc.

Row 24: Ch 1, turn; work beg dec, decrease; finish off: 2 sc.

Unravel tail and trim ends as desired.

Words

LETTER "T" (Make 2)

Horizontal Line: With rose, ch 10 *loosely*, (work Bobble, sl st) in second ch from hook, sl st in each ch across to last ch, (work Bobble, sl st) in last ch; finish off leaving a long end for sewing.

Vertical Line: With rose, ch 20 *loosely*, (work Bobble, sl st) in second ch from hook, sl st in each ch across to last ch, (work Bobble, sl st) in last ch; finish off leaving a long end for sewing.

LETTER "W" (Make 2)

With rose, ch 36 *loosely*, (work Bobble, sl st) in second ch from hook, * sl st in next 16 chs, (work Bobble, sl st) in next ch; rep from * once more, finish off leaving a long end for sewing.

LETTER "O" (Make 2)

With rose, ch 23 *loosely*, (work Bobble, sl st) in second ch from hook, sl st in each ch across; join with sl st to top of first Bobble, finish off leaving a long end for sewing.

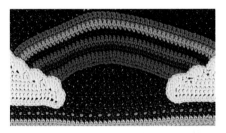

Rainbow

COLOR SEQUENCE

Work 2 rows of *each* color: purple, dark blue, blue, green, gold, rose.

With purple, ch 30 *loosely*.

Row 1 (right side): Working in back ridges of beg ch, sc in second ch from hook and in next 3 chs, (2 sc in next ch, sc in next 4 chs) across: 34 sc.

*Note: Mark row 1 as **right** side.*

Row 2: Ch 1, turn; 2 sc in first sc, sc in each sc across to last sc, 2 sc in last sc changing to next color in last sc: 36 sc.

Row 3: Ch 1, turn; 2 sc in first sc, sc in each sc across to last sc, 2 sc in last sc: 38 sc.

Rows 4–11: Rep rows 2 and 3, 4 times: 54 sc.

Row 12: Ch 1, turn; 2 sc in first sc, sc in each sc across to last sc, 2 sc in last sc; finish off leaving a long end for sewing.

Noah's Ark

Cloud (Make 2)

With white, ch 28 loosely.

Row 1: Sc in second ch from hook and in each ch across: 27 sc.

Row 2 (right side): Ch 1, turn; work beg dec, sc in each sc across to last 2 sc, dec: 25 sc.

*Note: Mark row 2 as **right** side.*

Rows 3–7: Ch 1, turn; sk first sc, dec, sc in each sc across to last 3 sc, dec, leave rem sc unworked: 5 sc.

Row 8: Ch 1, turn; 2 sc in first sc, sc in next 3 sc, 2 sc in last sc: 7 sc.

Row 9: Ch 1, turn; work beg dec, sc in next 3 sc, dec: 5 sc.

Row 10: Ch 1, turn; work beg dec, sc in next sc, dec: 3 sc.

Edging: Ch 1, do *not* turn; working in end of rows, sk first row, sc in next 2 rows, (5 dc in next row, sk next row, sc in next row) twice, 3 dc in last row; working in free loops of beg ch, 3 sc in ch at base of first sc, sc in each ch across to last ch, 3 sc in last ch; working in end of rows, 3 dc in first row, (sc in next row, sk next row, 5 dc in next row) twice, sc in next 2 rows, sk last row;

working across sts on Row 10, sc in first sc, 3 dc in next sc, sc in last sc; join with sl st to first sc, finish off leaving a long end for sewing.

Star (Make 4)

CENTER

Rnd 1 (right side): With gold, ch 2, 5 sc in second ch from hook; join with sl st to first sc.

*Note: Mark rnd 1 as **right** side.*

Rnd 2: Ch 1, 2 sc in same st and in each sc around; join with sl st to first sc: 10 sc.

Rnd 3: Ch 1, sc in same st, 2 sc in next sc, (sc in next sc, 2 sc in next sc) around; join with sl st to first sc: 15 sc.

Rnd 4: Ch 1, 2 sc in same st and in each sc around; join with sl st to first sc, do *not* finish off: 30 sc.

FIRST POINT

Row 1: Ch 1, sc in same st and in next 5 sc, leave rem 24 sc unworked: 6 sc.

Row 2: Ch 1, *turn;* work beg dec, sc in next 2 sc, dec: 4 sc.

Row 3: Ch 1, turn; sc in each sc across.

Row 4: Ch 1, turn; work beg dec, dec: 2 sc.

Row 5: Ch 1, turn; sc in each sc across.

Row 6: Ch 1, turn; work beg dec: one sc.

Row 7: Ch 1, turn; sc in next sc; finish off.

NEXT THREE POINTS

Row 1: With *right* side facing, join gold with sc in next sc on rnd 4 of Center from last Point made; sc in next 5 sc, leave rem sc unworked: 6 sc.

Rows 2–7: Work same as First Point.

LAST POINT

Row 1: With *right* side facing, join gold with sc in next sc on rnd 4 of Center from last Point made; sc in last 5 sc: 6 sc.

Rows 2–7: Work same as First Point; at end of row 7, do *not* finish off.

EDGING

Ch 1, do not turn; sc evenly around entire Star working 3 sc in end of each Point; join with sl st to first sc, finish off.

FINISHING

Use safety pins to hold crocheted pieces in place while sewing to Afghan Body.

Center and sew Rainbow and Clouds to Top Panel.

Using photos, pages 118-124, as a guide:

- Sew eyes on animals and people.

- For each spot on Giraffes, thread ends of a 5-in. length of gold up from back of Giraffe through holes in button and knot ends to secure. Unravel ends and trim as desired.

- Sew buttons to Stars in same manner as Giraffe spots.

- Sew Ark pieces together attaching House to Bottom and Roof.

- Sew Large Heart to House.

- Sew Ark to Center Panel.

- Sew Doves to Center Panel, lapping First Wing over Second Wing on Right Dove and lapping Second Wing over First Wing on Left Dove.

- Sew Noah, Mrs. Noah, Small Heart, and Words to Bottom Panel.

- Sew Elephants, Camels, Sheep, Giraffes, and Hippos to Side Panels.

- Sew one Star to each Corner Panel.

Compliments of Leisure Arts, Inc., USA. For a complete line of products, call Leisure Arts, Inc. @ 800-526-5111 or log on to www.leisurearts.com.

Country Sampler

Laura Pawlowski

Gorgeous alternating panels of aqua and white feature different stitches, creating a beautiful texture in Laura's afghan.

Country Sampler

Materials & Tools

Worsted-weight yarn, approximately:
24 oz. each of aqua and white

Crochet hook size K, or size to
match gauge

Gauge
Panel 1 = 6 in.; Panel 2 = 5¼ in.;
Panel 3 = 5½ in.;
Panel 4 = 5½ in.;
Panel 5 = 5¾ in.;
Panel 6 = 5 in; and
Panel 7 = 5 in.

Finished size
Approximately 44 x 60 in.

FAIR FACTS

Oregonians first marveled
at the phonograph and
the telephone at their
fair in 1877.

PANEL 1
With aqua, ch 24 loosely.

Row 1 (Right side): Dc in fourth ch from hook, FPtr in next ch, dc in next ch, (sk next 2 ch, 5 dc in next ch, ch 2, sk next 3 ch, dc in next ch, FPtr in next ch, dc in next ch) twice.

Note: Loop a short piece of yarn around any st to mark last row as right side.

Row 2: Ch 3, turn: dc in next dc, BPtr in next tr, dc in next dc, 5 dc in next dc, ch 2, sk next 4 dc, dc in next dc, BPtr in next tr, dc in next dc, 5 dc in next dc, ch 2 sk next 4 dc, dc in next dc, BPtr in next tr, dc in top of beg ch.

Rep row 2.

PANEL 2
With white, ch 21 loosely.

Row 1 (Right side): 5 dc in sixth ch from hook, sk next 2 ch, dc in next ch, * sk next 2 ch, 5 dc in next ch, * sk next 2 ch, dc in next ch; rep from * across.

Note: Loop a short piece of yarn around any stitch to mark last row as right side.

Row 2: Ch 3, turn; sk first 3 dc, 5 dc in next dc, sk next 2 dc, * dc in next dc, sk next 2 dc, 5 dc in next dc, sk next 2 dc; rep from * across, dc in top of beg ch.

Rep row 2.

PANEL 3
With aqua, ch 20 loosely.

Row 1 (right side): Sc in second ch from hook, and across. Ch 3, turn (19 sts). In next 6 sc, (ch 1, sk next sc, dc in next sc) 3 times, dc in each sc across (19 sts).

Row 2: Ch 1, turn; sc in first 7 dc, work popcorn as follows: 5 dc in next ch-1 sp, drop loop from hook, insert hook in first dc of 5-dc group, hook dropped loop and draw through, ch 1 to close—popcorn made, sc in next dc, sc in next ch-1 sp, sc in next dc, work popcorn in next ch-1 sp, sc in next 6 dc, sc in top of beg ch.

Note: Loop a short piece of yarn around any stitch to mark last row as right side.

Row 3: Ch 3 (counts as first dc, now and throughout), turn, dc in next sc, [work BPtr around post of dc below next sc, sk sc behind BPtr (now and throughout), dc in next sc] 3 times, ch 1, sk next popcorn, dc in next sc, ch 1, sk next sc, dc in next sc, ch 1, sk next popcorn, (dc in next sc, work BPtr around post of dc below next sc) 3 times, dc in last sc.

Row 4: Ch 1, turn; sc in first 7 sts, sc in next ch-1 sp, sc in next dc, work popcorn in next ch-1 sp, sc in next dc, sc in next ch-1 sp and in each st across.

Row 5: Ch 3, turn; dc in next sc, (work BPtr around the post of next BPtr, dc in next sc) 3 times, ch 1, sk next sc, dc in next sc, ch 1, sk next popcorn, dc in next sc, ch 1, sk next sc, (dc in next sc, work BPtr around the post of next BPtr) 3 times, dc in last sc.

Row 6: Ch 1, turn, sc in first 7 sts, work popcorn in next ch-1 sp, sc in next dc, sc in next ch-1 sp, sc in next dc, work popcorn in next ch-1 sp, sc in last 7 sts.

Panels 1 and 2

Panels 3 and 4

Panels 5 and 6

Row 7: Ch 3, turn: dc in next sc, (work BPtr around the post of next BPtr, dc in next sc) 3 times, ch 1, sk next popcorn, dc in next sc, ch 1, sk next sc, dc in next sc, ch 1, sk next popcorn, (dc in next sc, work BPtr around the post of next BPtr) 3 times, dc in last sc.

Rep rows 4–7 for pat.

PANEL 4
With white, ch 20 loosely.

Row 1 (right side): Sc in second ch from hook, * ch 2, sk 2 chs, sc in next ch, rep from * across, ending sc in last ch (7 sc each separated by ch 2.)

Row 2: Ch 1, turn. * Sc in next sc, ch 2, sk 2 ch, rep from * across, ending sc in last sc.

Row 3: Rep row 2.

Row 4: Ch 3, turn. 2 dc in sc, sk 2 ch, * 3 dc in next sc, sk 2 ch, rep from * across, ending 2 dc in last sc.

Rep row 2 (3 times, but sc into middle dc of 3-dc group), then row 4, then 3 more row 2, etc., for required length.

PANEL 5
With aqua, ch 19 loosely.

Row 1: Sc in second ch from hook and in each ch across (18 sc).

Row 2 (right side): Ch 3 (counts as first dc),turn; dc in next sc, work popcorn as follows: 4 dc in next sc, drop loop from hook, insert hook in first dc of 4-dc group, hook dropped loop and draw through ch 1 to close—popcorn made, dc in next sc, (sk next 2 sc, 5 dc in next sc, sk next 2 sc, dc in next sc, work popcorn in next sc) twice, dc in next sc.

Note: Loop a short piece of yarn around any stitch to mark last row as right side.

Row 3: Ch 1, turn; sc in each st and popcorn across (18 sc).

Rep rows 2 and 3 for pattern.

PANEL 6
With white, ch 22 loosely.

Row 1 (right side): Dc in fifth ch from hook, * sk next 3 ch, 5 dc in next ch, sk next 3 ch, (dc, ch 1, dc) in next ch—V-st made; rep from * once, dc in last ch.

Note: Loop a short piece of yarn around any st to mark last row as right side.

Row 2: Ch 3 (counts as first dc), turn; 2 dc in first ch-1 sp, sk next 3 dc, work V-St in next dc, * 5 dc in next ch-1 sp, sk next 3 dc, work V-st in next dc; 3 dc in last sp.

Row 3: Ch 4 (counts as first dc plus ch 1), turn; dc in same st, * 5 dc in next ch-1 sp, sk next 3 dc, work V-st in next dc; rep from * once.

Rep rows 2 and 3 for pat.

PANEL 7
With aqua, ch 18 loosely.

Row 1 (right side): Dc in fourth ch from hook and in next 4 ch, * sk next 2 ch, (2 dc, ch 2, 2 dc) in next ch—Shell made, sk next 2 ch, dc in next 6 chs.

Note: Loop a short piece of yarn around any stitch to mark last row as right side.

Row 2: Ch 3 (counts as first dc), turn; dc in next dc, BPtr in next 2 dc, dc in next 2 dc, Shell in next ch-2 sp, dc in next 2 dc, BPtr in next 2 dc, dc in next dc, dc in top of beg ch.

Rep row 2, but do FPtr around the tr of the previous row on the right side (but BPtr on the wrong side, so the raised tr always appears on front side of work.)

PANEL EDGING
Each panel is worked to desired length, then sc around for uniformity.

PANEL JOINING
Join by (sl st, ch 2, sl st, ch 2) across back and forth between panels.

AFGHAN EDGING
Two rnds of sc followed by a rnd of sc, * sk 2 st (dc, ch 1 dc, ch 2, sc in second ch from hook—picot made, dc, ch 1, dc) all in next st, rep from * around.

Tip: Although Laura lists a size K crochet hook, she cautions that she crochets much tighter than the average person, so a size H or I may be appropriate for others.

Original Design

Panels 6 and 7

Delphinium Dream

Lynne Walsh

This bouquet of crocheted flowers earned the top prize for Lynne; it was created for her eldest granddaughter, who asked for an afghan worked in shades of blue.

Materials & Tools
Worsted-weight yarn, approximately:
28 oz. ecru (color E)
12 oz. each of bright navy
(color N), medium powder
blue (color M), and light
powder blue (color L)

Crochet hook sizes G and N, or
sizes to match gauge

Tapestry needle

Gauge
Each motif = 5 in. square.

Finished size
Approximately 53 x 63 in.

MOTIF (Make 120)
Starting at center with color E and size H hook, ch 3. Join with sl st to form ring.

Rnd 1: Work 8 sc in ring; join with sl st to first sc. Fasten off.

Rnd 2: With color M, sl st in any sc, ch 3, work 3 dc in same sc, drop loop from hook, insert hook in top of ch 3 and draw dropped loop through loop on hook so that sts puff out toward you—popcorn made; * ch 1, work 4 dc in next sc, drop loop from hook, insert hook in first dc of group and complete popcorn as before. Rep from * 6 times more (8 popcorns), ch 1; join to top of first popcorn. Fasten off.

Rnd 3: With N, sl st in any ch-1 sp, work popcorn, (ch 2, popcorn in next ch-1 sp) 7 times, ch 2; join. Fasten off.

Rnd 4: With color E, sl st in any ch-2 sp, ch 3, work 2 dc in same sp, * ch 1, in next sp work (3 dc, ch 3 and 3 dc) for corner, ch 1, 3 dc in next sp. Rep from * twice more; ch 1, work corner in next sp, ch 1; join. Fasten off.

Rnd 5: With color L, sl st in a corner sp, ch 3, in same sp work (2 dc, ch 3 and 3 dc) for first corner, * (ch 1, 3 dc in next ch-1 sp) twice; ch 1, in next corner sp work (3 dc, ch 3 and 3 dc) for another corner. Rep from * twice more; (ch 1, 3 dc in next sp) twice, ch 1; join. Fasten off.

Rnd 6: With color E, sl st in a corner sp, work corner, * ch 1, 3 dc in next sp. Rep from * to next corner sp, ch 1, work corner in corner sp. Continue in pat, ch 1; join. Fasten off.

JOINING
Arrange motifs 10 wide by 12 long and sew together neatly, working through outer loops only of last rnd.

BORDER
With G hook, rep rnd 6 once each with colors E, L, M and N.

Reprinted from the WOMAN'S DAY Magazine. Permission granted by WOMAN'S DAY Magazine. Copyright 2002 Hachette Filipacchi Magazines, Inc.

Bright Waves

Lester, a crochet pattern tester, knows a winning design when she sees one. This colorful afghan will brighten the rainiest day.

Materials & Tools
Worsted-weight yarn, approximately:
28 oz. black
7 oz. each of gold, red, green,
and orange

Crochet hook size I, or size to
match gauge

Gauge
3 dc = 1 in.; 4 dc rows = 3 in.

Finished size
Approximately 54 x 61½ in.

INSTRUCTIONS
Row 1: With black, ch 212, 2 dc in fourth ch from hook, *[dc in next 2 chs, (dc next 2 chs together) 4 times, dc in next 2 chs], 5 dc in next ch; rep from * 14 more times; rep between [ ], 3 dc in last ch, turn (209 dc).

*Note: Work remaining rows in **back loops** only.*

Row 2: Ch 3, 2 dc in same st, *[dc in next 2 sts, (dc next 2 sts together) 4 times, dc in next 2 sts], 5 dc in next st; rep from * 14 more times; rep between [ ], 3 dc in last st, turn. Fasten off.

Row 3: Join gold with sl st in first st, ch 3, 2 dc in same st, *[dc in next 2 sts, (dc next 2 sts together) 4 times, dc in next 2 sts], 5 dc in next st; rep from * 14 more times; rep between [ ], 3 dc in last st, turn.

Row 4: Rep row 2.

Rows 5–82: Working in color sequence of black, red, black, green, black, orange, black, gold, rep rows 3 and 4 alternately, ending with black.

Pattern Courtesy of The Needlecraft Shop

FAIR FACTS

Officials at the Iowa State Fair recently instituted a new rule in their Ugliest Cake Contest: everything on or in an entry had to be edible. One recent winner? A skunk, complete with tire tracks down the middle.

Hugs & Kisses

Laura Pawlowski

Here's another winner for baby. As the name suggests, this design features hugs and kisses formed by crossed triple crochets.

Materials & Tools
Sport-weight yarn, approximately:
16 oz. white
12 oz. variegated

Crochet hook size G, or size to match gauge

Gauge
In pat, 16 sts = 4 in.;
Rows 2–5 = 1 ⅝ in.

Finished size
Approximately 42 x 42 in.

INSTRUCTIONS
With white, ch 168.

Row 1 (right side): Sc in second ch from hook and in each ch across changing to variegated in last st; turn (167 sc). Cut white.

Row 2: With variegated, ch 4 (to count as a dc and a ch-1 sp), sk first 2 sc; *[yo and draw up a loop, yo and through 2 loops] 4 times all in next sc, yo and through all 5 loops on hook*—puff st made; ch 1, sk next sc, * puff st in next sc, ch 1, sk next sc; rep from * across to last sc; dc in last sc changing to white; turn. (82 puff sts.) Cut variegated.

Row 3: With white, ch 1, sc in first dc, * sc in ch-1 sp, sc in top of puff st; rep from * to ch-4; sc in ch-4 sp, sc in third ch of ch-4; turn.

Row 4: Ch 4 (to count as first tr); *sk first 3 sc, tr in next sc, ch 1, working **behind** tr just made, sk 1 sc to the **right**, tr in next sc to the **right**—**beg crossed-tr** made; * sk next 2 sc, tr in next sc, ch 1, working **behind** tr just made, sk next sc to the **right**, tr in next sc to the **right**— **crossed tr** made; rep from * to last sc; tr in last sc; turn (55 crossed-tr groups.)

Row 5: Ch 1, sc in first tr, * sc in next tr, sc in ch-1 sp, sc in next tr; rep from * to ch-4; sc in top of ch-4 changing to variegated; turn. Cut white.

Rep rows 2–5 24 *more* times or until approximately 40½ in. from beginning, then rep rows 2 and 3 once more. Fasten off.

EDGING
With right side facing, attach variegated in first st of last row. Ch 1, 2 sc in first st; *ch 1, sl st in top of last sc made*—**picot** made; * sc in next 3 sts, picot; rep from * to last st; (2 sc, picot) all in last st; ** 2 sc over next ch, sc over next sc, picot; rep from ** along next edge; working in rem loop of beg ch, (2 sc, picot) all in first st; rep from * to last st; (2 sc, picot) all in last st; *** sc over sc, 2 sc over ch, picot; rep from *** across next edge; join with a sl st to first sc. Fasten off. Weave in ends.

Alteration: Laura substituted pink yarn for the white—she must have had a girl in mind when she made this afghan.

Pattern Courtesy of Coats & Clark

Bargello Afghan

This memorable prizewinner is reminiscent of bargello, the classic needlepoint stitch. Bonnie changed the color scheme to rich jewel tones when she created this afghan.

Bonnie Lineberry

Materials & Tools

Worsted-weight yarn, approximately:
- 20 oz. each of jade, light purple, and fuchsia
- 30 oz. natural

Crochet hook size H, or size to match gauge

Gauge

In pat, 6 blocks = 6½ in.; 8 rows = 4 in.

Finished size

Approximately 53 x 73 in.

*Note: To change color at the end of the second row of a color, yo, insert hook into the top of the ch-3 and draw loop through, yo and through 2 loops on hook, cut color in use leaving a 4-in. strand, with next color to be used yo and draw through 2 loops remaining on hook—**dc-color change** worked.*

BARGELLO PATTERN

Row 1 (Right Side): Dc in fourth ch from hook and in next 2 ch, * [sk 2 ch, sl st in next ch, ch 3, dc in next 3 ch] 3 times, [ch 3, sl st in next ch, sk next 2 ch, dc in next 3 ch] 3 times; rep from * to last ch, dc in last ch; turn—8 chevrons.

Now work all dc and sl sts into the back loop only of dc and ch on every row.

Row 2: Ch 3, sk first dc, * [dc in next 3 dc, sk sl st, sk 2 chs of ch-3, sl st in next ch, ch 3] 3 times, [dc in next 3 dc, ch 3, sl st in next ch, sk next 2 chs, sk sl st] 3 times; rep from * to last 4 sts; dc in next 3 dc and in top of ch-3; turn.

Rep row 2 for pat.

AFGHAN

With jade, ch 295. Work 2 rows of Bargello pat changing to light purple in last st of second row. Then work * 2 rows light purple, 2 rows fuchsia, 2 rows jade; rep from * once more (14 rows).

** Work 8 rows natural. Work 2 rows light purple, * 2 rows fuchsia, 2 rows jade, 2 rows light purple; rep from * once more.

Work 8 rows natural. Work 2 rows fuchsia, * 2 rows jade, 2 rows light purple, 2 rows fuchsia; rep from * once more.

Work 8 rows natural. Work 2 rows jade, * 2 rows light purple, 2 rows fuchsia, 2 rows jade; rep from * once more.

Rep from ** once more (146 rows). Fasten off. Weave in ends.

Alteration: Bonnie chose a different color scheme for this pattern.

Pattern Courtesy of Coats & Clark

Eastern Idaho State Fair Centennial Afghan

Betty Jean Perry

What an interesting idea—Betty Jean made this commemorative afghan for the centennial celebration of her state fair. Adapt this concept to make your own afghan for a very special occasion.

Materials & Tools
Worsted-weight yarn, approximately:
    48 oz. white

Sport-weight yarn, approximately:
    2½ oz. each of blue, black, and gold

2 skeins of gold embroidery floss

Afghan hook size K, or size to match gauge

Crochet hook size I, or size to match gauge

Gauge
11 afghan st = 3 in.

Finished size
Approximately 46 x 68 in.

INSTRUCTIONS

With afghan hook and white yarn, work 170 sc. Then work afghan stitch across for 223 rows. One loop rem on hook, at the right of afghan. To finish last row of afghan stitch: With loop on hook, sk first vertical bar and under next vertical bar pull up loop. Pull loop just made through loop on hook. Pull up loop under next vertical bar and through loop on hook for the rest of the row. With one loop on hook and now at left of afghan, change to crochet hook size I.

BORDER

Row 1 (edge): Sc around outside edges; put 1 sc in each st and end of row. Put 3 sc in each corner. Sl st to the 1st sc.

Row 2: Ch 3, 4 dc in st where sl st was just made. * Sk 2 sc, sc in next sc, sk 2 sc, 5 dc in next sc. Rep from * around ending sk 1 sc instead of sk 2 sc, sl st to top of ch 3. Finish off.

Hide threads and block after cross stitching.

CROSS-STITCH

Top Half

- 8 blank rows
- Eastern Idaho State Fair—7 rows
- 9 blank rows
- 1902–2002—7 rows
- 8 blank rows
- Affiliated With 16 Counties—5 rows (smaller letters)
- 21 blank rows

Stars

Large star—61 rows from top point to bottom points. Start large star on the 66th row from the top of afghan and 84 sps over from the edge to the center.

Small stars—8 rows from top point to bottom points.

- First set of small stars at top right and left of large star. Start on the 51st row from top of afghan and over 44 spaces from edges.
- Second set starts 3 rows from first star and over 20 spaces from edges.
- Third set starts 7 rows down from second star and over 29 spaces from edges.
- Fourth set starts 10 rows down from third star and over 33 spaces from edges.
- Fifth set starts 7 rows down from fourth star and over 17 spaces from edges.
- Sixth set starts 10 rows from fifth star and over 29 spaces from edges.
- Seventh set starts 9 rows down from sixth star and over 18 spaces from edges.
- Eighth set starts 3 rows down from seventh star and over 39 spaces from edges.

Lettering

Inside large star—Start 24 rows down from point at the top of star and over 23 spaces from right top star point.

- 100 Yrs.—5 rows, 3 spaces between "100" and "YRS."
- 4 blank rows
- Of Wow— 5 rows, 4 spaces between "OF" and "WOW."

Backstitch rays from star tips and around star, using yarn and embroidery floss.

Bottom Half

Bingham County—5 rows, start 21 rows down from bottom points of large star.

- 5 blank rows
- Home Of The Eastern Idaho—5 rows
- 5 blank rows
- State Fair—5 rows
- 6 blank rows
- Counties—5 rows and 3 blank rows between each county name, three columns of county names. First column on the 23rd space from left edge, second column on the 72nd space from the left edge and third column on the116th space from the left edge.
- 8 blank rows to the bottom

Original Design

IDAHO Toyfair

Joyce L. Salavitch

Joyce's first great-grandson snuggles under this afghan, an adorable embroidered prizewinner featuring alternating panels of afghan stitch and filet squares.

Materials & Tools

Sport-weight yarn, approximately:
- 30 oz. light blue
- 2½ oz. each of aqua, gold, pink, and brown

Crochet hook size G (for filet squares), or size to match gauge

Afghan hook size J (for afghan stitch squares), or size to match gauge

Gauge

Size G hook—3 blocks and 2 sp or 2 blocks and 3 sp = 2 in., 3 rows = 2 ins.

Size J Afghan Hook—4 sts = 1 in., 8 rows = 3 in.

Each square = 6 x 6 in.

Finished size

Approximately 36 x 44 in.

INSTRUCTIONS

Light blue is used to crochet all panels, joinings, and borders; additional colors are for embroidery.

Note: Mark beg of each panel for lower edge.

First, Third and Fifth Panels

FIRST AFGHAN ST SQUARE—With afghan hook and light blue, ch 24 loosely.

Note: All rows of afghan st are worked from right side.

Row 1 (First Half of Row): With care not to twist ch, *retaining all loops on hook,* draw up a loop through single loop at top of second ch from hook and through each rem ch to end; 24 loops on hook.

Second Half of Row: To complete row, work off loops in following manner: yo hook, draw through first loop on hook, * yo hook, draw through next 2 loops on hook; rep from * until 1 loop remains on hook.

Row 2: Counting loop on hook as first loop of row, insert hook under second vertical bar from edge, yo and draw up a loop, draw up a loop under each rem bar to within 1 bar of end, insert hook under both vertical bars of last st and draw up a loop; 24 loops on hook. Work off loops as before to complete row.

Rep row 2 until 16 rows from beg have been completed.

Finish Afghan St Square by working a row of sl st in following manner: * draw up a loop under next vertical bar and draw this loop through loop on hook; rep from * to within 1 bar of end, draw up a loop under both vertical bars of last st and through loop on hook. *Do not fasten off.*

FILET SQUARE: Transfer rem loop on afghan hook to size G hook.

Note: When working dc, draw up loops to about ¾ in.

Row 1 (wrong side): Turn, sl st into first st, ch 3, work 1 dc in next st, * ch 2, sk 1 st, 1 dc in each of next 2 sts; rep from * to end; 8 blocks and 7 sps.

Row 2: Ch 5, turn, sk first 2 sts, work 2 dc in next sp, * ch 2, sk next 2 sts, 2 dc in next sp; rep from * 5 times, ch 2, 1 dc in top of ch 3; 8 sps and 7 blocks.

Row 3: Turn, sl st into first sp, ch 3, 1 dc in same sp, * ch 2, sk next 2 sts, 2 dc in next sp; rep from * 5 times, ch 2, 2 dc in last sp; 8 blocks and 7 sps.

Rep rows 2 and 3 until 9 filet rows have been completed, end on wrong side with row 3.

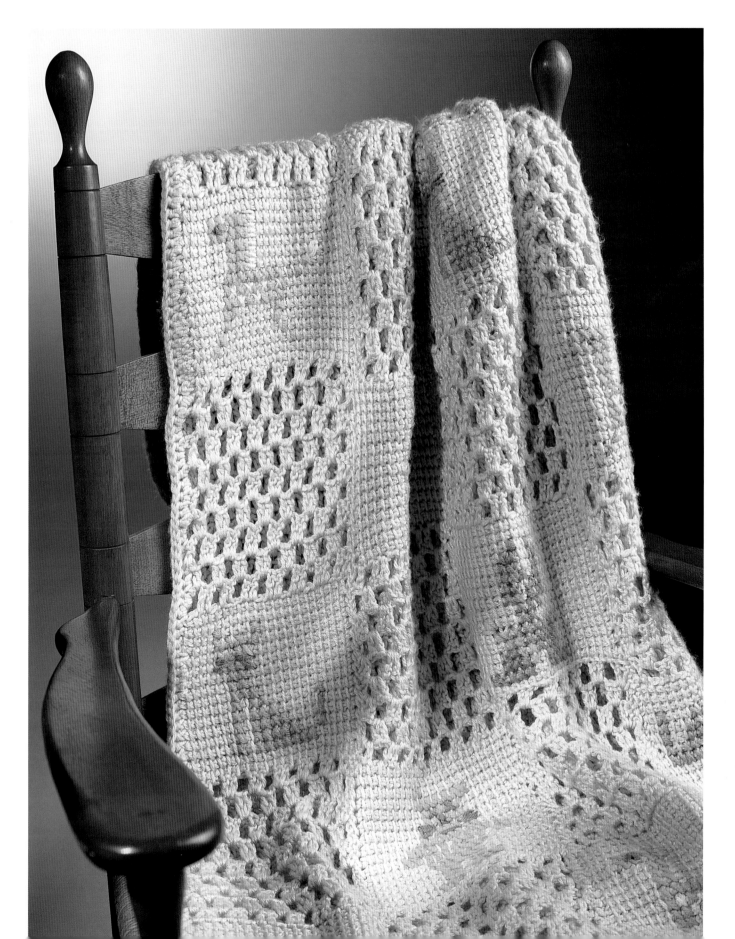

Toyfair

SECOND AFGHAN ST SQUARE: Transfer rem loop on hook to afghan hook.

Row 1 (First Half—right side): Turn, pick up and retain on hook 1 loop in each of first 2 sts, * 1 loop in next sp, 1 loop in each of next 2 sts; rep from * 6 times; 24 loops on hook.

Work off loops as before. Complete as for first Afghan St Square. Continue to alternate Filet and Second Afghan St Squares until 7 squares have been completed, end with Afghan St Square. Fasten off.

Second and Fourth Panels

FIRST FILET SQUARE—With size G hook and light blue, ch 25 loosely.

Row 1 (wrong side): Work 1 dc in fourth ch from hook, * ch 2, sk 1 ch, 1 dc in each of next 2 chs; rep from * to end; 8 blocks and 7 sps.

Rep rows 2 and 3 of filet square on first panel until 9 rows from beg have been completed.

Work Afghan St Square same as for Second Afghan St Square on first panel.

Work Filet Square same as for first Filet Square on first panel.

Continue to alternate Afghan St and Filet Squares until 7 squares have been completed, end on wrong side with Filet Square.

FINISHING
Block each panel to 6 x 42 in. having each of the 7 squares measure 6 x 6 in.

EMBROIDERY
Working from embroidery charts (figures 1–6), using colors as indicated. Keep work flat and embroider animals on each panel as shown on arrangement chart (figure 7).

With following exceptions, all embroidery is worked in cross-stitch.

- Giraffe eye: brown French knot, winding yarn twice around the needle.
- Mane: pink straight stitches
- Tip of tail: pink lazy daisy stitch

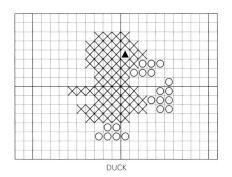

DUCK

Figure 1

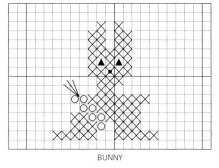

BUNNY

Figure 2

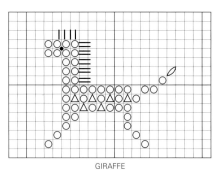

GIRAFFE

Figure 3

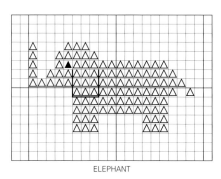

ELEPHANT

Figure 4

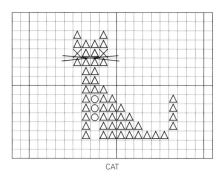

CAT

Figure 5

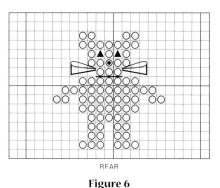

BEAR

Figure 6

Key

◎ Gold	⊠ Aqua	⟋ Lazy Daisy Stitch
▲ Brown	△ Pink	● French Knot

PANEL 1	PANEL 2	PANEL 3	PANEL 4	PANEL 5
DUCK		BEAR		ELEPHANT
	ELEPHANT		DUCK	
GIRAFFE		CAT		BUNNY
	DUCK		GIRAFFE	
CAT		BUNNY		BEAR
	BEAR		ELEPHANT	
BUNNY		GIRAFFE		CAT

Figure 7

- Cat whiskers: brown straight stitches
- Bunny nose: pink French knot, same as for giraffe
- Top of carrot: brown straight stitches
- Elephant—outline of ear: brown straight stitches
- Bear—nose: brown French knot, same as for giraffe.
- Bow: aqua lazy daisy and straight stitches.

Arrange panels as shown on arrangement chart (figure 7).

All joinings and borders are worked with size G hook.

LOOPS FOR JOINING

First Panel, Right Edge Only: From right side, with loop of light blue on hook, sl st into first row of afghan stitch at lower right corner of panel; working along long edge, † * ch 6, sk 2 rows, sl st into next row *; rep between * 4 times, ** ch 6, sk next dc block, sl st into next sp **; rep between ** 3 times, ch 6, sl st into first row of next Afghan St Square; rep from †, end last rep with sl st in last row of last Afghan St Square (35 loops). Fasten off.

Third Panel, Right Edge: Work same as on first panel.

Left Edge: From right side, beg at upper left corner of panel, work same as on right edge.

Fifth Panel, Left Edge Only: Work same as for left edge on third panel.

JOINING

From right side, with loop of light blue on hook, sl st into top of ch 3 at upper left corner of second panel, ch 3, sl st into first loop on upper right edge of first panel, ch 3, sk first dc block on second panel, sl st into next sp, * ch 3, sl st into next loop on first panel, ch 3, sk next dc block on second panel, sl st into next sp *; rep between * 3 times, end last rep with sl st in first row of next Afghan St Square on second panel, † ** ch 3, sl st into next loop on first panel, ch 3, sk 2 rows of afghan st on second panel, sl st into next row **; rep between ** 4 times, rep between * 5 times, end last rep in first row of next Afghan St Square on second panel, rep from †, end with sl st into lower left corner of second panel. Fasten off.

From right side, with loop on hook, sl st into end st of foundation ch at lower right corner of second panel and join to left edge of third panel in same manner.

Join fourth panel to third and fifth panels.

BORDER

Lower Edge: From right side, with loop of light blue on hook, sl st into lower left corner st of afghan, working along lower edge, * ch 4, sk next 2 sts, 1 sc in next st *; rep between * 6 times, † ch 4, 1 sc in first joining loop, ch 4, 1 sc in next joining loop, ** ch 4, sk next dc block, 1 sc in next sp **; rep between ** 6 times, ch 4, 1 sc in first joining loop, ch 4, 1 sc in next joining loop, ch 4, sk first st on next Afghan St Square, 1 sc in next st, rep between * 7 times †; rep between †

once, end last rep with 1 sc in corner st (45 loops across lower edge).

Side Edge: Working along right side edge, * ch 4, sk 1 row of afghan st, 1 sc in next row *; rep between * 7 times, † ch 4, 1 sc around end dc of next row, ** ch 4, 1 sc in next sp, ch 4, 1 sc around dc of next row **; rep between ** 3 times, rep between * 8 times †; rep between † twice, end last rep with 1 sc in upper right corner st (59 loops along side edge).

Work along upper and left side edges to correspond. Join with sl st in first st.

For Lower Edge: From right side, ch 3, 1 dc in first ch 4 loop on lower edge, * ch 3, work a dec dc in following manner: yo and draw up a loop in same ch 4 loop, yo and through 2 loops on hook, retaining the rem 2 loops on hook, yo and draw up a loop in next ch 4 loop—4 loops on hook—yo and through 2 loops, yo and through rem 3 loops; rep from * to end, completing last dec dc in sc at corner. Fasten off.

For Upper Edge: From right side, with loop of light blue on hook, sl st into first sc at upper right corner, ch 3, 1 dc in first ch 4 loop on upper edge, complete same as for lower edge. Fasten off.

Block completed afghan to 36 x 44 in.

Alteration: Joyce added a backing composed of dc, which required an additional 15 to 20 oz. of yarn.

Pattern Reprinted with Permission from Bucilla

Popcorn Stitch Afghan

Diana L. Snow

Here's another design that attracted two blue ribbon winners. Diana's interpretation included altering the shell panel of this darling pattern.

Materials & Tools

Worsted-weight yarn, approximately:
- 72 oz. white
- 12 oz. variegated

Crochet hook size H, or size to match gauge

Tapestry needle

Gauge

7 dc = 2 in.; 4 dc rows and 4 sc rows = 3 in.; 1 fan = 1 in.; 2 dc rows = 1 in.

Finished size

Approximately 56½ x 65½ in.

Note: Use white unless otherwise stated.

SPECIAL STITCHES

Front post stitch (fp) and back post stitch (bp): Yo, insert hook from right to left around post of st on previous row, complete as dc.

HEART PANEL (Make 3)

Row 1: Starting at *bottom*, ch 31, dc in fourth ch from hook, dc in each ch across, turn (29 dc).

Row 2: Ch 1, sc in each st across, turn (29 sc).

Row 3: Ch 3, dc in next 13 sts; for *popcorn st, 4 dc in next st, drop loop from hook, insert hook in top of first dc of group, pull dropped loop through st;* dc in last 14 sts, turn (1 popcorn st, 28 dc). Ch 3 at beginning of row is counted as first dc. Front of row 3 is right side of work.

Row 4: Rep row 2.

Row 5: Ch 3, dc in next 11 sts, popcorn st in next st, dc in each of next 3 sts, popcorn st, dc in last 12 sts, turn (2 popcorn st, 27 dc).

Row 6: Rep row 2.

Row 7: Ch 3, dc in next 9 sts, popcorn st, dc in next 7 sts, popcorn st, dc in last 10 sts, turn.

Row 8: Rep row 2.

Row 9: Ch 3, dc in next 7 sts, popcorn st, dc in next 11 sts, popcorn st, dc in last 8 sts, turn.

Row 10: Rep row 2.

Row 11: Ch 3, dc in next 5 sts, popcorn st, dc in next 15 sts, popcorn st, dc in last 6 sts, turn.

Row 12: Rep row 2.

Row 13: Ch 3, dc in each of next 3 sts, popcorn st, dc in next 19 sts, popcorn st, dc in last 4 sts, turn.

Row 14: Rep row 2.

Row 15: Ch 3, dc in each of next 3 sts, popcorn st, (dc in next 9 sts, popcorn st) 2 times, dc in last 4 sts, turn (3 popcorn st, 26 dc).

Row 16: Rep row 2.

Row 17: Ch 3, (dc in next 5 sts, popcorn st) 2 times, dc in each of next 3 sts, popcorn st; rep between ( ), dc in last 6 sts, turn (4 popcorn st, 25 dc).

Row 18: Rep row 2.

Row 19: Ch 3, (dc in next 7 sts, popcorn st, dc in next st, popcorn st) 2 times, dc in last 8 sts, turn.

Row 20: Rep row 2.

Row 21: Ch 3, dc in each st across, turn.

Popcorn Stitch Afghan

Rows 22–161: Rep rows 2–21 consecutively. At end of last row, do not turn.

Row 162: Working in ends of rows on side, sc in end of each sc row and 2 sc in end of each dc row across (242 sc). Fasten off.

Row 163: With right side facing you, working in ends of rows on opposite side, join with sc in first row, sc in end of each sc row and 2 sc in end of each dc row across (242 sc). Fasten off.

SHELL PANEL (Make 2)

Row 1: Starting at *bottom,* ch 39, dc in fourth ch from hook, dc in next ch, * sk next 3 chs; *for shell, 5 dc in next ch or st;* chs 2, sk next 3 chs, dc in each of next 2 ch, popcorn st in next ch, dc in each of next 2 chs; rep from *, sk next 3 chs, shell, ch 2, sk next 3 chs, dc in each of last 3 sts, turn (2 popcorn st, 3 shells, 14 dc).

Row 2: Ch 3 dc in each of next 2 sts, * [sk next ch sp, shell in first dc of next shell, ch 2, sk next 4 dc], back post (bp) around next st, dc in each of next 3 sts, bp around next st; rep from *; rep between [ ], dc in each of last 3 sts, turn (3 shells, 4 bp, 12 dc).

Row 3: Ch 3, dc in each of next 2 sts, * [sk next ch sp, shell in first dc of next shell, ch 2, sk next 4 dc], front post (fp) around next post st, dc in next st, popcorn st in next st, dc in next st, fp around next post st; rep from *; rep between [ ], dc in each of last 3 sts, turn.

Rows 4–121: Rep rows 2 and 3 alternately. At end of last row, *do not turn.*

Row 122: Working in ends of rows on side, 2 sc in end of each row across (242 sc). Fasten off.

Row 123: With right side of work facing you, working in ends of rows on opposite side, join with sc in end of first row, sc in same row, 2 sc in end of each row across, turn (242 sc). Fasten off.

PANEL EDGING

Row 1: For Heart Panel 1, with right facing you, working on long edge, starting at *bottom,* join variegated with sc in first st, sc in each st across, turn.

Row 2: Working this row in *back loops,* sl st in each st across, turn.

Row 3: Working this row in unworked *front loops* of row 1, sc in each st across. Fasten off.

For Heart Panel 2, work same as Heart Panel 1. Starting at *top,* rep on opposite side.

For Heart Panel 3, starting at *top,* work same as Heart Panel 1.

For each Shell Panel, work same as Heart Panel 1. Starting at *top,* rep on opposite side.

ASSEMBLY

Sew Heart Panels and Shell Panels together as in photo on page 42.

BORDER

Rnd 1: With right side facing you, working around outer edge, join white with sc in any st, sc in each st and in end of each row around with 3 sc in each corner st, *do not join* (910 sc).

Rnd 2: Working this rnd in *front loops,* sl st in each st around.

Rnd 3: Working in unworked *back loops* of rnd 1, sc in each st around with 3 sc in each center corner st (918 sc). Fasten off.

Rnd 4: Join variegated with sl st in any center corner st, (ch 3, popcorn st, dc) in same st, * (dc in next st, popcorn st, dc in next st) around to next center corner st, (dc, popcorn st, dc) in corner st; rep from * 2 more times, (dc in next st, popcorn st, dc in next st) across, join with sl st in top of ch 3 (926 sts). Fasten off.

Rnd 5: Join white with sc in corner st on first Heart Panel, 2 sc in same st, sc in each st around with 3 sc in each center corner st, join with sl st in first sc (934 sc).

FAIR FACTS

North Carolina's fair hosted the world's largest exhibit on space in 1972, when an estimated 250,000 people piled through the gates to learn a little more about blastoff and splashdown.

Rnd 6: Rep rnd 2, join with sl st in first sl st.

Rnd 7: Ch 1, * 3 sc in next st, (sc in next 62 st, 2 sc in next st) 3 times, sc in each st across to next center corner st, 3 sc in next st, sc in each st across * to center corner st; rep between first *, join with sl st in first sc (948 sc).

Rnd 8: Sl st in next st, ch 5, (dc, ch 2, dc) in same st, sk next 3 st, *(dc, ch 2, dc, ch 2 dc) in next st, sk next 3 sts; rep from * around, join with sl st in 3rd ch of ch 5.

Rnd 9: Sl st in first ch sp, *(ch 3, sc, ch 3, sc, ch 3) in next st, sc in each of next 2 ch sps; rep from * around to last ch sp, ch 3, sc in last ch sp, join with sl st in first sc. Fasten off.

Alterations: Diana changed the shell panel to sc and dc, to match the rest of the pattern design, and she used only off-white yarn.

Pattern Courtesy of Annie's Attic

Profiling the Winners

Kenneth B. Allen
Woodinville, Washington

Ken started crocheting in 1974, while serving aboard ship as a Coast Guard officer. The exacting nature of the work appealed to him, and he quickly began winning awards at local county and state fairs. Ken says, "Imagine the surprise of needlework superintendents upon discovering that their blue ribbon winner was a man!"

He experimented with several techniques before adapting the afghan stitch to his original plaid designs. Each afghan Ken makes is a gift for a family member or friend. He partners with his wife, Candy, as they design each afghan, spending hours planning the pattern and choosing the colors that best suit the special recipient. Ken feels that the unique pattern and fine craftsmanship create an afghan that is both warm and beautiful.

In addition to many blue ribbons, Ken has won several Best of Class, Best of Show, and Judge's Award of Excellence ribbons at fairs in Virginia, California, and Washington.

Kathy Antus
Viola, Arkansas

After wanting to learn to crochet for years, Kathy and her neighbor signed up for a class through the local high school's adult education program. "That was 30 years ago and I haven't put down my hook since," she states.

As for her prizewinner on page 58, Kathy says she "fell in love" with an alphabet afghan she saw at a baby shower.

"It was kind of like doing a counted cross stitch," she relates. "I really enjoyed making it and loved the end result. On graph paper I charted out the numbers 0 through 9 to go with the alphabet, and when my first grandbaby was born I crocheted a birth announcement for him using the letters and numbers as my guide.

"That's the beauty of crocheting," she adds. "It is so versatile; once you find a pattern you like, you can adapt it to whatever design you want."

Laura Bareuther
Reno, Nevada

Laura's blue ribbon entry, shown on page 90, was her very first afghan. A senior in high school, Laura learned to crochet just two years ago, when she was 15.

"My cousin and aunt were crocheting and I decided that I wanted to learn," Laura explains. "My cousin showed me how to chain, and then how to single and double crochet." At home, her mother showed her how to make the basic granny square pattern.

"I practiced and made a couple of squares, but there wasn't enough scrap yarn around to make anything." So, she says, "My mom and I went to the store and bought enough white and blue yarn to make an afghan. I finished just in time to enter it into the Nevada State Fair," Laura continues, where her blanket won not only the blue ribbon, but a championship ribbon, too. And now, Laura's at work on a second afghan, a pink and burgundy creation, in a six-sided granny square pattern.

Thelma H. Berkley
Lewisburg, West Virginia

Born on a family farm near her present-day home, Thelma says she and her brother Carl "learned early what farm chores were all about."

"My mother was an accomplished seamstress," Thelma shares, "who loved to crochet, sew, quilt, and tat. She thought I should learn these skills." By age six, Thelma had pieced her first quilt, and by age 12, she was creating intricate projects: embroidered pillowcases and dresser scarves, crocheted doilies and edgings.

She worked with the local telephone company for 33 years, advancing to a group chief operator. Though she made her first afghan many decades ago, she finally had time to really pursue crochet, as well as her other crafts, after retirement. She's won blue ribbons at the State Fair of West Virginia for her doilies, quilts, jellies, and pickles, as well as her afghans.

Thelma's sister-in-law, Elizabeth Willis, gave her the pattern for the afghan featured on page 24. Thelma says she's made other patterns, but this is her favorite.

Frances Burgess
Stuart, Iowa

Frances has been crocheting for 35 years and says she is always excited to see her finished work. "I really enjoyed making this afghan and I love doing this stitch," she says of her entry, shown on page 72. "It makes a nice afghan to cuddle up to."

Now that her two daughters are grown, Frances has more time to devote to crocheting, and in recent years, she's been entering the Iowa State Fair. "I'm always hoping I get Best of Show," she shares. Though that hasn't happened yet, Frances is an optimist. "There's always next year!" she adds.

Loi Tra Carter

Concord, North Carolina

"I learned to crochet at age ten," says Loi, a professional seamstress. "Over the years I have made many things to share with family and friends."

Loi finds crochet relaxing and has learned that it's rewarding to display and share her work. Her patriotic afghan, on page 56, was a natural for the blue ribbon, which she was thrilled to receive. She has also adapted this original design to a smaller size, suitable for display on a wall.

"I have greatly enjoyed crocheting different things over the years," she concludes.

Janice Trautman Cook

Salem, Oregon

For a girl who grew up "not very interested" in crocheting (she preferred hiking and bowling to working with yarn), Janice certainly took to the craft later in life. By age 20, she was a fairly adept knitter. "But," she laments, "most knitted articles needed to be finished with a row or two of crochet, and I couldn't do that."

By age 40, Janice decided once and for all that she was going to learn to crochet. Armed with a couple of library books, a ball of yarn, and a large crochet hook, she finally figured out how it was done.

Janice's mother-in-law commissioned—then rejected!—a solid, off-white afghan that would become both her first state fair entry and her first blue ribbon winner. Janice says her mother-in-law decided "it was too bulky [and] wasn't what she had in mind." Not knowing what else to do with the piece, Janice entered it in the Oregon State Fair. When it won, she was hooked. ("Pun intended," she says.)

These days, Janice always keeps in mind the advice she read in an article several years ago: "If you want to win a blue ribbon on your state fair entries, you should make them for someone you love." Now that she's retired from a 43-year career in bookkeeping and accounting, Janice plans to spend even more time creating prize-winning afghans for her friends and family.

Jacquelynn A. Copenhaver

Fayetteville, West Virginia

By profession, Jacquelynn works as the human resources director for a rural health-care clinic in southern West Virginia. Her life's work, though, she says, is "to live my life in love and service while pursuing the highest good and greatest growth for all." In that spirit, Jacquelynn is involved with the Sydney Banks Institute for Innate Health at West Virginia University, and she conducts workshops throughout the state. She still makes time for her friends, family, and "energetic" dog, Katie.

Jacquelynn is also an avid crocheter, learning the craft from her aunts, Phyllis and Norma, more than 20 years ago. Although Jacquelynn has created everything from scarves, slippers, and baby outfits to toys and ornaments, afghans remain her favorite projects.

She made the afghan featured on page 36 for her sister and brother-in-law, Barbara and Jeff. The couple is on a waiting list to adopt a baby, and Jacquelynn "wanted them to have a lovely blanket to wrap their new addition in when she or he arrives.

"Now we have a blue ribbon blanket waiting on the arrival," Jacquelynn says. "I hope others can enjoy this pattern and share it with babies they love, too."

Loretta Coulson

Florence, Colorado

Loretta grew up on a wheat farm in Oklahoma during the Great Depression. When she was about 14 or 15, her mother tried—to no avail—to teach Loretta the art of crocheting. Instead, Loretta graduated from business college before getting married and moving to Colorado. She raised three children and spent 30 years working for the state of Colorado before she revisited crochet. This time around, Loretta was determined to learn. She purchased a book and has been making afghans ever since.

"I find crocheting a very good source of therapy and relaxation," Loretta shares, "and [I] love the challenge of putting together beautiful afghans and competing to be one of the winners." She has won three grand awards in the state fair.

Millie Crawford

Tampa, Florida

A native of Michigan, Millie learned to quilt, embroider, and crochet from her mother when she was about eight years old. But eventually, she says, she "kind of dropped the crochet."

She picked it back up about 12 years ago, with great success. Most of the 36 ribbons she's earned at the Florida State Fair—half of them blue—have been for crochet projects. Millie retired a few years ago, and with the extra time to work on her crafts, she says, "I'm entering 10 projects in this year's state fair, and eight of them are crochet."

Millie says she picked the *Baby Rings* afghan pictured on page 54 "because it was different, and I used the jewel-toned yarns for their brightness."

When she's not creating prize-winning projects, Millie enjoys travel. She has visited Germany, France, China, England, Scotland, Wales, Ireland, Turkey, Canada, Mexico, Puerto Rico, and the Dominican Republic.

Lisa Donald
Albuquerque, New Mexico

Lisa finds that crocheting is the best form of relaxation.

"It calms you," she says. "You are creating something to give; it is a lasting reminder to the recipients of gratitude for their kindness. But best of all, [afghans] contain many good thoughts, some tears, lots of prayers, and are made with love."

Lisa says the first afghans she made were simple, but her "wonderful friends and family paid for them to help put [her] son through school." Later, she began giving her creations to the families who opened their homes to her husband, a traveling minister. As a result, her afghans can be found in homes in many of the 50 states.

Carol Joan Fritz
Cicero, New York

"I was taught how to crochet by a very dear friend 26 years ago," says Carol. She has won dozens of ribbons from her entries in fairs in Pennsylvania and Florida.

Carol works for the Syracuse City School District, but she has many interests in her spare time. Crocheting is still one of her favorite hobbies, but she also enjoys gardening, working jigsaw puzzles, spending time with her grandchildren, and traveling with her husband; they've been married 35 years.

Viola M. Heaton
Indianapolis, Indiana

Viola and her husband, Sam, were married in June 1941. Just five months later, Sam was inducted into the army. It was during this time that Viola taught herself how to crochet, knit, tat, and embroider, using books. (In those days, she relates, the books were just 10¢ and 25¢ each.) "I also made most of my clothes," she says, and in fact, she still does.

For years, Viola gave away many of her handmade items as gifts. She sold many of the things she made, too, although she has been known to keep a few for herself.

It was Sam who encouraged Viola to exhibit her work, and about 20 years ago, he entered her in the Indiana State Fair. She's been exhibiting on the state and county level ever since and has taken just about every prize there is.

"Sam passed [a few years ago]," shares Viola, "but at age 82, I'm still entering."

Shirley R. Henry
Reno, Nevada

When Shirley was 12 years old, her maternal grandmother taught her the basic stitches of crochet. "However, being a tomboy and probably hyperactive, I didn't do anything with it until after I was married," she recalls. Then she and her husband moved to a small farmhouse apartment, miles from town. They didn't have television and her husband needed their car to drive to and from the air force base where he was stationed.

"On a trip to town, I bought a ball of thread, a hook, and a how-to book, and I was on my way," she says. "Crocheting has been both my hobby and my 'therapy,' through being an air force wife, having and raising four children, transfers, overseas assignments, and 46 years of marriage to the one and only love of my life.

"Now that I'm alone and unable to do many physical activities," she continues, "I rely on 'putting knots' in thread and yarn more than ever."

The Medford County Fair in Oregon was Shirley's first fair. She entered 15 pieces in 15 different categories—and took home 14 ribbons! "Needless to say, I was thrilled," she says. That was over 20 years ago. Since then, Shirley has racked up nearly a dozen more ribbons, entering state and county fairs wherever she's lived.

LeAnn Hill
Salt Lake City, Utah

LeAnn taught herself to crochet, starting with her very first project, a baby blanket for her oldest son. A full-time registered nurse, LeAnn says her craft hobbies are an essential creative outlet. She also quilts, cross-stitches, sews, and paints ceramics—an accomplished crafter, she's also won ribbons for crocheted clothing, quilting, wreath making, and painting.

She feels that the "handcrafted home arts need to be passed on to our daughters and sons, otherwise they will be lost." LeAnn is trying to keep them alive, passing along her love for handcrafts to male and female students alike. She taught her husband, her sons, and one of her male colleagues to cross-stitch.

LeAnn says she likes to work with "natural yarns, like cotton and wool." The afghan featured on page 99, for instance, is made from 100 percent cotton. And like most of her projects, it was created and given away as a gift.

Sara Janzen
Buhler, Kansas

"I like to crochet," Sara says. "The problem is finding the time."

"When I was young," she shares, "my mother taught me the chain stitch. I didn't really do any more with it until I was married and expecting my first baby." Eventually, she completed a full-sized Navajo afghan, which she took to the fair. "To my amazement, I won a blue ribbon!" she exclaims.

(Sara Janzen, cont'd)

Later, she came across a beautiful white afghan pattern that she felt would be perfect for a little girl's bed. Being the mother of three boys, she filed it away until her first grandchild was born—a girl! She remembered that white afghan, shown on page 85. "I dug out the patterns and started working on it," she recalls.

Since Sara is a part-time nurse, teaches piano lessons, and plays organ and piano at her church, she's busy. It takes her a while to finish a big project, she adds. "I enjoy watching the patterns form as the work progresses and eventually would like to develop my own designs," she concludes.

Mary Johnson
Pelion, South Carolina

Mary admits that she's crazy about crochet.

"It became an obsession!" she exclaims. Once she got the bug, Mary sought out new and different patterns and felt compelled to try them all. Needless to say, everyone in her family has one of her afghans. Mary now has a collection of some 2,000 patterns that she is bound and determined to make someday.

"When I find a stitch I like, I incorporate it into everything," she says, adding that she sometimes adapts afghan designs to other items like scarves and hats.

She and her husband have three dogs and a cat, but the cat, she says, "rules" the entire household. Mary works at the local senior citizens' center and plans to hold a crochet class there this summer, so she can share her love of the craft.

Samantha Kline
Paxinos, Pennsylvania

Samantha's mother taught her to crochet 15 years ago, when she was eight years old. "My personality drove me to better my technique," she says, feeling "blessed" with pattern ideas. She confesses that she had a hard time reading patterns, so she began to design her own, resulting in the two prizewinners included here.

Samantha particularly enjoys crocheting in purple, "probably because it was my grandmother's favorite color as well," she speculates. *Grape Arbor* (page 22) and *Purple Shades* (page 29) both reflect her love of the color.

Samantha is grateful to her parents, brother, family, and friends "for the interest, encouragement, suggestions, and admiration they have given for my work."

Ruth Ellen Klug
Lewiston, Minnesota

Two of Ruth Ellen's favorite crafts, crochet and counted cross-stitch, are both on display in her prize-winning afghan, shown on page 80.

Like many of her fellow blue ribbon winners, she started crocheting as a young girl. Her mother, who had no pattern books, taught her the stitches from memory, and only later did Ruth Ellen learn to read pattern instructions.

"My inspiration is to make something useful for my 14 grandchildren," she says, and the lucky recipient of this prizewinner will be a grandson who graduates from high school soon. "His mother probably won't let him take it to college, though," she chuckles.

Ruth Ellen makes an afghan for each grandchild as a graduation gift, and also creates one for each new great-grandchild—four to date, with one on the way. After her own children were grown, she studied accounting and reentered the workplace. Ruth Ellen retired after 20 years of bookkeeping, and now, she says, "I have more time for all my craft projects."

Bonnie Lineberry
Idaho Falls, Idaho

Bonnie says she "shudders to think" of some of her past craft hobbies. Even her early forays into crochet, she relates, may not have been terribly well received; her first afghan, which she completed in high school, consisted of "ghastly shades of orange."

Obviously, Bonnie's eye for color has improved dramatically. She has inspired many of her friends to take up the craft, and earned the nickname the "rip-out queen" for her habit of "ripping out their projects and helping to restart them along the right path."

"If you're going to do something," she says, "you might as well do it right."

It was this philosophy that probably helped Bonnie conquer the Idaho State Fair. At age 50, she decided to enter for the first time, submitting three of her favorite afghans. She was shocked to discover that she won three first-place ribbons, including one Best in Class. "Now I'm really energized to find or create a new pattern for next year's fair!" she says.

Karen Marie Massey
Orgas, West Virginia

Karen has been crocheting since she was 21, and entered the State Fair of West Virginia for the first time 13 years ago. She's won 25 ribbons since then! Karen gives some of the credit for her state fair success to her husband of 32 years, who she says "supports me all the way at fair time.

"Crocheting," adds Karen, "is like having a small child within."

Her *Sunbonnet Sue* afghan, featured on page 33, reminds her of her two granddaughters: "So pretty," she says.

Lois W. McLeod
West Columbia, South Carolina

Lois was born into a musical family, her father a minister and her mother a musician in the church. "Our home was filled with singing and instruments of every kind," she says. Lois inherited this talent and subsequently earned undergraduate degrees in music and psychology and advanced degrees in music and public administration. She is now the director of training and special projects for the United States District Court for the State of South Carolina.

Her love of crafts and needlework began early. She shares, "Mother taught me to sew on a sewing machine (to make my own doll clothes and later my clothes) and to crochet, which has remained my passion. Fortunately, I have a wonderful husband who indulges, and even encourages, my projects and my many crochet magazine subscriptions."

About 10 years ago, Lois made a baby afghan for a friend, who suggested it be entered in the state fair. "Well," Lois concludes, "it won a blue ribbon and the rest, as they say, is history. Too many ribbons later to count, I love to crochet unusual projects and always have multiple projects going on simultaneously."

Andrea Murphy
Tampa, Florida

Andrea earns her living as an accountant, but she unwinds by crocheting. She first learned the craft while growing up on a farm in Ohio. "My mother was very skilled at all types of needlework and taught me how to knit, crochet, and [do] needlepoint."

Andrea married Wayne, a deputy sheriff, in 1975, and the two moved to Tampa a year later. She has more time for crafting now that her son has entered his twenties and her two stepsons are grown and raising their own families. Over the years, Andrea has tried her hand at doll making and cross-stitching, but crochet has remained her favorite.

She says she entered the Florida State Fair "to validate" her crochet skills. The first year, she was rewarded with a second-place prize. The next year, she received the ultimate validation with a blue ribbon for her afghan, shown on page 50.

Ravon L. Noble
Afton, Minnesota

"Crocheting is a passion for me," says Ravon. "I feel it is a stress reliever after a long day at work. I always have a project in my sewing basket, and it takes only a moment to transfer it to a travel bag."

Ravon has been crocheting her entire life; as a young girl, she would make rugs for her dollhouse. When she was a bit older, she and her mother would make cotton-thread bedspreads as special gifts for relatives. Now, she especially enjoys making baby afghans, in soft pastel colors, and always has a few on hand to welcome a new arrival.

A mechanical design drafter by trade, Ravon spends her spare time gardening, reading, and doing genealogical research, in addition to crocheting. She and her husband enjoy the company of their three grown children, and they also like to cruise in their classic 1958 automobile.

Laura Pawlowski
Casper, Wyoming

Laura was born and raised in Casper, where she learned to crochet at a young age from her mother, Betty Pawlowski. Her mother says Laura has far surpassed the skills she passed on to her daughter! Both women are prolific blanket makers, and every year, they donate at least 20 afghans (and toys, also) to a local shelter that temporarily houses abused women and their children. Laura crochets baby caps and afghans to donate to other charitable organizations, as well as to the local hospital.

After attending local schools, Laura received an associate's degree in art from Casper College. Today, she puts her creative education to use adapting existing patterns to suit her needs, as well as creating her own patterns. She was recently named the second-place Sweepstakes winner in the needlework division at the Wyoming State Fair; Laura has also won many blue ribbons, Judge's Choice, and Sweepstakes ribbons for sewing and drawing.

Though she has chronic neck problems, Laura continues to crochet and create artwork almost every day.

Betty Jean Perry
Blackfoot, Idaho

Like many of our prizewinners, Betty Jean learned to crochet from her mother. Because her mother didn't read patterns, Betty Jean and her sister learned by a different method. "She would look at the picture of our project and tell us in her own crochet terms how to do it. For example, double crochet was one wrap around and treble was two wrap arounds."

Over the past 30 years, Betty Jean has received several blue ribbons, Best of Show ribbons, and trophies for her projects at the Eastern Idaho State Fair. In fact, she has a nickname there—the Afghan Lady. Betty Jean's prize-winning afghan, on page 136, commemorates the centennial edition of the Eastern Idaho State Fair. Her work has also been featured in a Herrschners publication, when she won a red ribbon in their national contest.

Betty Jean is planning to pass along her love for the craft: "To keep the tradition going, I am now teaching my eight-year-old granddaughter to crochet. She can't wait to enter something in the fair."

Julie Roberts
Magna, Utah

At 16, Julie is already a veteran of the craft of crochet. She's been making afghans since she was nine years old, and she gives her handiwork as gifts for birthdays, holidays, and baby showers.

Julie didn't realize the afghan featured on page 102 was in the running for any kind of ribbon, let alone the coveted blue. She had been asked to make a special piece for a birthday gift. Unbeknownst to Julie, her father entered it in the 2001 Utah State Fair. With a little friendly trickery, her father took her to the fair and she was amazed to see her afghan among the entries. "To my surprise, I got a blue ribbon," she says happily.

Jean M. Roush
Zanesfield, Ohio

Jean feels that she has really been blessed. She says, "I've been happily married to Don Roush Jr. for 24 years and have two wonderful daughters, Aubrey and Brandy."

Jean first picked up a crochet hook at 15, and she counts crocheting and designing among her favorite pastimes. She loves to share her passion for crochet and enjoys interesting others in "this beautiful art form."

Jean was absolutely thrilled when she won a blue ribbon at the Ohio State Fair in the original design category. "I've placed in fairs before, but never with one of my own designs. Then being selected to appear in this book was another wonderful surprise!"

Her love of crochet is evident, and she concludes, "I hope to continue designing and crocheting for many years to come."

Joyce L. Salavitch
Meridian, Idaho

This blue ribbon winner on page 138 was made especially for Joyce's first great-grandson, and she took extra care to see that it kept him toasty.

"I double crocheted a piece to fit on back, to cover the cross-stitch ends, and to make it warmer," she says. This piece was also awarded Best in Show—on her first attempt!

Joyce relates that the state fair in her home state, Illinois, was too far away for her to enter her handiwork, but she and her husband retired to Idaho some 10 years ago. Now, she says happily, she can take advantage of the fair and enters five or six pieces each year, usually bringing home a ribbon. A family friend first encouraged her to enter the fair.

The Salavitches still love their adopted home, and she's happy they were able to take full advantage of all the opportunities available to them there, like river rafting and horseback riding. Joyce keeps busy crocheting, which she learned on her own, and she also enjoys cross-stitch.

Sadie H. Sanchez
Pueblo, Colorado

"One of the ways I have improved my skills and techniques is by attending the judging and hearing strong/weak points of all my afghans, as well as of others'," states Sadie. She's applied this knowledge well, having won a ribbon every time she's entered the competition at the Colorado State Fair.

Sadie began crocheting at 11 and quickly learned to read patterns by "trial and error." She has been named both the Junior and

Senior Grand Champion during the years, and she continued to enter the competition in her home state while pursuing an undergraduate degree at Harvard College and later attending medical school. While she's been off at school, her parents have taken over the administrative tasks of her entries. "Interestingly enough, [neither] my mother nor my father knows how to crochet, but [they] are nearly experts on the subject," she says.

Sadie has many other interests, including knitting, cross-stitch, tatting, and scrapbooking. She also sings and plays five instruments.

Anne R. Scharf
Lincoln, Nebraska

Anne remembers watching her grandmother crochet when she was a little girl growing up in Nebraska. Even so, she didn't try her hand at the craft until her four daughters were grown. After 30 years working as a psychiatric medical technician at the Lincoln Veteran's Hospital, where she garnered many service awards, Anne retired at the age of 71. Now she has more time than ever to devote to her crochet, and at 77, she crochets almost every day.

Anne "never sold any of her afghans because she gets so much enjoyment from giving them as gifts." Her five grandchildren each received an afghan in the colors of their choice upon graduating from high school, and her three great-grandchildren look forward to warm, crocheted birthday gifts.

After years of entering her *kaloches* (a sweet dessert bread) and baked rolls in the Nebraska State Fair, Anne—at her daughters' urging—decided to enter the afghan shown on page 74. Sure enough, it was blue ribbon material.

Nancy Sheck
Greenville, North Carolina

"I wish I had a nickel for every granny square I have done over the years," chuckles Nancy.

She has a real love of yarn and an entire closet full of bins stuffed with every type imaginable. "My friends know that if they need just a little more of any one color that I probably have it," she says. Nancy is also a collector of patterns, storing them all in a special bookcase.

Her husband, Robert, retired from the United States Navy after 23 years, and her children have followed in his footsteps. Their son, Scott, is a Green Beret in the United States Army, and daughter Stephanie is married to a navy officer. At the couple's first overseas station, Nancy found the pattern she used to win this blue ribbon. She worked on it for years until she mastered the combination of stitches that resulted in her prize-winning project.

In addition to crochet, Nancy has another passion: she and Bob do volunteer work with their therapy dogs at the local hospital.

Charliene B. Smith
Lexington, South Carolina

"When my daughter was born," shares Charliene, "my mother-in-law crocheted and made my daughter some really lovely things. I wanted to learn so she taught me," she says simply. "That was 32 years ago."

Her afghan featured on page 62 was her first try for a state fair ribbon. She started the *Red, White, and Blue* as a Christmas gift for a family friend in the service. "I love the old granny square," she says, so she decided to make that her pattern and finish it with a star border.

She began work on the blanket in July. Then her daughter reminded her that Charliene had been talking about entering an afghan in the fair for years. Why not this one?

Charliene says the blanket became her constant companion, putting the finishing stitches in place the morning of the entry deadline. She's still in a state of shock over having won the blue ribbon, but she's positive the friend for whom she made the blanket will truly love it.

Kathleen M. Smith
Tampa, Florida

A native of Tampa, Kathleen has had a busy life. After graduating from high school in 1940, she married her first husband, U.S. Air Force Sergeant Ralph F. Carey. They raised six children, three girls and three boys, before Ralph passed away in 1964.

In 1972, Kathleen married Robert M. Smith, and the couple has been together ever since. After Kathleen retired 20 years ago, her older sister, Mary Ann Martinez, taught her to crochet.

At 82, a grandmother and great grandmother many times over, she still keeps her own house, cooks for her husband, takes care of her yard, and participates in two seniors groups, her local women's garden club, and a church group. Oh, and she "crochets as a hobby."

Kathleen says, "I plan to keep active and on the go as much as possible."

Diana L. Snow
Cascade, Colorado

Diana, who taught herself to crochet, has been practicing the craft seriously for about three years. She makes as many as 12 afghans annually, always seeking to create unique, warm, and inviting patterns.

The pattern she submitted for this book, shown on page 142, is her favorite. "I have made seven of them so far and can finish one in three weeks," she says.

It was also her first entry in a state fair. She was "quite surprised" when it took the blue ribbon. "It was the highlight of my day," she says. Diana entered several more pieces in subsequent state and county fairs and won two more ribbons. "Now I have the bug," she declares.

Dee Stanziano
New Fairfield, Connecticut

Now an advanced crocheter, Dee learned the craft in early childhood. She is constantly learning and experimenting, becoming a crochet instructor several years ago. Dee became the president and cofounder of the Crochet Guild of America's first Connecticut chapter, "The Happily Hooked on Crocheting Club."

Dee designed a baby afghan to display in her employer's store to showcase some of the stitches she teaches. Her husband encouraged her to enter it in the Bridgewater County Fair, one of Connecticut's largest. Unfortunately, when Dee came to pick up the blanket, she discovered that it had been sold! With just two weeks until the entry deadline, Dee quickly crocheted a much more detailed replacement. She spent 100 hours on the *Sweet Baby Afghan Sampler*, shown on page 38. In addition to 26 different stitches, she created the border in a stitch design that she calls "Rainbow Speckles."

Dee volunteers to teach crocheting to children at a local daycare facility. Of course, she has also started teaching her own young children how to crochet.

Vickie P. Story
Sandston, Virginia

Vickie says she enjoyed needlework even when she was a young child. "Mama has always said that she didn't know where I got my love for needlework," she shares. While her mother and her maternal grandmother embroidered and quilted, Vickie loved it all, especially crochet.

She made afghans for weddings and baby showers and had always been interested in entering her work in the State Fair of Virginia. It took some encouragement from a coworker to convince Vickie to do it, but in 1987, she submitted her first afghan. "I didn't win, but I was excited about the next year," she remembers. "In 1988, I won my first blue ribbon."

Since then, she's won eight more blue ribbons, two reds, and one white, almost all for patterns she created herself. Vickie has also received awards for knitting and candlewicking.

"Win or lose, just competing is a thrill," she says. "I strongly encourage anyone who has ever thought about entering into any competition to do so. You won't be disappointed."

Lester Vaughn
Kirkland, Washington

At 82, Lester says she's been crocheting "for more years than [she] cares to remember." While in her mid-seventies, she decided to share her love of crochet by becoming a Craft Yarn Council of America certified instructor. To complete her certification, Lester was required to volunteer 25 hours of her time teaching. She learned through the grapevine that a local elementary school was looking for a crochet instructor for its children's enrichment classes. Lester signed up and has been teaching the class ever since.

She meets with her students, who range in age from six to 11 years old, once a week. "We begin by teaching the basic stitches and then progress to small 'make-it-take-it' projects. The children love being able to take something home," she says.

She delights in teaching kids, including her 11-year-old grandson, Sean, and her eight-year-old granddaughter, Shannon. "My wish is to get more teachers to work with children so we can carry on the crochet traditions that are such a part of our heritage."

Lynne Walsh
Silverton, Oregon

Lynne says she is "still waiting for retirement to really begin so I can spend more time crocheting and knitting," even though she is almost 77! She loves both crafts, but has "only been able to find time to do an occasional project." When her oldest granddaughter, Tammy Lynne Ellis, asked for a special afghan, though, Lynne made the time.

Tammy said she liked blues, which made Lynne remember a pattern she had saved from a magazine. Lynne worked on the blanket during the winter, and when it was time for her husband, a blue ribbon-winning dahlia grower, to enter his flowers in the Oregon State Fair, she thought, "I might enter my afghan, too."

Although Lynne thought it would be fun to tell her granddaughter that her afghan had been in the fair, she "never thought it would have a blue ribbon on it when I sent it to her! We were both delighted."

Jeanney Whitney
Boise, Idaho

A native of southern California, Jeanney learned to work with yarn when she was just five years old. "A woman in our parish, Irene Betts, who was passionate about all handwork, decided to teach children and adults how to knit and crochet at no charge," Jeanney says. "She was so energetic and exciting to be with that I knitted my first sweater at the age of eight." By age 10, Jeanney was making dozens of hats, sweaters, and mittens every year, which she donated to a local charity for needy children.

A mother of three grown children, Jeanney says that she has tried to follow Irene's example by "teaching knitting and crocheting to anyone interested in learning the skill." She loves color and design, and believes that "every home should have a handmade afghan to provide warmth and comfort."

Since she and her husband of 32 years moved to Boise nine years ago, Jeanney has found that "the wide open spaces and four seasons" help her "budget" her time for all her hobbies, including crocheting, gardening, and horseback riding.

Beverley Hite Young
Leesville, South Carolina

"Never underestimate the power of a 13-year-old," advises Beverley, who learned to crochet at that age from another 13-year-old, her cousin Cathy Cinnamon. In fact, 13 seems to be Beverley's lucky number; she made the prize-winning afghan shown on page 48 for the youngest of her four children, her 13-year-old daughter, Angela.

Beverley was no stranger to the state fair scene when she entered this afghan. As a young bride, she made several passes at the blue ribbon, but it wasn't until she approached 40 that she became truly determined. "Instead of having a midlife crisis and leaving my husband, I just wanted blue," she says. And blue she got, several times over, including a ribbon for the ABC baby afghan on page 60. "It's just waiting for grandchildren," she hints.

State Fair Information

Alabama

Alabama National Fair
P.O. Box 3304
Montgomery, AL 36109-0304
Date(s) of Operation: October
www.alnationalfair.org
334-272-6831

Greater Gulf State Fair
1035 N. Cody Rd.
Mobile, AL 36608
Date(s) of Operation: October
www.mobilefair.com
251-344-4573

Alaska

Alaska State Fair
2075 Glenn Hwy.
Palmer, AK 99645
www.alaskastatefair.org
Date(s) of Operation: Late August through
early September
800-850-3247

Tanana Valley State Fair
1800 College Rd.
Fairbanks, AK 99709
www.tananavalleyfair.org
Date(s) of Operation: August
907-452-3750

Arizona

Arizona State Fair
1826 W. McDowell Rd.
Phoenix, AZ 85007
Date(s) of Operation: October
www.azstatefair.com
602-252-6771

Arkansas

Arkansas State Fair
2600 Howard St.
Little Rock, AR 72206
Date(s) of Operation: October
www.arkfairgrounds.com
501-372-8341

California

California State Fair
1600 Exposition Blvd.
Sacramento, CA 95815
Date(s) of Operation: Mid-August through
early September
www.bigfun.org
916-263-3010

Colorado

Colorado State Fair
1001 Beulah Ave.
Pueblo, CO 81004
Date(s) of Operation: August
www.coloradosfair.com
719-561-8484

Connecticut

Connecticut Agricultural Fair
Goshen Fair Grounds, Rte. 63
Goshen Center, CT 06756
Date(s) of Operation: July
www.ctagriculturalfair.org/index.shtml
(Note: Connecticut has several major state
events. For more information, see the
Association of Connecticut Fairs at
www.ctfairs.org/index.html.)

Delaware

Delaware State Fair
South Dupont Hwy.
P.O. Box 28
Harrington, DE 19952-0028
Date(s) of Operation: July
www.delawarestatefair.com
302-398-3269

Florida

Florida State Fair
Florida State Fair Grounds
4800 US Highway 301 N.
Tampa Bay, FL 33610
Date(s) of Operation: February
www.floridastatefair.com
813-621-7821

Georgia

Georgia State Fair
P.O. Box 4105
Macon, GA 31208-4105
Date(s) of Operation: September
www.georgiastatefair.org
478-746-7184

Hawaii

Hawaii State Farm Fair
2343 Rose St.
Honolulu, HI 96819
Date(s) of Operation: Weekends, mid-July
through early August
www.hawaiistatefarmfair.org
808-848-2074

Idaho

Eastern Idaho State Fair
P.O. Box 250
Blackfoot, ID 83221
Date(s) of Operation: Late summer, beginning Labor Day weekend
www.idaho-state-fair.com
208-785-2480

North Idaho Fair and Rodeo
4056 N. Government Way
Coeur d'Alene, ID 83815
Date(s) of Operation: August
www.northidahofair.com
208-765-4969

Western Idaho Fair
5610 Glenwood
Boise, ID 83714
Date(s) of Operation: August
www.idahofair.com
208-376-3247

Illinois

Illinois State Fair
State Fairgrounds, Emmerson Building
801 Sangamon Ave.
P.O. Box 19427
Springfield, IL 62794-9427
Date(s) of Operation: August
www.agr.state.il.us/isf
217-782-6661

Indiana

Indiana State Fair
1202 E. 38th St.
Indianapolis, IN 46205-2869
Date(s) of Operation: August
www.state.in.us/statefair
317-927-7500

Iowa

Iowa State Fair
P.O. Box 57130
Des Moines, IA 50317-0003
Date(s) of Operation: August
www.iowastatefair.com
515-262-3111

Kansas

Kansas State Fair
2000 N. Poplar St.
Hutchinson, KS 67502-5598
Date(s) of Operation: September
www.kansasstatefair.com
620-669-3600

Kentucky

Kentucky State Fair
937 Phillips Ln.
Louisville, KY 40209-1398
Date(s) of Operation: August
www.kystatefair.org
502-367-5000

Louisiana

State Fair of Louisiana
3701 Hudson Ave.
Shreveport, LA 71109
Date(s) of Operation: Mid-October through
early November
www.statefairoflouisiana.com
318-635-1361

Maine

Bangor State Fair
100 Dutton St.
Bangor, ME 04401
Date(s) of Operation: Late July through early
August
www.bangorstatefair.com
207-947-5555

Skowhegan State Fair
P.O. Box 39
Skowhegan, ME 04976-039
Date(s) of Operation: August
www.skowheganstatefair.com
207-474-2947

Maryland

Maryland State Fair
P.O. Box 188
Timonium, MD 21094-0188
Date(s) of Operation: Late August through
early September
www.marylandstatefair.com
410-252-0200

Massachusetts

The Big E: Eastern States Exposition
1305 Memorial Ave.
West Springfield, MA 01089
Date(s) of Operation: September
www.thebige.com
413-737-2443

Michigan

Michigan State Fair
1120 W. State Fair Ave.
Detroit, MI 48203
Date(s) of Operation: August
www.michigan.gov/mda
313-369-8254

Upper Peninsula State Fair
2401 12th Ave. N
Escanaba, MI 49829
Date(s) of Operation: August
www.upstatefair.net
906-786-4011

Minnesota

Minnesota State Fair
1265 Snelling Ave. N
St. Paul, MN 55108-3099
Date(s) of Operation: Late August through
early September
www.mnstatefair.org
651-642-2200

Mississippi

Mississippi State Fair
P.O. Box 892
Jackson, MS 39205
Date(s) of Operation: October
www.mdac.state.ms.us
601-961-4000

North Mississippi Tri-State Fair
2800 S. Harper Rd.
Corinth, MS 38834
Date(s) of Operation: September
www.crossroadsarena.com
662-287-7779

Missouri

Missouri State Fair
2503 W. 16th St.
Sedalia, MO 65301
Date(s) of Operation: August
www.mostatefair.com
660-530-5600

Montana

Montana State Fair
Montana ExpoPark
P.O. Box 1888
Great Falls, MT 59403
Date(s) of Operation: August
www.ci.great-falls.mt.us
406-727-8900

Nebraska

Nebraska State Fair
P.O. Box 81223
Lincoln, NE 68501
Date(s) of Operation: Late August through
early September
www.statefair.org
402-473-4110

Nevada

Nevada State Fair
Reno Livestock Event Center
1350-A N. Wells Ave.
Reno, NV 89512
Date(s) of Operation: August
www.nevadastatefair.org
775-688-5767

New Hampshire

The Hopkinton State Fair
P.O. Box 700
392 Kearsarge Ave.
Contoocook, NH 03229-0700
Date(s) of Operation: Late August through
early September
www.hsfair.org
603-746-4191

New Jersey

New Jersey State Fair
Sussex County Fair Grounds
37 Plains Rd.
Augusta, NJ 07822
Date(s) of Operation: August
www.njstatefair.org
973-948-5500

New Mexico

New Mexico State Fair
P.O. Box 8546
300 San Pedro Dr. NE
Albuquerque, NM 87198
Date(s) of Operation: September
www.nmstatefair.com
505-265-1791

New York

New York State Fair
581 State Fair Blvd.
Syracuse, NY 13209
Date(s) of Operation: Late August through
early September
www.nysfair.org
1-800-475-FAIR

North Carolina

North Carolina State Fair
1025 Blue Ridge Blvd.
Raleigh, NC 27607
Date(s) of Operation: October
www.ncstatefair.org
919-821-7400

North Dakota

North Dakota State Fair
2005 Burdick Expressway E
P.O. Box 1796
Minot, ND 58702
Date(s) of Operation: July
www.ndstatefair.com
701-857-7620

Ohio

Ohio State Fair
Ohio Expo Center
717 E. 17th Ave.
Columbus, OH 43211
Date(s) of Operation: August
www.ohiostatefair.com
614-644-4000

Oklahoma

Oklahoma State Fair
500 Land Rush St.
Oklahoma City, OK 73107
Date(s) of Operation: September
www.oklafair.org
405-948-6700

Oregon

Oregon State Fair
2330 17th St. NE
Salem, OR 97303-3201
Date(s) of Operation: Late August through
early September
www.fair.state.or.us
503-947-3247

Pennsylvania

Pennsylvania Farm Show
2301 N. Cameron St.
Harrisburg, PA 17110-9408
Date(s) of Operation: January
www.farmshow.state.pa.us/farmshow
717-787-5373

South Carolina

South Carolina State Fair
1200 Rosewood Dr.
Columbia, SC 29201
Date(s) of Operation: October
www.scstatefair.org
803-799-3387

South Dakota

South Dakota State Fair
P.O. Box 1275
Huron, SD 57350-1275
Date(s) of Operation: Late July through early
August
www.sdstatefair.com
605-353-7340

Tennessee

Tennessee State Fair
Tennessee State Fairgrounds
P.O. Box 40208, Melrose Station
Nashville, TN 37204
Date(s) of Operation: September
www.tennesseestatefair.org
615-862-8980

Texas

State Fair of Texas
Fair Park
P.O. Box 150009
Dallas, TX 75315
Date(s) of Operation: Late September
through mid-October
www.bigtex.com
214-565-9931

Utah

Utah State Fair
Utah State FairPark
155 N. 1000 W
Salt Lake City, UT 84116
Date(s) of Operation: September
www.utah-state-fair.com
801-538-8400

Vermont

Vermont State Fair
175 S. Main St.
Rutland, VT 05702
Date(s) of Operation: Late August through
early September
www.vermontstatefair.net
802-775-5200

Virginia

State Fair of Virginia
Atlantic Rural Exposition, Inc.
600 East Laburnum Ave.
P.O. Box 26805
Richmond, VA 23261
Date(s) of Operation: Late September
through early October
www.statefair.com
804-228-3200

Washington

Central Washington State Fair
P.O. Box 1381
Yakima, WA 98907
Date(s) of Operation: Late September
through early October
www.fairfun.com/index.shtml

Evergreen State Fair
14405 179th Ave. SE
P.O. Box 129
Monroe, WA 98272
Date(s) of Operation: Late August through
early September
www.evergreenfair.org
360-805-6700

West Virginia

State Fair of West Virginia
P.O. Drawer 986
Lewisburg, WV 24901
www.wvstatefair.com
Date(s) of Operation: August
304-645-1090

Wisconsin

Wisconsin State Fair
Wisconsin State Fair Park
8100 W. Greenfield Ave.
West Allis, WI 53214
Date(s) of Operation: Late July through mid-
August
www.wistatefair.com
414-266-7188

Wyoming

Wyoming State Fair
400 W. Center
P.O. Drawer 10
Douglas, WY 82633
Date(s) of Operation: August
www.wystatefair.com
307-358-2398

Pattern Credits

American School of Needlework, Inc.
DRG Publishing
1455 Linda Vista Drive
San Marcos, California 92069

Annie's Attic
DRG Publishing
102 N. Tyler Street
Big Sandy, TX 75755
903-636-4303
www.AnniesAttic.com

Bucilla
3225 Westech Drive
Norcross, GA 30092
800-392-8673
www.plaidonline.com

Caron International
Post Office Box 222
Washington, NC 27889
www.caron.com

Coats & Clark
30 Patewood Drive
Greenville, SC 29165
www.coatsandclark.com

Craft Yarn Council of America
Post Office Box 9
Gastonia, NC 28053-0009
800-662-9999
www.craftyarncouncil.com

Lion Brand Yarn Co.
34 West 15th Street
New York, NY 10011
www.lionbrand.com

Leisure Arts, Inc., USA
Post Office Box 55595
Little Rock, AR 72215-5595
For a complete line of products, call Leisure
Arts at 1-800-526-5111 or log on to
www.leisurearts.com

The Needlecraft Shop
DRG Publishing
102 N. Tyler Street
Big Sandy, TX 75755
903-636-4303
www.needlecraftshop.com

Shady Lane
114 Shady Grove Street
Big Sandy, TX 75755
903-636-4884
If you like the pattern featured in this book,
look for similar ones using the same technique at www.shadylane.com.

Woman's Day
A Publication of Hachette Filipacchi Media
U.S., Inc. (HFM U.S.)
1633 Broadway
New York, NY 10019
212-767-6000

Photo Credits

Arizona State Fair: Cover (second from bottom and bottom), 32 (left), 94 (left), 96, 143 (right)

Delaware State Fair, Inc.: 36, 53, 91, 145

Indiana State Fair: 7, 15 (bottom left), 35 (left), 45 (center), 84 (right), 89, 132 (right), 141 (right)

Indiana State Fair, photographer Michael Vaughn: Cover (second from top), 5 (left), 25 (left), 84 (left), 87, 111, 128 (left), 146, 147

Iowa State Fair: 10 (top), 11 (top), 12 (top), 14 (bottom), 15 (top and center), 19 (right and bottom), 70 (left), 72, 79, 118, 132 (left)

The State Fair of Louisiana: 11 (bottom), 13 (center), 14 (top)

Middle Georgia Archives, Washington Memorial Library, Macon, Georgia: 10 (bottom), 13 (bottom), 15 (bottom right)

Minnesota State Fair: 54 (left), 68 (right), 94 (right), 128 (right), 134 (left and right)

New York State Fair, photographer Michael J. Okoniewski: 6, 21, 22, 25 (right), 29, 41 (left), 42 (left and right), 47, 48 (left), 57, 65, 82 (left), 103 (left), 106, 115, 127 (right), 137, 143 (left), 152

N.C. Office of Archives and History: 8 (top), 9, 12 (center), 13 (top)

N.C. State Fair/N.C. Department of Agriculture: Cover (top and middle), 5 (second from right), 17 (left and right), 19 (top), 26, 32 (right), 35 (right), 41 (right), 48 (right), 54 (right), 59 (left and right), 60, 63, 66, 68 (left), 74, 82 (right), 113 (left and right), 124, 127 (left), 131 (left), 138, 150, 151

Oregon State Fair & Expo Center: Cover (back), 8 (bottom), 50, 141 (left)

Utah State Fair: 70 (right), 101, 131 (right)

The State Fair of West Virginia, photographer Steve Shaluta: Cover (spine), 16, 19 (left), 45 (left and right), 93, 103 (right), 148, 149

Acknowledgments

Blue Ribbon Afghans from America's State Fairs is the culmination of many months of work and is truly the result of a focused group effort by the staff at Lark Books. The state fair organizations were extremely important to the success of the book, and we were often helped by more than one person in each group. First, we contacted them to obtain the names of their blue ribbon winners, and the following individuals were very helpful during this process:

Pamella Meekin Troutman, Alaska State Fair; Kathleen Browning and Val Miller, Arizona State Fair; Jeannie Molter, Arkansas State Fair; Marci Slinski, The Big E; Sandi Hurtgen, California State Fair; Deb Wallace, Colorado State Fair; Pam Oddi, Crochet Guild of America; Bonnie Kendall and Anne T. Minner, Delaware State Fair; Karen Miner and Anja Publicover, Evergreen State Fair; Lois Duffey, Florida State Fair; Laurie Schafer, Eastern Idaho State Fair; Evelyn Legg, Western Idaho Fair; Andy Klotz, Indiana State Fair; Andrea Gersesma, Iowa State Fair; Debbie Anderson, Kansas State Fair; Mary Herbert, Kentucky State Fair; Sandra Grady Hart, The State Fair of Louisiana; Susan Yoder and Pat Herbert, Maryland State Fair; Alice Diefenthaler, Michigan State Fair; Jill Nathe, Minnesota State Fair; Heather Bruns, Nebraska State Fair; Liz Williams, Nevada State Fair; Marty Bruner, New Mexico State Fair; Jodelle C. Fletcher, New York State Fair; Betty Shaw, North Carolina State Fair; Mandy Nelson, North Dakota State Fair; Sande Haldiman, Ohio State Fair; Sharon Gates, Oklahoma State Fair; Joanne Robinson, Oregon State Fair; Judy Heise, South Carolina State Fair; Jodi Kloss, South Dakota State Fair; Barbara Jones, State Fair of Texas; Judy Duncombe, Utah State Fair; Marge Christie, Vermont State Fair; Reagan Simms, State Fair of West Virginia; and Darlene Hageman and Peggy Hopkins, Wyoming State Fair.

After we received submissions from the blue ribbon winners, we obtained permission to reprint many patterns that had first appeared in other publications. My gratitude to these individuals or companies that assisted us:

Rita Weiss, American School of Needlework; Bucilla; Kathleen Sams, Coats and Clark; Mary Colucci, Craft Yarn Council of America; Delesia Hudson, DRG Wholesale Division, representing Annie's Attic and The Needlecraft Shop; Sandra Case and Debra Nettles, Leisure Arts, Inc., USA; Nancy Thomas, Lion Brand Yarn Company; Carol Hegar, Shady Lane; Melina Martocci, *Woman's Day* Magazine, HFM U.S., and Terry Kimbrough.

During the production of the book, we relied heavily on the state fair organizations for background information and imagery. These folks provided invaluable assistance in this endeavor:

Natalie Macdonald and Kristi Meyer, Arizona State Fair; Randy Hooker, Delaware State Fair; Andy Klotz, Indiana State Fair; Jessica O'Riley, Steve Pope, and Kathie Swift, Iowa State Fair; Paige Howell, State Fair of Louisiana; Danyl Zamber, Minnesota State Fair; Peter Cappuccilli, New York State Fair; Steve Massengill, North Carolina Division of Archives and History; Tiffany Budd and Heather Overton, North Carolina State Fair; Diane Childs, Oregon State Fair; Adam Holt, Tennessee State Fair; Judy Duncombe, Utah State Fair; Muriel Jackson, Washington Memorial Library, Macon, Georgia; and Pamela W. Edwards, West Virginia State Fair.

Now, back to those hard-working professionals at Lark Books. Art Director Kathleen Holmes had the formidable task of designing this book that is overflowing with words and images, and she really took to heart the essence of the project and created a fabulous tribute to our American craftspeople that captures the palpable excitement of our state fairs. Before Kathy worked her visual magic, though, there was a lot of hard work involved in developing the content for the book. Cindy Burda, Delores Gosnell, Jeff Hamilton, Rebecca Lim, Nathalie Mornu, Rain Newcomb, Marissa Y. Thompson, and Nicole Tuggle all made editorial contributions, while Avery Johnson and Shannon Yokeley helped with technical matters. Barbara Zaretksy designed a terrific cover, and the folks at keithwright.com (Wendy and Keith Wright) did their usual superb job of capturing the beautiful afghans on film.

I wanted to offer a special, heartfelt thank-you to Assistant Editor Veronika Alice Gunter and Editorial Assistant Anne Wolff Hollyfield, who were simply amazing as they cheerfully dealt with the complex photographic and copyright issues involved in the book. Without months of their unflagging support, there would have been no book. Words cannot express my gratitude for all their help.

My technical consultant, Marilyn Hastings, was a true gift and her profound appreciation for the talents of the blue ribbon winners was an inspiration to me. To the winners—she provided the lavender sachets! Thank you, Marilyn.

Finally, a dedication: To each of the blue ribbon winners, and to every person who has ever made a gift from the heart.

Abbreviations

beg	beginning
BPdc	back post double crochet
BPtr	back post triple crochet
ch(s)	chain(s)
ch-	chain made previously
dc(s)	double crochet(s)
dec	decrease
dtr	double triple crochet
FPdc	front post double crochet
FPdtr	front post double triple crochet
hdc	half double crochet
inc	increase
pat	pattern
rep(s)	repeat(s)
rnd(s)	round(s)
sc(s)	single crochet(s)
sk	skip
sl st	slip stitch
sp(s)	space(s)
st(s)	stitch(es)
tr	triple crochet
tr tr	triple triple crochet
yo	yarn over

Index